# SIMON & SCHUSTER'S

# Guide to
# DOGS

by Gino Pugnetti
Edited by
ELIZABETH MERIWETHER SCHULER

**A FIRESIDE BOOK**
**PUBLISHED BY SIMON & SCHUSTER INC.**
New York London Toronto Sydney Tokyo Singapore

A Fireside Book
Published by Simon & Schuster Inc.
Simon & Schuster Building
Rockefeller Center
1230 Avenue of the Americas
New York, New York 10020

Printed and bound in Spain by Artes Gráficas Toledo, S.A.
D.L.TO:1804–1992

12 13 14 15 16 17 18 19 20

Published in Italy under the title, CANI
Library of Congress Cataloging in Publication Data

Pugnetti, Gino
    Simon & Schuster's guide to dogs.


    Translation of Cani.
    Includes index.
    1. Dogs.   2. Dog breeds.    I. Schuler, Elizabeth
Meriwether.   II. Title.   III. Title: Guide to dogs.
SF426.P8313          636.7                  80-12906

ISBN 0-671-25527-4

Layouts and symbols by Giorgio Seppi.

# TABLE OF CONTENTS

# EXPLANATION OF SYMBOLS

dog adapted to
living in the city

dog adapted to
shepherding

gentle dog

cowherd

definite tendency
to bite

watchdog or
guard dog

dog that can live
and sleep outdoors

dog can be trained
for defense

**dog that should
sleep indoors**

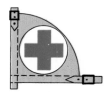

guide dog for
the blind

mountain
rescue dog

water
rescue dog

sled dog

Swiss cart-
pulling dog

dog adapted
to pointing

retriever

scenting hound

fox hunter

hunting dog for marshy areas

needs clipping

dog that must be
protected from the cold

sport racing dog

7

### Descent from the wolf

Opinions about the origins of man are vague and subject to disagreement. So, too, are those concerning the origins of his friend the dog. Archeological findings dating back 25 to 30 million years are the first glimmerings we have of the presence of the dog on earth. We may therefore say that in the so-called Age of Mammals, alongside the primitive apes there lived a being with canine characteristics. This animal's scientific name is *Cynodesmus,* and we know (or rather surmise) that after millions of years of evolution—via an intermediate wolflike animal called *Tomarctus*—it was the ancestor of the wolf, the jackal, the fox, the coyote, and all the canines.

The first dog domesticated by man was a wolf. It is possible to date its appearance in most parts of the world to about twelve thousand years ago. The remains found in the Beaverhead Mountains of Idaho and those found in Europe, Asia, and pre-Columbian America all belong to the same epoch. The friendship between man and dog is one of the oldest and most lasting in history. In all the vicissitudes of life—in peace and in war, in misery and in wealth, in art, hunting, defense, sport, in companionship and in scientific discovery—man has been accompanied by the dog. Recently, an English philosopher, wishing to confer a long-deserved tribute, defined the dog as "an honorary human being."

## Cooperation with man

Human beings and wolves reached such a quick accord because they have the same social organization and, on the whole, the same instinctive mental structure. Wolves live in couples and the whole pack cooperates under a single leader in the hunt. Duties are clearly divided: one wolf picks out the track trampled down by the prey; another blocks the way; while the boldest one goes for the throat. If the prey travels in groups, there is also a wolf whose job it is to isolate the victim. The leader of the pack feeds first. When his hunger is satisfied, the rest of the pack is allowed to finish the banquet.

It is probable that men who lived in more or less settled family groups threw the bones and scraps of their meals to the hungry animals that prowled around the villages. The wolves gradually realized that the men had "superior arms" for catching game: stone tools, arrows, and snares. They sensed his superiority in hunting and began treating him as a leader, following him at a distance during the hunt and returning with him to the villages to get their share of the spoils.

It is easy to presume that in time man began to take some interest in the wolf cubs, that he adopted some, and that in the course of generations individuals developed that took part in the hunt, no longer as observers, but as willing helpers, flushing and isolating the gazelle or the caiman for the man to kill.

In order to domesticate the horse, the reindeer, or the elephant, man had to capture them (that is, conquer them), imprison them, and win them over by force. Alone among animals, the dog acceded to the authority of man without constraint. Theirs was a friendship between colleagues, based on a mutual interest: hunting, which allowed them both to satisfy their hunger.

In some remote villages of Paraguay and Peru, it is still common for a puppy that has lost its mother to be nursed by a woman. Such practices may have occurred even at the beginning of the dog-man relationship and may have played a major role in cementing the closeness between man and animal.

## The Arabs and the first breeds

The dog is thus a tamed wolf, the first of the many animals domesticated by man over the centuries. Its evolution was very rapid. According to some scientists the dog has reproduced in domesticity more than five thousand times, and all the physical and psychological qualities which it has today come from the wolf or from accidental mutation, while the effects of cross-breeding with the jackal are negligible.

Wolf and dog, therefore, have common antecedents but have followed two different paths: one has remained wild and ferocious; the other has become domesticated. Their basic characteristics have, however, remained the same through the centuries: both dog and wolf wag their tails as a sign of contentment; they put them between their legs when they are afraid; they curl their lips and growl when they are angry; they mark out their territory with their scent; they have the same gestation period; and they are subject to the same illnesses and the same parasites.

Ever since the so-called "peat bog dogs" raised by the Neolithic palafitte dwellers, the appearance of new types of dogs and breeds similar to those we know today took place without pause. Whether due to natural mutation, climate, environment, or crossings engineered by man in the process of domesticating them, the breeds became ever more numerous and specialized until they reached the point of modern classification, which is based on the aptitude of the breed and the use to which it is to be put: hunting, shepherding, guarding, work, company.

Perhaps the first fully distinct breed was the Saluki, an Arabian greyhound whose name means "noble." Indeed, the concept of breeds was defined by the Arabs, first in relation to horses and later to dogs: "a breed is a group of animals raised by man so that it possesses certain hereditary qualities, including a uniform look which distinguishes it from other members of the same species."

## A guard dog, five thousand years old

In order to have certain knowledge of the physical existence and, above all, of the social function of the dog, it is necessary to wait until the time when man painted its image or described it in his ideograms. In the grand spectrum of the history of civilization, man certainly would not fail to mention Canis familiaris.

Prehistoric painters, however, were at first more readily inspired by animals that called up the emotions associated with hunting and appetite. In the caves they decorated, one finds stag, bison, wild boar, and reindeer, while the dog is missing. Probably, household friend that it was, it was such an everyday element that it did not offer inspiration to the artists. But, like every other art, so-called prehistoric art underwent an evolution in subject matter and eventually the painters began depicting the jackal and the hyena. Around 4500 B.C. the first figure of the dog appeared. It was, naturally, in the act of helping a hunter; but its aesthetic lines do not correspond to any breed known today. Not only hunting dogs appeared in the art of this ancient period: on the handle of a knife four to five thousand years old is inscribed the outline of a dog with a collar. This may be the first real proof that dogs were also used as guards.

For dog lovers, pharaonic Egyptian art has the merit of having transmitted the first images of dogs belonging to breeds similar to those of today. Here, one can see hounds and dachshunds. Later, mastiffs, perhaps imported from the Orient, appeared; and still later, greyhounds. Those famous merchants, the Phoenicians, who traded in all sorts of goods in the Mediterranean and Middle Europe, played a large part in the appearance of new dogs in Egypt, Rome, and Athens.

### Dog as a cult object

Opinions regarding the dog, so deeply a part of human life, have also been expressed by various religions. In Egypt, tombs were raised and tearful epigraphs were written to deceased dogs. Killing a dog was a crime meriting severe corporal punishment, and cases of certified cruelty were even punishable by death. The Persians, too, considered killing a dog a crime. There, the dog was officially defined by the state as "guardian of the herds and protector of man."

According to the Greeks, the dog was forged by Vulcan, and its role in mythology is abundantly expressed in Greek pottery, sculpture, and literature.

In pre-Columbian cultures the dog also assumed a supernatural function, so much so that at a man's death his loyal canine friend was killed and buried with him.

The Hebrews, however, did not show any particular tenderness for the dog. Not being hunters, they did not feel any positive attraction for the canine species. In the Old Testament, the dog is considered a pariah among animals, a dirty, emaciated being, nourishing itself on the garbage in the roads. In the Bible, there are some forty references to the dog, almost all of them derogatory.

Turning to the Orient, one does not find much consolation. It is true that in China "sleeve dogs," tiny enough to be kept in the cuff of a kimono, were raised as pets; but three centuries before Christ, the dog was considered a delicacy and dog meat was never missing from many aristocratic menus. This sad habit has lasted even to this day.

### The first writing about dogs

Wherever there has been hunting, or malefactors to be kept at

Statue of Anubi, an Egyptian deity, half dog and half jackal, connected with the cult of the dead (Egyptian Museum, Cairo). The dog is frequently found in the mythology and religions of ancient peoples.

bay, there has been the dog, and men, who have tended continuously to the improvement of the species, creating new breeds, seeing to their training, and providing them with the proper foods.

Even before the Classical Period, the Greeks had wolf dogs as well as Egyptian hounds and the Persian Molossus. Aristotle, the Greek philosopher and zoologist, listed the various breeds of dog, giving them the names of the countries from which they came. Thus, we know that in 300 B.C. there existed dogs from Cyrenaica, India, Egypt, and Epirus. But since the author gave no clear descriptions, we cannot put faces or bodies together with these names.

In Rome, too, hunting dogs were held in high esteem. The Latin poet Ovid gave precise instructions on how to insure that the dam would produce good pups. And the writer M. T. Varro offered the first advice on acquiring a dog. He counseled in particular that one not trust a dog fed on scraps. These dogs, he felt, accustomed to licking blood, would end up by attacking live animals. The Greek Oppian, author of *Cynegetica*, in his turn was personally involved in breeding dogs of small size, which he considered to be most adapted to hunting in the woods.

One can therefore assert that two thousand years ago there was already an interest in, perhaps even a love of, dogs. The plaques on the houses in Pompeii saying *"Cave Canem"* (∴"Beware of Dog") show explicitly that dogs were also used as

Clay cast of a Pompeian dog that died in the eruption of Vesuvius in 79 A.D., struggling desperately to free itself from its chain. The lava and the ash preserved forever its last convulsion.

guards. These guard dogs were usually ferocious Molossuses of powerful size and frightening teeth. In the daytime they were kept chained up. At night they were allowed to run free on the property. It was the fashion to keep ferocious animals in the house or the garden. The poor had to content themselves with a goose.

### From the Romans to the medieval period

Since very early times the dog has also been used in war. The Romans, for example, used dogs as message carriers and attack dogs. For attack and defense, the Molossus, with its pincer-like fangs, was equipped with iron collars bristling with blades. In the face of such an apparition, the enemy was often put to flight before the battle was joined. The most unfortunate animals were the so-called messenger dogs. The military orders were put in a small copper tube which the dog was made to swallow. When it arrived at its destination, there was no time to wait for the dog to expel the tube naturally. To get the orders delivered quickly, the unknowing messenger had to be slaughtered.

In the first years of the fall of the Roman Empire, after the invasion of the barbarians, the dog was abandoned and regressed to its prehistoric state. Hordes of hungry dogs that had followed the invaders remained wandering sadly in the towns and countryside, united in dangerous wild bands in search of food.

In truth, the dog never suffered the troubled existence of the cat, which medieval superstition accused of witchcraft and personification of the devil; but during this period, its presence was just as poorly tolerated. Perhaps it was at this time that such negative expressions as "dog's world," "dog-tired," "dog's life," "son of a bitch," and "die like a dog" originated. However, the dog's existence during the medieval period was saved once again by hunting. During periods of severe famine, in order to put something in the pot besides roots from the garden, there was no alternative but to go hunting. Everyone, rich and poor, began to hunt, armed, as war had taught them, with bows, crossbows, lances, and blades of every description, but also with snares and nets. In pursuit of this bloody enterprise, man turned once again to the indispensable aid of the dog, which could manage in the great forests and marshes of the time. In England, a good hunting dog was worth as much as a slave.

## The beginning of specialization

During the Middle Ages, dogs were also raised at monasteries, perhaps to provide company for the monks, but also for their protection. The bloodhound, for example, was created by the monks at the Abbey of St. Hubert in the Belgian Ardennes. Similarly, according to reliable sources, the German shepherd originated from breeding carried out by German monks who wanted to have a dog capable of protecting the monastery from the attacks of bandits.

It was during this same period that the first true specialization of hunting dogs began. Some hunting dogs, such as pointers and setters, were channeled into the search for prey; scented hounds were used to flush stag; greyhound-type dogs were used for following; while the Molossus was reserved for attacking bison and bear. Small dogs called beaver dogs also began to be used at this time for burrowing into the lairs of foxes and wild rabbits. There were the very first terriers.

As if inspired by the stories of the great traveler Marco Polo, who recounted how the Great Khan of the Tartars went hunting preceded by packs of five thousand dogs, the rich feudal lords joined their noble friends in the hunt accompanied by one thousand to fifteen hundred hounds.

With a force of at least eight hundred dogs, the soldiers of Elizabeth I fought the Irish rebels, and big dogs harnessed with armor and spikes participated en masse in the Spanish occupation of America.

The dog became ever more important in civilian, military, and sporting life. Already, there were treatises on dog care which recommended such things as keeping the packs warm when they returned tired from the hunt, keeping their wooden feeding bowls clean, and currying the dogs every day, as well as giving information regarding proper nutrition and the treatment of eczema with seawater baths.

Ideas of veterinary science were sketchy during the Middle Ages. On the other hand, dogs were used empirically to cure man's ills. It was believed that the blood of a white dog would calm madness and that the blood of a black dog would help a

One of the numerous pictorial representations of the dog. This one was reproduced from a fifteenth-century treatise on falconry and hunting (Bibliothèque de Chantilly).

woman bring to completion a painful childbirth. The first veterinary and surgical information to reach Europe came by way of Arabic science.

## A luxury during the Renaissance
As the Middle Ages progressed, customs became gentler and prosperity became more widespread; affection for the dog grew as well. Clearly, the cruelty to animals which is found even today is the heritage of dark periods of misery, ignorance, and evil superstition. At the threshold of the Renaissance, owning a beautiful dog had even become a sort of snobbism. Hunting was still practiced, but it was also considered pleasing to have a walking dog and a companion dog. One went out escorted by a Molossus. Races were organized in which the greyhound, imported all over Europe from England, triumphed.

Women, especially aristocratic women with no interest in hunting, gave their affections to small companion dogs which they petted and decorated with ribbons, creating the fashion for the luxury dog. Often in order to enter into the good graces of a noblewoman, it was necessary first to gain the affection of her little favorite.

## The dog in art
The number of breeds of dogs grew——especially of hunting dogs. The foremost country for hunting dogs in the seventeenth century was France. All the kings Louis loved hunting, and they knew how to go about it with royal majesty. The famous *chiens blancs du roi*, elegant, full-blooded, unequaled for hunting in packs, date from this period. Exchanges, sales, and contests among the various European states led to widespread respect for this noble, modest animal, so beautiful and friendly, unmatched by any for loyalty, strength, and intelligence. It was destined to be immortalized by the greatest painters, who depicted it lying at the feet of its most genteel patrons.

For several centuries, paintings illustrated man's love for the dog and offered an indication of the most favored breeds. The paintings of the Renaissance are full of beautiful dogs. Among the famous painters who depicted this subject are Dürer, Botticelli, Piero della Francesca, Mantegna, Titian, Bosch, Brueghel the Elder, Rubens, Canaletto, Velásquez, and Goya. And the list will never end.

Poetry and theater also resounded with love of the dog: one need only mention Lorenzo de' Medici and Shakespeare.

In the nineteenth century, the consolidation of democracy in England and the coming of the French Revolution changed the life of the dog as they did the lives of men. The great dog packs of the nobility disappeared, but not the individual's passion for hunting. The middle-class hunter was content with one or two dogs, provided they were quick and had a fine sense of smell. Above all, pointing and setting dogs were highly regarded, and English breeders created the pointer, a breed that became famous.

## The first dog shows

The new attitude required that the dog, besides being skilled in hunting, appear aesthetically attractive and be physically well adapted to its multiplicity of activities. Breeders quickly set to work with intelligence and passion to fulfill these demands. In 1859, in the town hall of Newcastle upon Tyne in England, the first dog show took place. It was for hunting dogs only, and fifty pointers and setters took part. Standards and genealogy were not held to be of much account; and more than anything, dog lovers thought of the dog show as a new and original sporting event without regulations. Fourteen years later, however, on April 1, 1873, the English Kennel Club was founded in London, and compilation of the *Studbook* began. In this book, which today is known as the *Book of Origins*, data concerning dogs belonging to the different breeds were recorded.

The English example was followed in other countries. The American Kennel Club dates from 1884 and the Italian Kennel Club from 1898. The first dog shows in the United States date back to 1875. While a little more than a century ago barely fifty dogs participated in a show, today in the most important shows as many as seven thousand dogs may be entered.

By the end of the 1800's the animal lovers' movement in England had achieved some success in controlling, among other things, the cruel practices common to dog trainers. For example, the useless practice of docking a dog's ears still remained

**19**

The picture of a dog on a French sign indicating that dogs are not allowed to enter.

in use, retained from the barbarians. This operation had been justified in the past because in combat the ear flap was easy prey to the enemy. In 1898, however, cutting of dogs' ears was abolished in England and no dog so mutilated (even for aesthetic reasons) is admissible in dog shows. In the United States the AKC rules that "any dog whose ears have been cropped or cut in any way shall be ineligible to compete at any show in any state where the laws prohibit the same, except subject to the provisions of such laws."

This surgery is still required by the standards of some breeds where it refers only to the tips of the ears. It should be performed by a veterinarian when the dog is about three months old and the ear cartilage has acquired some consistency.

### Changing fortunes in peace and war
In the early years of the twentieth century, the popularity of the dog was at a high point. Besides the role the dog played in dog shows, in family life, in army units, in all the most important areas of defense, guarding, herding, and hunting, the dog's image also appeared on lucky charms, wood carvings, toys, greeting cards, the trademarks of records, in advertising, and in heraldry. In this respect, it should be remembered that since the Middle Ages, hunting dogs, greyhounds, mastiffs, and Great Danes found a place of honor in the coats of arms of all the great families. They provided beautiful symbols of the hunt and of combat, important arts during the Dark Ages and the Renaissance.

As it has in the past, war led to the decimation of the dog. Times of poverty and misery do not allow for the feeding of nonhuman mouths. In 1871 during the siege of Paris by the Prussians not only dogs but horses, cats, birds, and mice disappeared from the French capital. Likewise, during the two World Wars, a great many dogs died or lost their homes and masters. In addition to its use in the ranks of armies, in times of war the dog has continued to be the friend of the poorest: of the soldiers at the front, of prisoners. In the great retreat in Russia in 1943, among the fleeing soldiers were mutts who even in the worst of times would not abandon those who had thrown them a crust of bread.

### Vivisection: stronger laws

It is calculated that the canine population of the world today numbers 120 to 150 million. In the United States alone there are approximately 35 million dogs, and it is estimated that 7 to 8 million live in France, 5 to 6 million in Germany, 4 million in Italy, 1 million in Belgium, and 400,000 in Switzerland.

Not all of them are happy dogs. Many are victims of abandonment by ungrateful masters, of street traffic, and of vivisection. Pages of fiery condemnation of the practice of vivisection have been written by such authors as Goethe, Schiller, Voltaire, Schopenhauer, Tolstoy, Twain, Shaw, and Malaparte as well as many philosophers, scientists, and journalists. Among those whose writings contain words of love and esteem for the dog are Jerome K. Jerome, O. Henry, D'Annunzio, Ada Negri, Gra-

**21**

zia Deledda, Thomas Mann, Jack London, Katherine Mansfield, John Steinbeck, Mikhail Zoshchenko, and Eric Knight.

Despite the fact that public opinion is decidedly against vivisection, 100 million animals, of which several hundred thousand are dogs, are sacrificed each year. Less ambiguous laws and more careful controls are needed to govern experimentation made in the name of science.

## A dog for every kind of hunting

After this rapid glance at the origins and social history of the dog in its collaboration and friendship with man, let us examine in more detail its mental and physical gifts for work, beginning with hunting. Not everyone is in agreement about the practice of this sport, and this is not the place to argue the question. Man and dog, however, met and developed a mutual respect, even a love, on the field of the hunt. If hunting had not existed, this bond, which has remained indestructible for centuries, would never have been formed.

There are many different ways of hunting and many different animals in the forest. There are predatory animals and flying animals, those that can run fast and those that live in dens, those that flee and those that attack, those that hide in hedges and those that camouflage themselves. It is said that from ancient times the dog has possessed the same hunting instincts as man. But when the hunting dog has assimilated a certain level of general training, it is necessary to begin specialization. Biologically and genetically, the dog has been an animal that has allowed itself to be molded more than any other mammal. Not only was it adapted to obeying and learning, but generation after generation it has transmitted to its progeny not only that which it has assimilated but also new physical characteristics. It has been like a lump of clay in the hands of man, slowly assuming the form desired by the artist. Physically and psychologically, it proceeds through the centuries with an even tread.

By vocation the dog was first of all a hound. Its instincts were for finding game, flushing it out of the underbrush, and driving it into open terrain where the hunter could by some means capture it. All this was, however, not enough, and man taught the dog other skills. He created, for example, the standing dog. By both inclination and training, the dog should stop suddenly the moment it senses the presence of game. In these moments of suspension, it should be as motionless as a statue, every muscle vibrating, one paw lifted. This is the signal, the so-called "stand," which indicates to the hunter that the game is just there in the direction indicated by the dog's muzzle. Among the standing dogs of today are the pointing breeds, spaniels, and griffons; among British breeds, the pointer and the setter.

Man also taught the dog to retrieve. It sometimes happened that an animal hit by a hunter's arrow (or today, a bullet) ran away and concealed itself in some hidden place. For this reason, the retriever was developed. As its name implies, this dog specializes in retrieving game that has been hit from wherever it may fall, be it brambles or the waters of the marsh.

The terrier, too, has a specialty, that of flushing game from its

Some hunting dogs are courageous and able enough to confront even the strongest, most aggressive adversaries. In the photo, two hounds have forced a lynx to seek shelter at the top of a tree.

den. Many woods or hill animals (foxes, badgers, stone martens, weasels) have for refuge a hole in the ground, in the hollow of a tree, or among rocks. The proud, aggressive terrier, with its short legs and dangerous teeth, penetrates the tunnels made by these wild animals, overcomes them in hard-fought battle, and flushes them from their holes.

Especially at the time of the monarchy in France when hunts such as stag hunts or fox hunts were transformed into worldly events with vast and gorgeous staging, great and noble breeds such as the Grand Bleu de Gascogne, the Poitevin, and the Chien d'Artois were developed. They worked in packs accompanied by horns and rows of huntsmen, beaters, and horsemen.

Under the reign of Charles I of Lorraine, seventy forests and almost eight hundred royal parks were created on land confiscated to raise and train the king's dogs. And Louis XI of France was such a passionate hunter and such a methodical man that he scheduled everything for the appropriate season: war in summer and fall, stag and bear hunting in winter, and hunting with falcons in the spring. So great was his love of hunting that when he was near death, so sick he could no longer move, he spent his last hours diverting himself by watching dogs catching mice in the royal bedroom.

Among all the kings who have been crazy about hunting, Canute the Great of Denmark and England should not be forgotten. In 1016, this king issued a degree ordering the breaking of the legs of any dog not belonging to the nobility that was found wandering in the royal hunting preserve.

## The need for training

Although gifted with instincts for venery, the hunting dog always needs to be trained. The period in which these dogs learn most quickly is from six months to one year of age. However, even at three months, they may be taken to the hunt along with their dams. They will, to be sure, have a great desire to play; but, at the same time, by imitation, they will learn to behave like their parents.

Dog trainers recommend that one always use the same command and the same gestures for each order and that brief lessons given in a spirit of play, never of constraint, be repeated until the task is learned.

Training in the sport of hunting has developed considerably in dogs of various breeds the latent capacities of their ancestors. However, the Sunday hunter may not know that for specialized hunting there are specialized dogs of good lineage adapted to the regions in which they must work. Mating of dogs belonging to friends or acquaintances in order to get free puppies is to be discouraged because the results are dogs of general ability, good at everything but excelling at nothing, and lacking in personality.

At the end of the hunting season, the hunting dog must become for several months a companion dog. It must be protected from the damp, nourished without being allowed to become fat, and taken often for training sessions so that it will quickly return to its accustomed good form during the next hunting season.

## The evolution of the sheepdog

From ancient times, dogs have had other skills besides hunting. Among their more valuable latent instincts has been that of guarding. If raising livestock provided supplies of food and skins and a convenient means of transportation for early nomadic peoples, there was always the impending possibility that their herds might be attacked by predators. The forests of Lebanon, the Nubian desert, the woods of Italy, and the plains of the Euphrates were filled with the danger of wild animals. Just as it was ready to involve itself in the business of hunting, so the dog became the sentinel of the herds, repulsing all aggressors, both man and beast. The first sheepdogs were, therefore, big, courageous, and mordant, ready to go for the throat of bears, wolves, or any other intruder, whatever it might be.

Herd dogs, it is supposed, first appeared thousands of years ago in the service of nomadic shepherds in Asia. Phoenician merchants then brought them to Europe where they mated with local dogs and over the course of centuries developed into numerous famous breeds. Early herdsmen preferred their herd dogs to have white coats. This made it easier to see them at night. More important, it distinguished them from the brown color of bears or wolves, so the herdsman could enter the struggle swinging his club without injuring his loyal companion. It is for this reason that there are today such light-coated sheepdogs as the kuvasz, the Maremmano-Abruzzese, the Tatra, the Great Pyrenees, and the Bergamasco.

The Romans took with them these excellent breeds to all those areas of Europe where pasturing flourished. And in each country, individual breeds developed that adapted to the terrain, the climate, and the type of work. For centuries, these dogs were used purely and simply for the defense of the herd with differing specialization depending on whether the herd consisted of sheep or cows. Only in the last century, when the menace of bears and wolves has become less likely, has the sheepdog been entrusted first and foremost with the job of finding lost animals and bringing them back to the fold.

### Competitions for sheepdogs

The training of a sheepdog is almost always accomplished by means of imitation. To accomplish this, one, therefore, puts a good-natured puppy that clearly has an instinct for its future job with an old herd dog. In a few months the puppy too will become a proven professional. Besides herding sheep and cows, the sheepdog should be able to herd geese, ducks, hens, and domestic rabbits without any of the temptations of hunger.

In England today there are still competitions organized exclusively for sheepdogs. In these, the sheepdogs must demonstrate their atavistic instincts by finding ten sheep placed eight hundred meters away and herding them into an enclosure via one or more prescribed paths. Points are added to the dog's score if it has worked silently, with concentration, speed, and mastery. A dog may be disqualified if it is slow in its work or if, overly authoritative, it makes itself obeyed by biting the sheep.

Every country has its own breeds of sheepdog. Not all these breeds, however, have continued to practice their original skills. Some, like the German shepherd, the Belgian shepherd, and the Norwegian buhund, have become specialized in guarding and defense. Others, such as the collie, the bobtail, and the corgi, prefer the advantages of being companion dogs.

Many shepherds, even today, use sheepdogs that are not pure-blooded—so-called mutts. These dogs can never reach the perfection of performance of purebred dogs. It does not cost much for farmers and shepherds to obtain dogs of good lineage, and the advantages will repay them tenfold.

### The instinct for guarding and defense

Just as the dog has an instinct for protecting the sheep in its care, so, once it feels responsible for them, it will protect the house, objects, and its master. In ancient Greece, some dogs, probably descended from the Molossus, were set apart as guardians of sacred places. Plutarch recounts that one dog followed a thief who had robbed the Temple of Aphrodite for 21 miles and then captured him. There is no dog, who will not by ancient instinct react and wake the house should a stranger lay hands on its master's things. Even the smallest terrier knows how to make itself heard by growling and barking.

The grandfather of all guard dogs was the Molossus, with its great size and aggressive instincts. The modern guard dog, however, is the result of specialized breeding effected by expert breeders. The dog used for guarding or defense must be

**27**

trained to overcome difficult obstacles such as stairs, quays, and ditches. It must be taught to guard objects, to attack people without injuring them, to remain indifferent to the sound of gunshots, to refuse food offered by strange hands, not to become nervous in the face of other animals' provocations, and to run for long distances—even as much as 25 miles (40 km.).

Extremely well trained guard dogs are used by the police. The breeds they use most are the German shepherd, the Belgian shepherd, the Doberman, the Airedale, the giant schnauzer, the Rottweiler, the bloodhound, and the Labrador. Training begins during the dog's first year, and once the dog has been enlisted in police service, it remains in the hands of its instructor for its professional life, usually 6 to 7 years.

Guard dogs for private homes are also trained in schools where they may remain for four to eight months, depending on how well they respond. Of course, training may be done at home, but only for elementary behavior: not barking; sitting, lying down, and staying; not running after other animals; not jumping on visitors, even out of friendship; responding immediately to being called; and eating only out of its own bowl.

All training should be given with patience and energy, never with constraint, yelling, and blows. The dog should find it a joy to execute its master's orders. Therefore, all training and especially the perfect execution of a command should be rewarded with praise. It is better to avoid rewards of food that tomorrow might be accepted from another hand.

The practice common in some work yards, small factories, and dairy farms of keeping an untrained dog chained up with the intention of using it as a guard dog is to be condemned. It only produces a snarling, unhappy dog, good for nothing.

On the other hand, robbers fear small companion dogs that bark at the first creak. They may not go for the throat or the robbers' calves, but they will sound the alarm; and there is no calming them. In contrast, an outside guard dog may be poisoned or drugged with a bit of treated meat.

### Rescue dogs

The first rescue dogs (of the Molossian type) were used centuries ago for tracing paths that disappeared in snowstorms. In addition, for 300 years, dogs raised by the Cenobite Brothers in the Hospice of St. Bernard in Switzerland have been used to find lost people. These St. Bernards, the result of felicitous crossings between German Great Danes and Newfoundlands, are often pictured with casks of brandy around their necks.

Rescues attributed to St. Bernards number in the thousands. And the story of one particular St. Bernard, Barry, has become a legend. Barry, so the story goes, saved forty-four people from the snow before being killed by the forty-fifth, who, in the night, mistook him for a bear. The irony is that the name Barry comes from *bari*, which in German dialect means "little bear." A statue to Barry was raised in Paris, and for many years the St. Bernard was also known as the Barryhund.

Today, the dog most preferred for rescue work following avalanches and earthquakes is the German shepherd, which is

capable of undergoing particularly rigorous training. For water rescues, the most popular breed is the Newfoundland, which can operate successfully even during severe storms at sea.

### Use of the dog in war

Since the earliest wars, dogs have been used as sentinels, messengers, and scouts. Later they also carried munitions, medicines, and telephone equipment and located mines and sought out the injured. During World War I, dogs were armed with gas masks.

Modern armies have always preferred their own national breeds. Thus they have used the German shepherd, the collie, the Doberman, and the Rottweiler. Breeds with white coats are avoided since they are easily spotted by the enemy.

In World War II, Germany had an army of 200,000 trained dogs guarding the Nazi concentration camps. The Americans used dogs most especially in the conquest of the Japanese-held Pacific islands, to flush out snipers and search for wounded in the jungles. The Soviets trained dogs to expect food under ammunition wagons. They then put TNT charges on the backs of the poor hungry dogs and sent them toward the enemy, exploding the charges as the dogs advanced.

### Guide dogs for the blind

One of the most glorious of canine activities has been acting as guides for the blind. The first centers for this humanitarian and compassionate training arose more or less contemporaneously in France and Germany in 1915. They were designed to

A team of sled dogs in Alaska.

help soldiers returning from the front with impaired vision. Other centers followed immediately all over the world.

The German shepherd became the preferred dog for this training. With its intelligence, obedience, loyalty, precision, and perfect movement, it was like a light for the extinguished eyes of its human companions. Good results have also been achieved with the Belgian shepherd, the Labrador, the boxer, and the collie (especially good for blind children). Bitches are preferred for their greater docility and obedience. Male dogs are too likely to become distracted by a bitch in heat.

## The importance of the working breeds

Until 1500, dogs were also trained to pull carts loaded with heavy goods. It was tiring work, but finally laws were passed in the dogs' favor, prohibiting their excessive exploitation. Today in Switzerland, for the sake of tradition and folklore, the strongest of the dogs used for herding cattle are also used to draw little carts filled with milk and cheese.

Indispensable as a working dog, however, are the sled dogs. There are situations where even those who have the mechanical means for crossing ice or shifting snows must, of necessity, use sled dogs as the only possible means of crossing great areas of frozen land. Teams of Alaskan Malamutes have participated in the glorious polar expeditions of Amundsen and the Duke of the Abruzzi. Only with the sleds pulled by these dogs was it possible to carry supplies and maintain communication between the expedition and the inhabited villages.

A dog fight in Afghanistan, where this sport is very popular. The fight often ends with the death of one or both of the combatants. Great sums of money are bet on the outcome of these fights.

In arctic countries, sled dogs such as the Eskimo are hitched to the sleds either in a fan-shaped formation or in pairs side by side. The Eskimos and the Siberians also use different systems of yoking.

In Alaska, sled-pulling contests are very popular. In Anchorage, Alaskan Malamutes compete periodically over courses 500 miles (800 km.) long. Of course, the teams are changed at predetermined way stations.

## A cruel sport: combat

On the subject of more or less sporting uses of the dog, one should not forget the combats in the amphitheaters of ancient Rome between dogs and tigers, dogs and lions, and dogs and dogs. Most often used for these combats was the Epirean Molossus, a beast weighing 177 pounds (80 kg.), which often succeeded in overcoming notoriously ferocious wild animals while the enthusiasm of the peasantry and the nobility united in the joy of the blood sport.

Rome was not the only place where this cruel sport, in which even men were sometimes sacrificed, thrived. In Britain powerful combat dogs known as Pugnaces Britanniae were raised and sold even overseas. The bulldog, for example, is an English dog created specifically to fight bulls. Its nose is pugged so that it can breathe easily even when it has the bull tightly by the throat.

Organized combat between dogs and dogs and between dogs and wild animals took place practically everywhere, even in Japan and China. The first country to prohibit combat between animals by law was Holland in 1689. France and England followed 150 years later. Even today, however, such combats take place secretly.

## A civilized sport: racing

More noble and civilized is the sport of racing. Greyhounds and whippets, natural runners, are raced on dog tracks, and spectators bet on the results as in horse races.

Dog races were organized as far back as pre-Roman Gaul, but only in Elizabethan England were the rules stabilized, organizing societies founded, tracks built, and dogs bred for their racing abilities.

In the past, racing dogs were led on by a real hare, behind which the dogs were unleashed. The first dog to capture the prey was the winner. Animal lovers protested; so in 1876, the first mechanical rabbit was constructed. However, it worked badly. It broke down during the biggest racing events and caused quite a commotion. The device was perfected in the early 1900's by an American engineer, Owen Smith. From then on in both England and the United States race tracks began to spring up and the number of fans and bettors grew. This is a sport to be encouraged. Above all, it has been a means of preserving and improving one of the oldest and purest breeds of dog.

The dogs run over sand tracks for distances ranging from 400 to 600 or even 1,000 meters. Training begins when the dog is about nine months old, and at a year and a half the dog is ready to race. The dog should not weigh more than 13.6 pounds (30 kg.) and must be able to run 400 meters in 22 seconds. A greyhound can run 43 miles (70 km.) per hour.

A good breeder must care for a champion dog as he would a pure-blooded horse, controlling its feeding and supervising its training. In the sprint which follows the launching of the mechanical rabbit, the dog may strain its muscles. So, before the race the greyhound's thighs are rubbed with camphored alcohol, as is done to warm the muscles of athletes.

Certain Anglo-Saxon and Spanish countries have retained the practice of using a live rabbit, not only in open courses where the rabbit has a chance, however small, of escaping death, but also on closed tracks without exits. However, this is a black mark against man, not dog.

## The scenting abilities of truffle dogs

The dog has performed many jobs during its long existence. One is the finding of truffles in certain areas of Italy and France. The truffle is a rare, delicious, and expensive mushroomlike fungus that grows in symbiosis with the roots of the oak. It can be found only through the scenting abilities of specially trained dogs (pigs are no longer used, as they tend to eat the truffles). The search for truffles is carried out only with mongrels or with terriers that do not allow themselves to become distracted by small game wandering in the woods, but rather go directly to their objective.

Louis XV used to amuse himself in the mornings by searching for truffles under the trees in the park at La Muette with dogs given to him by his grandfather, the King of Sardinia.

Dogs, particularly terriers, bassets, and small schnauzers, are also used to catch mice in fruit and vegetable markets and in food stores. But the use of chemical pesticides and the fear that the dogs will catch leptospirosis (which is widespread among rats) have recently discouraged this use of dogs.

**Good for a thousand tasks**

Dogs have turned the wheels of the mills in Scotland and the butter churns in Wales, spits in Central Europe and the "sacred wheels" of monks of the Far East. In Holland and Denmark, German shepherds are used to detect small leaks in gas pipes, even a number of feet underground. Dogs drew off the parasites of their masters at a time when washing was infrequent and warmed the abdomens of those with bad digestion as well as the feet of the faithful in cold churches. They have kept sheep away from railroad tracks, entertained in the circus, and been used (often abused) in medical research, especially in experiments concerning rickets and diabetes. The dog even preceded man into space.

**The value of the companion dog**

The dog has made a great contribution simply in offering its own disinterested companionship and affection. How many

**33**

Performing dogs in a circus.

people have been loved by a little dog? How much warmth has such a dog brought to a bereaved family? People who no longer believed in affection have given up suicide because of a dog. The dog has brought value to the lives of the emotionally impoverished with its gift of devotion, its living presence, and its tail wagging with a love of life.

Many companion dogs popular today come from working breeds. They are the ex's, like the poodle, ex-pointing breed and water dog; the Dalmatian, ex-hunter; or the fox terrier, ex-hunter in dens and lairs. But whatever the dog, whatever breed it may belong to, large or small, purebred or mongrel, over and above its instincts for hunting and guarding, it knows how to give company, warmth, and honesty.

Almost all companion dogs are medium-sized, small, or miniature. Some breeders, in order to make the so-called toy breeds more appealing, have reduced size excessively, obtaining little dogs weighing 2½ pounds (1 kg.), which are delicate and neurotic.

From 1600 to the present, companion dogs have earned an ever-growing popularity. The kings and queens of England especially have added to their appeal. It is enough that a sovereign obtains a puppy and is seen with it in public. The press will pick up the story and suddenly the breed will become fashionable, and the breeders will be busy filling all the requests. In this way, periods of popularity arose for the collie, the poodle, the Scottish terrier, the basset, and others.

Three famous characters from the first feature-length animated cartoon in CinemaScope, *The Lady and the Tramp* (1955) by Walt Disney.

## The success of canine actors

Over the last fifty years, the movies have been an effective vehicle of propaganda for dogs. Since ancient times, dogs have shown themselves to possess the curious instincts of the actor. It is sufficient to think of the story told by the Greek author Plutarch about a poodlelike dog called Zoppico, which, two thousand years ago, performed for the emperor Vespasian. The dog-actor bit a piece of meat and chewed it, but suddenly, opening its eyes wide, it had a nervous seizure, gave a death rattle, and lay limp on the ground, as if poisoned to death. Only the applause revived it, returning liveliness to its cheerful tail.

There are poor but happy dogs that accompany street acrobats, and important dogs that are paid like divas. The most celebrated of the screen dogs are Rin Tin Tin and Lassie.

The first Rin Tin Tin was an extremely intelligent German shepherd that had served as a messenger in World War I. He had been found wounded by an American sergeant named Lee Duncan. The war was over, and Duncan took the dog back to California. His earliest training showed that this dog was an exceptionally gifted student and within a year he landed in Hollywood. He had a brilliant fourteen-year career in which he played in twenty-two extremely popular films. Producers preferred that Rin Tin Tin sign his own contracts, which he did with a paw print. When Rin Tin Tin died in 1932, United Press International sent out the following message: "The most cele-

**35**

The affection between children and dogs is spontaneous and reciprocal.

brated dog in the world has left to go to the hunting grounds in the Elysian fields.''

The original Rin Tin Tin has been followed by more than six generations of German shepherds (and the series is not finished yet), each of which has played new adventures on the screen.

### Lassie cost $5

In 1941, the spotlight fell on another canine actor, a male collie. His name was Pal, and his master could not keep him because he was too lively for his household. The person who bought him for $5 responded to an advertisement for a film test for *Lassie Come Home*. The $5 dog was chosen from among three hundred competitors. He became Lassie. The film was a big success and others followed. Lassie lived the life of a star, with an apartment, a huge salary, a contract that limited his work to seven hours per day and short weeks. Besides this, a double was to be used for dangerous sequences. When Lassie died, in order not to upset the children who loved him, the substitution of one of his offspring was not announced. As in the case of Rin Tin Tin, the movies continued for a while with other collies that more or less resembled the first fortunate Lassie.

Canine stars, both past and present, have also been created by animated cartoons. Among the most famous are the Disney creations Pluto, Tramp, and the fabulous Dalmatians in *One Hundred and One Dalmatians*, as well as Charles Schulz's Snoopy.

## A quick look at canine psychology

Of all domestic animals, the dog is the one that adapted most easily to living with man, becoming used to his presence and learning to obey him. If a reciprocal understanding and affection have grown up between man and dog, it is because the domestication of the dog took place through an agreement on work and the division of food and lodging. This resulted in an affectionate and intelligent cooperation and the integration of the dog into human society. If the dog cannot live without man, human life would also be poorer without the dog.

What kind of memory does the dog have? Psychologists agree that the ability of the dog to "recall" is of short duration, possibly only a few hours. But the dog's associative memory is surprising. The dog probably never asks itself where its master is at any given moment, but let it hear the sound of its master's car and instantly the memory of its master will jump into its mind.

The dog has chosen human society as its "pack" and its master as the leader of the pack. With the instinct of the higher social animal, the dog has sensed the leadership of human being-master-perfect leader. The house is its territory. When the dog loses master and home, it loses its sense of equilibrium. The abandoned dog suffers, as does the dog put into a kennel. Losing its master throws the dog into turmoil, and the dog that has lost its master must find another in order to regain its balance.

Despite the fact that it possesses a powerful physique and strong sensorial powers, the dog is always a childish creature. Perhaps this is the reason for the tacit accord between dogs and children and the disarming confidence that the smallest child seems to reserve for the largest, most ferocious looking dogs. A small child might say to its parents who have just given him a powerful and threatening-looking bull mastiff: "Is he for me, or am I for him?"

The horse, the cat, the bird, and many other animals have tolerant and submissive temperaments, but they remain passive, without initiative. The dog, on the other hand, loves to play; it gets excited, pretends, participates. Even the most skittish of dogs will often put up with anything from babies: the finger in the eye, the pulling of the tail. When the baby grows up, however, and tries to impose his supremacy over the dog, the rapport changes mysteriously. But for that matter, the bitch will reject her own puppies when they are grown. One explanation for this behavior may be that babies and puppies have more potassium and magnesium in their bodies than do adults and thus have a particularly attractive or pleasing odor which inspires the dog's attention and indulgence.

One of the most obvious sentiments in the psyche of the dog, however, is jealousy. This reaction may appear when a baby is born into a house where a dog has lived and been petted for some time. If the animal seems to suffer from a sense of rivalry, be sure to control its reactions and its meetings with the newcomer, and be careful not to leave them alone in the same room. Don't send the dog away but continue to treat it with the same affection as before, until it can approach the infant. When the baby grows up and begins to walk, usually the greatest understanding will develop between the two.

Babies, however, must understand that a dog is not a toy, but a living being. It must, therefore, not disturb the dog when it is eating or sleeping, must not strangle the dog with too much affection, must not share its food with the dog, or allow it to lick him in the face. Fortunately, the dog is very patient. With an old dog, set in its ways, and probably not eager for new and lively friends, it is necessary to be a bit more careful.

### How dogs "talk" to each other

Dogs play together, fight with each other, and sometimes ignore each other completely. When they meet, they have a whole ritual of pricking up their ears, wagging their tails, sniffing, and barking. Dogs that have a high proportion of wolf blood are less likely to fight among themselves but are always ready to attack others, especially those of predominantly jackal type, like the Basenji.

We must be careful not to judge the behavior of the dog according to a human model. This would be no more sensible than comparing the behavior of a dog with that of a bird. Each has the intelligence and instincts of its own species. There is between the intelligence of animals and of humans an unbridgeable abyss based on the inability of animals to think conceptually and logically, and above all on their lack of language, which allows people to express themselves.

But even dogs "speak." They express themselves in a code made up of a complex of signs, perceptions, and odors that allows them to understand each other. Thus, lowered ears denote preoccupation and fear; pricked ears mean attention; ears held forward, alarm; a raised and wagging tail, joy and security; a set, rigid tail, disquiet; a lowered tail, insecurity; a tail between the legs, fear; and lips raised in a snarl, intimidation.

The dog that offers its paw is immature or insecure, unless it is simply obeying a command. The dog that lies on its back is passive and surrenders to a greater authority or it is wise and is asking for an alliance.

As has been said before, the dog, like the wolf, has lived in a pack and recognizes a hierarchic order; therefore, it submits to its master as a leader. If, however, it no longer esteems its master because of unjust treatment, it will stop recognizing his superiority.

The cat does not obey human beings and will not allow itself to be trained. This is because it has never lived in a pack. From primordial times, it has led an isolated existence. Thus, it does not recognize anyone, cat nor human, as its leader. Its mentality is opposite to that of the dog.

### Defense of territory

Many living beings try to be masters of a territory that they hold as their exclusive domain. Wild animals delineate their territory by scratching against trees, marking the bark, and leaving their scent at strategic points. Wolves circumscribe their territory, marking it with urine to proclaim their possession. This rit-

Two typical kinds of canine behavior.
*Above:* A sled dog submits to one of its pack mates.
*Below:* Manifestation of aggressiveness.

For a dog, urinating also serves to mark the boundaries of its territory.

ual has been assimilated by the dog. When walked in the street to perform a physiological function, but it intends also to leave along its path its odoriferous visiting card, urinating frequently, almost always in the same places, leaving a message and a warning to others of its species.

Having established its territory, the dog will defend it; and having made the territory of its master its own, it will defend that too with the same passion. If a dog is chained up, one should never invade the area to which it is limited. Likewise, if a dog is in a kennel, one should never approach it, but should pass by it calmly and at a distance.

Before lying down to sleep, the dog will turn around several times. This, too, is a ritual action that dates back to ancient wild dogs, which trod down the grass and leaves both to mat them into a bed and to delineate the dogs' place.

### The need for play
Among all animals, the dog plays the most, both as a puppy and as an adult. It is descended from a predatory species, and it is precisely the predatory animals that can allow themselves the luxury of playing, because they do not fear the attack of other animals. Herbivores and basically nonaggressive species must always remain alert and thus cannot permit themselves to be distracted by play. One may see a lion playing, not a gazelle.

The dog, however, needs to play. Lack of play may cause

**40**

behavioral disturbances and may negatively affect its hunting and fighting ability and even its mating.

In bad weather when the dog cannot go out, it nonetheless needs diversion and exercise. Besides its necessary walks, it needs to still play indoors. Be careful to select the proper toys for the dog: not so small that it may swallow them and not pointed so that it might injure itself. The ideal toy is made of hard, solid rubber in the shape of a bone, a ball, or a stick. Children's rubber balls should be avoided because eventually the dog will bite off some bits which it will swallow, causing intestinal difficulties. A good outdoor toy is an apple, since its pulp cleans the dog's teeth.

### The norms of civilized life

The dog must be trained. Training signifies teaching it all the norms of a good civilized life among people. That is, not to soil the house, to bark only when the situation demands it, to get used to a leash, to remain alone for several hours, not to jump on or growl at visitors, to stay off the furniture, and to obey commands. In the course of training, one must remember that the basis of a successful education is repetition.

Two elements must act as the mainspring to memory for the training of a young dog: reward and punishment. The first may consist of a caress, an affectionate word, or even a biscuit. The punishment may be a reproof delivered in a severe tone of voice or a smack on the backside with a rolled-up newspaper.

**41**

But the fundamental rule for training a dog is that the punishment must be given immediately after (or shortly after) the mistake takes place. One should never punish a dog a long time after the misdeed because it will not understand the reason for the punishment and will begin to fear its master's hand.

The dog is glad to obey. If, in principle, it should obey, then it wants to and shows itself glad to execute its master's commands. It is true that some dogs have difficult and recalcitrant temperaments, but this is rather rare.

Dogs get along well with humans, but they are not always in tune with other animals. There are dogs that are mordant from puppyhood and have an aversion to horses, geese, and spring-loaded toys. It is, therefore, imperative to train the dog early, putting it in contact immediately with other animals, grasping it by the skin of the neck and scolding it the moment it acts menacingly and then caressing it until it quiets down. To convince a grown dog to desist from aggression is more difficult because its character is already developed.

If all dogs were well trained, dog owners would not have to undergo so many prohibitions. The presence of a dog is looked upon askance in stores or in the houses of friends. Very often, the fault is that of the master who did not teach it the right manners. In England, dogs are generally well trained. Certain English clubs allow dogs but not children, often the most undisciplined of animals.

Training must begin the very moment the dog enters the house, keeping in mind that only after three months of age will it begin to understand that the smack it receives with a rolled-up newspaper is punishment for soiling in the house instead of using the street. It is necessary to set up civilized behavior by taking the dog out right after it eats.

Once the dog has assimilated the most elementary training, it will not forget its lessons and will put the training into practice all its life. Naturally, there are puppies that possess innate good manners and are immediately receptive to training, and others from which one can get obedience only after trying and insisting patiently for a long time.

**Two kinds of behavior**

Dogs exhibit two kinds of behavior. The first is genetically inherited, like burying a bone to satisfy a future hunger. The other is learned, as when a dog avoids a road where it was once doused with water.

Thus the instincts for play, hunting, and aggression form a part of a dog's behavior, but they must be leavened by social interaction. Though intelligence will speed learning, it must be stimulated by rewards.

**Its guide is its sense of smell**

Its sense of smell is the most developed of the dog's senses. The dog's life is to a large extent guided and conditioned by odors: for a dog the world is composed of dozens of odoriferous trails that overlap, intersect, and change continually. In this confusion of good and bad smells, the dog can differenti-

ate perfectly odors that man cannot even notice. For example, any dog can detect the presence of a drop of blood in five liters of water and can easily pick up and differentiate the smells of the meat of the pig, cow, horse, sheep, rabbit, and so forth, even though they are very similar to one another. In the same way, the dog can easily distinguish the odors of different people, even though they may be as closely related as twins, and can follow the tracks of animals even when overlaid by foul-smelling substances. (Some experts contend that the act of wagging the tail has the practical function of spreading the dog's own olfactory signals in moments of joy.)

A tracking dog follows the trail of smells left by the individual (man or beast) it is following. If a man at a certain point begins to ride a bicycle, the dog will be able to continue following his smell without hesitation. If, however, the man unexpectedly climbs onto a cable car that lifts him several inches off the ground, even the best hound will stop, having lost the trail at the point at which the man ceased walking. This will also happen when a trail is interrupted by a body of water.

One may deduce that the isolated odor of a man will not help to guide a dog without the help of the ground and grass on which he treads. This medium serves to hold for several hours the smell of the prey, and the combination constitutes what is commonly known as ''a fresh trail.''

### The stimulus of fatty acids
Besides the admirable apparatus inside the dog's nose, the outside of the dog's nose also contributes to its sense of smell.

43

An innate, and so far inexplicable, sense of orientation allows dogs to find their way home even from great distances.

This nose tip in a healthy dog is always damp, and this damp surface absorbs the odors that float in the air and holds them on the perceptive papillae.

In man, the olfactory cells cover a total area of about 4 square centimeters; in a German shepherd this area is 150 square centimeters. Man has about 5 million olfactory cells; the basset has 125 million; the fox terrier, 150 million; the German shepherd, 200 million. This suggests that the dog's sense of smell is some forty times greater than man's, but experts contend that the difference is even greater than that.

The dog is particularly able to pick up the smell of the fatty acids of the individual it is seeking, acids that form a part of the food of a carnivore. If the dog is not fed meat, its sense of smell will be heightened, and it will more easily and enthusiastically be able to help pick up even old trails that have almost disappeared. Some hunters, therefore, have adopted the custom of leaving their dogs without food the day before the hunt. In such case, however, one runs the risk that the dog, having found the prey, will devour it.

### The dog's highly developed sense of hearing

Also highly developed is the dog's sense of hearing, which can pick up even ultrasonic vibrations. These are vibrations of the highest frequency, which the human ear cannot detect. In war and in police work, man has often had recourse to ultrasonic signals to give orders at a distance to a trained dog. An enemy, of course, is unable to hear these signals. In addition, the same sound that a man can barely hear at thirteen feet a dog can hear at more than eighty feet and can locate its source.

Also noteworthy is a dog's ability to discriminate between different sounds, even when the differences are almost imperceptible. A good example of this is the dog's ability to pick out the sound of its master's car from among all others of the same make and model.

## The dog sees the world in black and white

The dog has good vision, although some say it sees only the movement of shadows, without color. At any rate, let us say the dog sees the world in black and white. Breeders, however, have improved the vision of the dog, especially in certain breeds. It is clear that the dog sees better at night than man does.

Sheepdogs have a 180-degree field of vision and can clearly understand their masters' gestures even from a distance of hundreds of yards. Likewise, the greyhound, used to hunting by sight, has excellent vision.

## The sense of smell takes precedence over taste

The element in a dog's physiology about which we know least is its sense of taste. Taste and smell are closely connected. However, smell takes precedence over taste. This is easy to see: when one gives a dog a morsel of food, the dog first smells it and then takes it in its mouth. In fact, the dog does not "taste" it, but swallows it without chewing. To teach a dog not to take food from strangers, it is sufficient to have a friend not known to the dog give it a piece of bread in which are wrapped a couple of hot chilies: they will serve as ample lesson to the dog. Likewise, for training a dog accustomed to robbing eggs from the hen house, putting a hot hard-boiled egg in its mouth should dissuade it from this practice in the future.

If a dog eats dirt, pebbles, or manure, it is an indication that its instincts are encouraging it to take in vitamins and mineral salts that are in insufficient supply in its body. In such cases, it is often wise to administer the missing elements under veterinary supervision.

## The dog's mysterious senses

As for the dog's sense of touch and external sensitivities, we know that it can perceive caresses and blows. The tactile, temperature, and pain sensations must be collected in the skin and the mucous membranes, but our understanding of these tactile sensations remains rudimentary, bristling with secrets. We know that the dog feels even a light touch on its coat, because the hair, attached to erectile muscles, will straighten. We also know that when the outside temperature goes down, the hair reacts by becoming thicker. It is for this reason that Nordic dogs can sleep in the snow and wake up covered with ice without discomfort. We know that rocks, sharp pebbles, and bits of coal will injure a dog's plantar cushions. But we have much to learn about the exact role of the vibrissae (whiskers similar to a cat's) and the modifications of the hair and the skin.

Puppies suckling. For dogs, the period of nursing lasts about a month.

Another enigma that has yet to be resolved is that of the faculty which permits a dog far from home to return there even after weeks of physical and mental hardship. This could be explained if the dog merely had to retrace streets with which it was already familiar, but its ability to return home from places hundreds of miles away, where it has never been before, remains a mystery of science.

### Parental care of the puppies
The male dog does not seem to have paternal instincts. Accustomed for centuries to count on the assistance of human beings, it has little by little lost its sense of familial obligation. The bitch, however, is full of tenderness, and for the entire time that she has the puppies, she will defend them, clean them, nurse them, and educate them until they are able to live on their own. In the end, however, even the mother is indifferent to her young once they are grown.

The male dog does feel a certain benevolence for the puppies. He respects them, is unlikely to attack them, and will even protect them from external attack.

### Deciding to buy a dog
The acquisition of a dog should be considered seriously. Often, the desire to have a dog stems from a passing infatuation, from snobbism, from the ambition to win prizes at dog shows, or from a longing for affection by people seeking in an animal object a surrogate for something lacking in their human

relationships. What is worse, many times, people buy dogs to please their small children. But the dog is not a mechanical toy, or a pair of shoes that one can take back because they are too tight. In deciding to buy a dog, people all too often picture the pleasure that a lovable puppy will bring to their homes and almost never the sacrifice and worry that it may cause. Then, they soon tire of the dog, and with the same ease with which they bought it, they give it away or abandon it. And thus the unpleasant relationship is ended.

Fortunately, there are also people who are able to institute solid, friendly relationships with their dogs, reciprocal and fair, satisfying and serene. There are those who, having bought a dog, hold on to it and love it for all its life, taking into account its hygienic needs, its susceptibility to illness, the fact that it is sensitive but cannot reason like a person, its need for preventive veterinary care (vaccinations, etc.), licensing, and appurtenances (collar, leash, muzzle, bed). The acquisition should thus be a decision taken after much thought by all the members of the family into which the dog will be brought, and a purely emotional choice should be avoided.

This may sound a bit pessimistic, but it is better to recognize a poorly rooted enthusiasm immediately than to become party to wishful thinking and unforeseen failures. Too often people tire of a puppy after a few days because it dirties the rug or chews on the legs of chairs. One should remember that puppies are likely to soil carpets and chew on shoes and furniture for several months. Only those who know how to train a dog

**47**

patiently can make this difficult period run smoothly and can quickly become the masters of obedient, intelligent, affectionate dogs that are without complexes and that can bring them much joy.

## The difficulty of selecting a puppy

Despite his personal preferences, the would-be dog owner should consider carefully the practical adaptability of the dog to a particular environment or to the company of certain people. Thus, a boxer would not be the ideal companion for an elderly woman; a dachshund would not be the right dog to defend one's property against robbers; and an Eskimo would suffer in a warm climate. There are small, medium-sized, and large dogs. The Irish greyhound standing on its back legs is taller than a man; the St. Bernard is one of the heaviest dogs; the Chihuahua, one of the smallest and most fragile. There are smooth-coated dogs, wirehaireds, long-haireds; dogs that need a lot of exercise and others that are content with short walks; dogs that prefer the heat, others that thrive in cold weather; quiet dogs and lively dogs; silent dogs and barking dogs. All these characteristics should influence one's selection of a puppy as much as one's aesthetic preferences.

Before deciding on a hunting dog, for example, one should take into account the fact that even if it is destined to be an apartment dog, it needs long daily walks and must run free twice a week so that it does not become fat and lazy and lose its natural verve. Among hunting dogs that are better adapted to home life are the cocker and the basset. Also well adapted to apartments, terraces, and traveling are all the terriers, the poodle, and the dachshund. Large dogs, on the other hand, like the German shepherd, the boxer, the Belgian shepherd, and the Airedale, require, besides daily walks, the space of a patio or a small yard.

The following is a brief list, organized by size, of dogs that are easy to find or import all over the world.

*Small dogs*: affenpinscher, dachshund, Bolognese, poodle, pug, Chihuahua, Welsh corgi, Dandie Dinmont, fox terrier, Belgian griffon, Yorkshire, Maltese, Pekingese, small Italian greyhound, pinscher, miniature schnauzer, Sealyham terrier, Skye terrier, Scottish terrier, spitz.

*Medium-sized dogs*: medium poodle, basset hound, beagle, Bedlington, bulldog, bullterrier, chow chow, Cyrenaico dell'Etna, cocker spaniel, spaniel, griffon, Kerry blue, medium schnauzer, hound, Irish terrier.

*Large dogs*: Airedale, great Dane, bloodhound, boxer, all the pointing breeds, Dalmatian, Doberman, golden retriever, great Swiss mountain dog, Labrador, Afghan, Saluki, Belgian shepherd, Bergamasco, Maremmano-Abruzzese, collie, German shepherd, pointer, riesenschnauzer, Rottweiler, St. Bernard, setter, Spinone.

## The puppy awaits a master

Puppies may be bought when they are two or three months old. Bitches are normally more affectionate, but they go into heat every six months, for which reason a male dog is probably

Children looking at puppies in a pet-store window.

Mongrels in a municipal pound.

preferable if one plans to have only one dog in the house. This is, however, a subjective decision.

One may also buy an older puppy, one of six to eight months of age, which will already have had its vaccinations. Both puppies and young dogs coming from a breeding kennel are just waiting for a master to love, and there should be no problem integrating them into their new lives.

Buying a dog is easy. They are sold by breeders (whom one can meet at dog shows), by specialized stores, by private individuals, and even by street vendors. One can also get a dog free from a dog refuge or pound. There is no law that obliges one to have a dog, but there are laws (often forgotten or too lightly enforced) that forbid their maltreatment.

Purebred or mongrel, titled or less royally born, the dog comes into the world to be a loyal companion and to give affection, and to be, in its turn, loved, protected, and included. It does not expect its master to equate differences of moral worth with physical beauty or perfection of line.

The mongrel is often lovable, intelligent, mild-mannered, hardy, and unpretentious. But only good luck will gain it the protection of a master. The majority of these poor animals ends up pitifully on the streets, in the gas chambers, used for vivisection in clinics, or, in the best of cases, unwelcome inmates of kennels or pounds.

**Pedigree, guarantee of purity**
Pedigree is a term meaning genealogical tree. It is used to in-

dicate the complete list of paternal and maternal antecedents of a purebred animal, whether horse or dog. Today, it has the same meaning even in botany.

The pedigree thus serves to identify the dog. By looking at its name, the breeder will know the dog's blood lines, and the owner will at the same time have a guarantee that he has a purebred dog.

All dogs registered by various kennel clubs are identified with the name of the breeder from whom they came (like a last name) and by an individual name.

The name becomes part of the personality of the dog. It is, therefore, necessary to train the puppy to obey immediately when its name is called, without waiting until it is more mature. Although purebred dogs may come from their breeders with rather complicated names, in the home they should be called by simple private names of one or two syllables which are easier for them to recognize.

The puppy should learn right away that it has a name, and that when it hears that name, it should pay attention. Training should begin by connecting the puppy's name with little enjoyable events that its sound will remind the puppy of treats, games, walks, and food. Thus, at the beginning, one should never call the puppy by name when one is going to punish it.

### The standard is the ideal model

For each breed, organizations of fanciers have established an ideal model. This ideal model is called the breed's standard, and giving weight, height, color, coat, the type is described in the most detailed manner.

The standard must first be perfected by breeders of a particular breed. Such breeders, as we have pointed out, develop and stabilize the various physical characteristics of the dog as well as qualities that relate to its duties or uses. If in subsequent years, the club of the various breeders considers it opportune, the breeders may institute variations in the standard, taking into account new exigencies and new aesthetic orientations of the breed.

The principal job of dog shows is to verify the continuation of the breed introduced by the breeders and to confer a valuation on the individual dogs (up to the title of champion) that will continue the reproduction of the breed. Genealogical books, shows, and field trials are all used by kennel clubs to improve the breeding of dogs, regulate their use, and improve their commercial value.

### Distemper, killer of puppies

The dog is basically a healthy animal. The most vulnerable period of its life is infancy, although it also needs special attention in its old age. The three illnesses that can kill a young dog are distemper, leptospirosis, and infectious hepatitis. In order to protect the dog against these mortal diseases, as soon as the puppy is weaned and thus loses the natural defenses that the mother transmits through her milk, its owner should take it to a veterinarian for a three-way vaccination.

Distemper is caused by a virus, similar to human influenza, that was brought from Asia in the 1700's. (Humans cannot catch distemper.) Besides the dog, animals that are subject to this disease include the wolf, the hyena, the fox, the lion, the tiger, the lynx, the bison, the ermine, and the weasel.

The virus may be contracted via either the digestive or the respiratory tracts. It remains in incubation for several days and then spreads through the entire organism, localizing itself in the digestive, respiratory, and nervous systems. The symptoms are tremors, listlessness, red eyes, coughing, and a very high temperature. Hopefully the owner will have immunized the dog before things reach this point.

### The danger of leptospirosis
Leptospirosis has been known since 1886. The bacteria have the form of springlike spirals and from this derives the disease's strange name. The infection can be transmitted by mice and by their urine (Leptospirosis icterohemorrhagia) or in pools of water. Ticks may also be carriers. Particularly susceptible are hunting dogs or dogs that live in the country. With this disease too, one will notice a general debilitation, excessive thirst, vomiting, and high fever. Vaccination should be given in the first months of the puppy's life.

### The third illness: hepatitis
The third serious infectious illness to which dogs are prone is infectious hepatitis. This disease attacks only dogs and foxes, with a preference for those individuals under one year of age. An infected dog carries the virus in its saliva, its urine, its feces, and its tears, and the contagion can thus easily be spread to any dog it is accustomed to sniffing on any street corner. The infection can also be spread by chronically ill dogs and by so-called healthy carriers, dogs who have recovered but still may carry the virus, which are nonetheless dangerous.

The hepatitis virus localizes in the liver and causes abdominal pain, yellowish diarrhea, convulsions, and fever. The disease can be avoided by a shot of antihepatitis serum when the puppy is two months old.

### Antirabies vaccination
Distemper, hepatitis, and leptospirosis are diseases that attack dogs but not people; the latter has been known in rare instances to infect humans. People are therefore more concerned about rabies, a disease that besides attacking dogs and other mammals may also attack man. Rabies is transmitted through bites, and for this reason it mainly affects carnivores that are used to biting in self-defense. However, it may also infect horses, cows, and swine.

After an incubation of several weeks, the rabies virus travels through the bloodstream to the brain, where it produces cellular degeneration. Rabies is also called hydrophobia (fear of water) because, among other things, the paralysis of the tongue caused by the disease makes it impossible for the animal to drink.

In many countries vaccinating dogs against rabies is mandatory. It is a good idea not to ignore this communal ordinance, especially if your dog frequents areas infested with foxes, which are great carriers of rabies. In countries such as the United States, England, Sweden, and Denmark, rabies has been nearly totally eradicated; therefore, dogs coming from other countries are subject to a six-month quarantine.

## Echinococcosis and tuberculosis

Another disease that can be transmitted from dog to man is echinococcosis. This is a larval infestation of the *Echinococcus* tapeworm. Human beings can become infested by drinking water, eating meat of dubious origins, or being licked on the face by a dog whose diet has not been properly controlled.

Dogs may also be subject to tubercular infection. If the dog's master has tuberculosis, the dog may catch it from him via airborne germs or its food. The tuberculosis bacillus can remain alive for four months in frozen meat, a month in spoiled meat, three months in dried foods, a month in salted or smoked foods (prosciutto and cheese), a month in butter, a minute at 194° F (90° C.), and several hours in sunlight. Since the bacteria are the same that affect man, the dog can also be cured with streptomycin.

In addition to having his animal vaccinated, the owner of a dog, whether puppy or adult, should always observe the strictest rules of hygiene, keeping the dog free of fleas and ticks, avoiding contagion from sick animals, and seeing to it that the dog is kept clean, especially during the summer.

## First aid

The vaccinations necessary to protect the dog from contracting and usually dying of distemper, hepatitis, and leptospirosis must be given by a veterinarian in the manner and at the time he considers best. Beyond this, however, it is a good idea for the dog owner to have some idea of the first aid necessary to alleviate more minor maladies that may affect his animal.

First, one should have in the house a first-aid kit equipped with all the materials necessary to cope with emergencies. It should contain a sterile plastic syringe with needle, disinfectants such as alcohol and peroxide, antibiotic powder, absorbent cotton and hemostatic cotton, gauze, a pair of blunt scissors, tweezers, an enema bag, eyewash, cotton swabs for cleaning the dog's ears, and, finally, a tourniquet and a thermometer.

In case of wounds, whether superficial, deep, or slightly torn, one must always cut away the hair around the wound, wash the wound with running water, disinfect it, and bandage it. If the wound is large, it may be necessary to have it stitched by a veterinarian. In cases of heavy loss of blood, it is necessary to stop the flow with the tourniquet applied above the wound.

If an injured dog has been frightened by the incident in

A puppy with broken leg that has been treated.

which it was hurt, it may have a tendency to bite, in which case the owner must muzzle it or at any rate keep its mouth closed with some kind of ligature. The injured dog should be moved as little as possible and not given anything to eat or drink before it is examined by the veterinarian.

### Medicine and injections

A dog's normal temperature is about 101.5° F. (38.5° C.). It should be measured with a normal rectal thermometer, being careful to hold the dog still.

The owner must know how to administer medicine to his dog and how to give it an intramuscular injection. Liquid medicine should be introduced into the sides of the mouth into the pouch formed by the lips with a spoon or a plastic syringe while the animal's head is held high. A capsule, on the other hand, should be placed firmly at the back of the mouth. If the dog is very reluctant to accept it, solid medicine may be administered wrapped in a bit of meat. In all cases, be watchful that the dog does not spit out the pill.

In order that salves may reach the depth of the skin efficiently, they must be spread and massaged into pre-clipped areas. To prevent the dog from licking the area and swallowing the salve, the area should be covered with gauze, and protected by a woolen sock when feasible. In extreme cases, it may be necessary to muzzle the dog.

The easiest area into which to give an intramuscular injection is the flat inside of the thigh, where there is usually no hair,

Dogs need specific veterinary care. In the photo: an intramuscular injection.

while the animal is kept lying down. But it may also be given in the muscles of the rump or the chest under the skin. The skin should always be disinfected before and after the injection, and should be massaged lightly after the injection is given to help the absorption of the medicinal liquid. It takes two people to give a shot: one to hold the dog and one to give the needle.

### The danger of poison

Among the serious dangers of a dog's life is that of being poisoned. Poisons can seriously damage the digestive, circulatory, and nervous systems. Besides rat poison, common causes of poisoning are overdoses of medicine, antiparasite preparations, herbicides, spoiled food, and household cleaning agents. Naturally, this list also includes intentionally administered poisons.

The dog will tend to vomit after ingesting a toxic substance. If it does not do so spontaneously, its owner must provoke vomiting by placing two teaspoons of salt on the back of its tongue or mix three to four tablespoons of activated charcoal in a glass of water and force it down the dog's throat. This should be followed by a visit to the veterinarian.

Hunting dogs may be bitten by snakes. One should be able to tell when this has happened by the reaction of the dog, which will rub and scrape the bitten area on the ground, most often the muzzle or the limbs. One should not waste time disinfecting the wound, but should immediately inject the dog with snake-bite serum, which the hunter should always carry with him (also for himself). If possible, one should cut the wound so that it bleeds freely and apply a tourniquet above it.

## The same illnesses as man
One illness frequent in dogs is tumor, either malignant or benign. The earlier a tumor is diagnosed, the easier will be the treatment, whether surgical or radiological. Tumors attack dogs, cats, and people, but are rare in ruminants and equine animals. It is possible that diet plays an important role.

The dog is subject to a variety of metabolic diseases that also attack people: rickets, diabetes, gout, and bone disease.

## The struggle against external parasites
A parasite is an organism that lives in or on another organism on which it nourishes itself, causing damage to its host while offering nothing in return. Dogs are often tormented by both internal and external parasites. The external parasites to which a dog is prone are fleas, lice, ticks, and mange mites; the internal parasites that attack dogs are so-called worms.

Everyone is familiar with fleas. They are jumping insects that suck blood, hop to a new site, prick, and suck again. The canine flea is *Pulex serraticeps* and will not infest man so long as it has a dog at its disposal. If it does not, however, it will not disdain human blood, although people are more likely to be bothered by *Pulex irritans*. Each flea can produce five hundred eggs and can remain without nourishment for months. The only true remedy is to wash the animal frequently and thoroughly, including its head, and to sprinkle it with a flea powder recommended by a veterinarian that will destroy both insects and larvae. This disinfection must also extend to all places frequented by the dog, such as the kennel, rugs, furnishings, and any corners in which the dog tends to linger. In severe cases call an exterminator.

Lice are less common than fleas and are especially prone to infest dogs kept in very dirty places. In this case, too, the dog should be treated with the appropriate powder. In particularly resistant cases, it may be necessary to shave the dog.

Ticks are a fairly common parasite among dogs, especially among country dogs that frequent areas inhabited by sheep. The tick is a very visible insect, looking somewhat like a small watermelon seed. It uses the beak on its little head to attach itself to an animal's skin in order to suck blood. Since the tick does not jump, but rather stays in one place, it is easy to remove. One need merely douse it with a couple of drops of gasoline or heavily salted water and remove it gently with a tweezers, being careful not to break the insect and thus release its eggs. When removed, the tick should immediately be burned or immersed in gasoline.

## Parasites that attack the ears
The worst of the external parasites to which the dog is subject

is the scabies mite, which causes sarcoptic mange. The skin becomes covered with red markings that develop into blisters. It is necessary to shave the animal and treat it with veterinarian-prescribed medicated baths and salves. Another type of mange attacks the dog's ears. This is demodectic mange. The dog will react by shaking its head, scratching, and complaining. One should take the dog to the veterinarian immediately in order to avoid irreversible otitis.

Besides these animal parasites, there is a vegetable parasite that should not be taken lightly: the fungus called ringworm. Ringworm attacks the animal's skin and destroys it, leaving it covered with exudation. The affected area should be shaved and washed with sulfur soap. Otitis can also be caused by ringworm, and for this reason, a veterinarian should be consulted.

### Various types of worms

Worms are the most common type of internal parasites in dogs. There are several kinds of worms and they can cause intestinal occlusions, inflammations, organic breakdown or decay, as well as lack of appetite (or insatiable appetite in the case of tapeworm), vomiting, diarrhea, epilepticlike attacks, and general itching. They are disastrous.

The presence of worms can be ascertained by examining the dog's stool. In case of doubt, a laboratory examination should be done by a veterinarian. To avoid infestations of worms, be careful that the dog does not come in contact with the feces of other animals, drink dirty water, eat dirt, or eat spoiled food. The dog's dish and water bowl should be washed daily with hot water and detergent. Despite all these precautions, however, dogs get worms. Many dog owners worm their dogs periodically whether or not they show symptoms of infestation. There are, however, different kinds of worms and therefore different kinds of worming medicines. There is an old medical saying to the effect that one cannot kill a tiger with a fishhook. In the same way, one cannot eliminate taenia with ascarid medicine. A veterinarian should prescribe the proper treatment.

### Heat and mating

The ideal age for the first mating of a male dog is a year and a half, when its structure is completely developed. For the female, it is advisable to wait until the second or third heat so that the uterus will have reached adult proportions.

The bitch goes into heat approximately every six months, but for city dogs, the period between heats may be reduced to five months. Sexual stimulus is always present in male dogs and is aroused by the secretions emitted by the female when she is in heat. The best time to achieve a fertile mating is toward the end of the second week when the bitch shows herself receptive to the approaches of the male, since this is the time when ovulation will be complete. For certainty, the mating should be repeated after twenty-four to forty-eight hours.

The attraction between the sexes is caused by sexual hormones produced respectively in the testicles and the ovaries. Fertility weakens with age and is completely lost first by the bitch and then the dog.

It is better to arrange matings so that puppies are born at the beginning of spring. They can thus take advantage of the good weather for development and healthy growth. Necessary walks and early training will also benefit from sunny days.

### Aborting the pregnancy

The most certain way to prevent mating is to keep male and female dogs apart during the entire period of estrus. There are so-called repellents on the market which applied to the outside genital areas of the bitch do not attract or at least weaken the instincts of the male; however, these products are not always sufficiently effective. Panties will avoid both vaginal leakage and coitus.

From the third to the tenth day after an unwanted mating it may be possible for a veterinarian to abort the pregnancy by administering hormones that stimulate the detachment of the fertilized egg. The bitch can also be spayed. This is accomplished by a veterinary procedure, today rather common, which requires the bitch to be totally anesthetized. Obviously, in this case, the bitch will be permanently infertile.

The gestation period for bitches is sixty to sixty-five days. Pregnancies will generally produce at least four to six puppies, or up to a maximum of twelve, depending on the breed.

### The moment of birth

The symptoms that signal the approach of the birth of the puppies are uneasiness on the part of the bitch, her loss of appetite, a lowering of her temperature to 98° F. (37° C.), and secretion from her breasts of a yellowish serum. Often the pregnant bitch will collect rags to make herself a sort of nest. It can be helpful to provide her with a basket or box in which to have her puppies, but normally it is wisest to let her do what she wants. The important thing is that at the chosen spot one places newspapers and a clean towel that can be replaced as it gets soiled. It is wise for you to be on hand as the time of whelping approaches.

At the moment of birth, the bitch will groan under the thrust of the labor pains. She will lie on her side and contort herself as the contractions become stronger and finally will expel the fetus. In normal births (the majority) the mother will extract the puppies from the natal sacks, sever the umbilical cord, clean the mucus out of the puppies' nostrils, and lick them both to stimulate them and to clean them. If she does not do so immediately you must open the sack, cleanse the mouth and nostrils, and stimulate breathing.

Prelude to mating between a miniature pinscher and a mongrel bitch. The differences in breed and size do not constitute obstacles.

Although adult dogs vary considerably in weight (a toy poodle weighs a little over 3 pounds (1½ kg.); a Great Dane weighs 155 pounds (70 kg.), the difference in the weights of newborn pups of different breeds is negligible.

Puppies will arrive at irregular intervals, anywhere from a few minutes to an hour. A novice breeder may well become anxious with a delay, but there is no need for alarm *unless* the bitch is obviously straining without result. In such cases, call the veterinarian. However, this is unusual except in the case of the toy breeds. Whelping may well take as long as eight or more hours. It is quite normal for the bitch to eat the afterbirth.

**The growth of the puppy**
Check the puppies frequently during the first twenty-four hours after whelping. Make certain they are warm; the room temperature must not fall below 75° F. Be sure that each puppy is nursing and check each one carefully for any physical defects. Other than watchful supervision your job is simple in the first ten days. Most dams are good mothers.

For the first two weeks the puppies' eyes and ears are closed but their sense of touch is very keen. As soon as the dam steps into the pen even a pup a few days old will instantly squirm its way over to her and fight for the best nursing station. Motor development starts in the third week, the eyes and ears are open, and the puppies are beginning to walk almost steadily. They are daily learning the pleasure of being held by a

*Below and right:* Despite having the dentition of a carnivore, a dog can live well and happily on a steady diet of packaged dog food.

human, will respond to sounds, and are barking and scrapping with their littermates.

The teeth come in when the pup is about two weeks old and the dam will start weaning them. She may continue to nurse them occasionally for close to a month, but the nursings will diminish and lessons in lapping from a bowl should begin at three weeks. By one month the puppies should be on three meals a day from a bowl and are ready to leave for new homes at eight weeks.

### Controlling the diet
An apartment dog that uses little energy should eat less than a dog that lives outside and runs around all day. In order to have a healthy, hardy dog, it is necessary to check its diet carefully, both for quality and quantity. There is no easy rule of thumb to judge how much to feed a dog. The best test is to watch the dog and its eating habits. If it consumes what you feel is a correct amount and still is obviously restless and unhappy, you may not be giving enough; if, however, it seems to be content, you are probably giving the right amount. Diets and amounts are based on the individual dog and the life it leads. When you find the diet your dog likes and thrives on, stick to it day after day; the dog does not need or really want variety. The correct diet supplies vitamins, fats, proteins, minerals, and carbohydrates in proper amounts. Be guided by your veterinarian and the way your dog responds.

If one meal is given, feeding in the morning is preferred. Feeding at night can result in the dog going to bed on too full a stomach. If two feedings are given, simply divide the day's rations between the two meals.

Water must always be available and the water dish must be kept clean. In extremely hot weather consult your veterinarian about the use of salt tablets in the water bowl.

If constipation is a regular problem add leafy vegetables to the dog's diet. Never experiment with laxatives that are prescribed for humans; some may be lethal for animals. For occasional constipation give one teaspoon of milk of magnesia for every ten pounds of body weight.

A dog sick for other reasons may require a special diet. Let your veterinarian determine what this should be.

**Protection from the cold**

No dog is able to endure the cold of a northern winter except sheepdogs, the St. Bernard, the chow chow, and the Siberian husky. This last breed is likely to become sickly if forced to live in the warmth of a house. There is the famous story of Boss, a husky that because of its courage and strength was used for ten years as head of the pack. Boss was then adopted by a Frenchwoman; and this venerable king of the ice then lived indoors and died two years later as a result of having injudiciously gone out in the rain one night.

The majority of companion dogs are permitted to sleep in-

A dog in the posture indicating an invitation to play in front of its rustic little house.

doors. The dog can be happy in any corner, in a hall, in the kitchen, even in a closet. All it needs is a little pad or an old blanket to lie on. Owners of large dogs, on the other hand, usually prefer their dogs to sleep outside on a terrace or in the yard.

The place in which one locates an outside kennel should be sheltered from the damp and the wind. The house should be in proportion to the size of its occupant, taking into account that the dog should be able to stand up and turn around comfortably inside. The classic kennel is made of wood in the shape of a little house with a roof sloping to the sides, possibly painted inside and out to protect the structure from the corrosive action of bad weather and to avoid the formation of parasite nests. It is also a good idea for the kennel to come apart easily to allow for thorough periodic cleaning.

The kennel should have only one opening, which should be large enough to allow the dog to enter and leave. During winter the opening should be covered with an old curtain or coverlet. This is the best way to protect the dog from rheumatism. Furthermore, the dog should sleep a few inches above the ground, and the roof should be protected by shingles or metal. The inside bed should consist of a good mattress stuffed with rags or wood shavings and should be aired weekly.

If the dog is subject to colds or leg problems, it should be allowed to sleep inside the house during the winter.

Two phases of grooming.

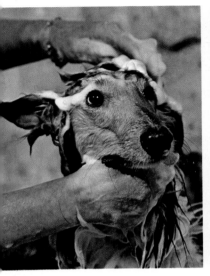

### Bathing the dog

There is no rule as to how often a dog should be bathed. In general, it should be brushed regularly and its coat checked for ticks and fleas, and it should be bathed about once a month. Naturally, it will also have to be bathed if it gets particularly dirty.

The water should be tepid. One should begin washing the dog from the tail, working toward its head, wetting it first and then lathering. It is a good idea to put cotton in the dog's ears and be careful not to get soapsuds in its eyes.

After a bath, the dog should be allowed to run around in a dry place indoors, not outside, until it is thoroughly dry.

Pregnant bitches and puppies under twelve weeks old should not be bathed unless absolutely necessary.

### Keeping the dog's coat clean

Dogs whose standard does not prescribe clipping should not be trimmed. The sun may burn the dog's skin, and insects will have a field day sucking the dog's blood. There are various tools for keeping the dog's coat clean: combs with long or widespread teeth, brushes of various degrees of hardness, little rakes, scissors, and knives. Sleek-haired breeds should be curried with a special ridged glove or a lightweight metallic brush. Long-haired and wirehaired breeds whose standards indicate it should undergo stripping, a procedure that elimi-

nates dead hair and gives the dog the proper shape, or trimming, in which the hair is only partially cut for aesthetic reasons. Both stripping and trimming are specialized operations, but they can be learned and performed by the owner himself if he has the time and the inclination. Poodles must be clipped on a regular schedule to keep their desired appearance.

### Eyes, ears, and mouth
All breeds of dog need careful and periodic care. From time to time, a couple of drops of eyewash should be put in a dog's eyes. Every week, the ears should be cleaned with cotton swabs ever so slightly dampened with denatured alcohol.

The teeth need veterinary care. The veterinarian will remove the accumulation of tartar, which can eventually cause loss of the teeth. The nails, if not sufficiently worn down with walking, should be trimmed with the appropriate clippers, being careful not to injure the live part. Finally, the anal glands, if they are itching, must be emptied. This is a veterinary procedure.

### Duration of life
The dog passes quickly from newborn puppy to older puppy to young dog. The dog then remains for several years in the prime of its maturity. The duration of its life varies according to a number of factors: its environment, its breed, the state of its

**65**

Six puppies for as many masters.

health, hygienic conditions, exercise, and feeding. Dogs of some breeds, such as the spitz and the fox terrier, are long-lived and may live to be eighteen to twenty years old. Others, such as the boxer and the German shepherd, are old at twelve to thirteen years.

It is not really exact to say that one can multiply a dog's age by seven in order to find the human equivalent. After all, a bitch one year old is already old enough to reproduce, while a seven-year-old child is far from old enough. The following table should show a more acceptable relationship between canine and human ages. The dog's age is multiplied by the coefficient to find the "human equivalent."

One can see from this table that on the average dogs live about twelve years and usually do not exceed fifteen years of age. This is too short a time for such a worthy animal. Nature has been stingy. Just think: a parrot lives one hundred years; a canary, twenty; a bullfrog, sixteen; and a sole, fifteen.

The dog reaches its full form between three and five years of age. In this period, its physique is completely developed and its energy is at a peak. Toward seven or eight years of age, a slow decline sets in. At this age, a companion dog will seek peace and quiet, will sleep more, and in winter will prefer the corner nearest the radiator. Defense dogs and hunting dogs will no longer show the resistance and aggressiveness of their younger years.

| Dog | Coefficient | Human |
|---|---|---|
| 2 months | 7 | 14 months |
| 6 months | 10 | 5 years |
| 8 months | 12.5 | 9 years |
| 12 months | 14 | 14 years |
| 18 months | 13.3 | 20 years |
| 2 years | 12 | 24 years |
| 3 years | 10 | 30 years |
| 4 years | 9 | 36 years |
| 5 years | 8 | 40 years |
| 6 years | 7 | 42 years |
| 7 years | 7 | 49 years |
| 8 years | 7 | 56 years |
| 9 years | 7 | 63 years |
| 10 years | 6.5 | 65 years |
| 11 years | 6.5 | 71 years |
| 12 years | 6.3 | 75 years |
| 13 years | 6.2 | 80 years |
| 14 years | 6 | 84 years |
| 15 years | 5.8 | 87 years |
| 16 years | 5.6 | 89 years |

In the process of aging, the dog will almost always become deaf; it may get cataracts; and its teeth will fall out, making chewing difficult. Males may also develop trouble urinating due to enlargement of the prostate. In terms of its character, it is likely to accentuate its contrariness and become very attached to its habits.

The good health of the aging dog is very dependent on the manner in which it was maintained and cared for in its youth. If it had a lot of exercise, fresh air, and sunshine, and was kept clean, well-fed, protected from the cold, and given regular veterinary care, it will be subject to much less infirmity.

The old dog needs care. It should be left in peace, given easily digestible food (more soup, less meat), kept from getting fat, and exercised but not tired.

Its death is often serene. Sometimes because of painful and incurable illness it is necessary to have recourse to euthanasia, death caused by a painless injection administered by a veterinarian. Ending useless suffering is a painful thing to do, but it is an act of love that the good master must perform when he knows that his dear friend has no more hope. The loss of the dog will leave a void. The days without its company will be sadder. But for those who want it, the void can be filled. There is always a puppy waiting.

# WORKING DOGS

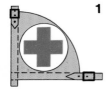

## 1 GERMAN SHEPHERD
### Deutscher Schäferhund

**Origin**   There are different theories regarding the origin of the German shepherd: that the breed was the result of crosses between the various breeds of sheepdog existing in Germany, or that it resulted from the spontaneous mating of shepherd bitches and wolves. The answer is lost in the darkness of time. However, it is known that the first German shepherds (long-haired) were presented at Hanover in 1882, and the short-haired variety was first presented in Berlin in 1889.

**Description**   Ideal height: dogs, 24 to 26 inches (60–65 cm.); bitches, 22 to 24 inches (55–60 cm.). Weight: 77 to 85 pounds (35–40 kg.). It has a sturdy, muscular, slightly elongated body with a light but solid bone structure. Its head should be in proportion to its body; forehead a little convex; strong scissors bite; ears, wide at the base, pointed, upright, and turned forward (the ears of puppies under six months may droop slightly). Eyes: almond-shaped, never protruding, dark, with a lively, intelligent expression. Its bushy tail reaches almost to its hocks and hangs down when the dog is at rest. Its front legs and shoulders are muscular; its thighs, thick and sturdy. It has round feet with very hard soles. Colors: black, iron gray, ash gray; either uniform or with regular shading of brown, yellow, or light gray. There are three varieties: rough-coated, long rough-coated, and long-haired.

**Personality**   Bold, cheerful, obedient, steady, loyal, affectionate with its master and with children, tolerant of other animals, wary of strangers, easily trained.

**Uses**   The breed came into being as a leader of flocks. Due to its intelligence and its outstanding character, it has also been used in time of war (carrying messages under fire and across mine fields), as a rescue dog (in water, in the mountains, and through fire), as a police dog (it can follow a trail several days old). But the German shepherd is unbeatable as a guard dog where it can display its fine reflexes and its lightning-quick attack. It always performs the work requested of it with good will and enthusiasm.

## 2  BELGIAN SHEEPDOG
### Groenendael

**Origin**  There have been Belgian sheepdogs for centuries, but the breed as we know it was isolated in 1891 by Professor Reul of the Belgian faculty of veterinary sciences. Professor Reul recognized three main types: long-haired, short-haired, and shaggy-haired. Later, in 1907, it was established that the long-haired variety should be black, the short-haired variety should be fawn and charcoal, and the shaggy, or rough-coated, variety should be ash gray. The Groenendael, a completely black long-haired Belgian sheepdog, was developed by the breeder Nicholas Rose, who lived in Groenendael, a few miles outside of Brussels.

**Description**  The Groenendael should have a sleek black coat somewhat thicker at the neck. Ideal height: dogs, 25 inches (63 cm.); bitches, 23 inches (58 cm.). Average weight: about 62 pounds (28 kg.). Ears: small and erect, triangular in shape. Eyes: brown, slightly almond-shaped. Legs: straight and muscular.

**Personality**  Continued selective breeding has attempted to eliminate excessive timidity from the Groenendael's personality. The majority of these dogs are endowed with intelligence and long memories. They are obedient, brave, and docile in the home.

**Uses**  The Groenendael is an outstanding herder and guard dog. It is adept as a police dog and is good with children.

---

## 3  BELGIAN TERVUREN

**Origin**  The Tervuren is one of the breeds developed in 1891 by the Belgian school of veterinary science under the direction of Professor Reul. It is an extremely close relative of the Groenendael, both physically and temperamentally, so much so in fact that a Tervuren pup can be born from the mating of two Groenendaels.

**Description**  The Tervuren differs from the Groenendael in the color of its coat, which is blackened fawn, abundantly thick and without curl. Average height: dogs, about 25 inches (63 cm.); 10% less for bitches. Weight should be about 62 pounds (28 kg.). Eyes: brown, slightly almond-shaped. Ears: triangular. Body: powerful but not heavy. Teeth: scissors bite. The Tervuren is the most robust of the Belgian sheepdogs and is therefore used by breeders to strengthen related breeds.

**Personality**  Like the Groenendael, the Tervuren is prized for its quick intelligence, its courage, and the ease with which it can be trained. It is deeply devoted to its owner and is very possessive, giving and demanding attention and affection. It should have a firm hand.

**Uses**  Originally used for guarding sheep, the breed is a fine devoted protector of its family and home.

**Note**  Belgian sheepdogs have formidable appetites. Their feeding should be watched carefully to avoid overweight.

## 4  BELGIAN MALINOIS

**Origin**  The breed was developed in 1891 by the Belgian Veterinary School, which was attempting to make some order out of all the breeds of sheepdog then known in Belgium, and by the Huyghebaert brothers. It is also known as the Malines sheepdog.

**Description**  It is the most rustic of the Belgian sheepdogs. It has a short coat of blackened fawn and a black mask. The Malinois resembles a small German shepherd. Height: under 24 inches (60 cm.). Weight: 55 to 60 pounds (24–27 kg.). Ears: upright. Eyes: brown and not protruding. Its hind legs are perfectly straight. There is another variety of Belgian sheepdog called the Laekenois that has a hard fawn-colored coat with dark markings.

**Uses**  The Malinois is a hardy dog, resistant to bad weather and adaptable to all sorts of work. It is first and foremost an excellent sheepdog, but it has also shown itself to be a fine guard dog in open areas, proving even more energetic than the German shepherd. If one wishes to use a Malinois as a guard dog, it is important to train it carefully to control its instinctive aggressiveness. Like its cousins the Groenendael and the Tervuren, the Malinois needs long walks and carefully controlled feeding to keep in shape.

## 5  BEAUCERON

**Origin**  Prior to 1889, which was the year the breed was named and its standard was set, the Beauceron was a rustic sheepdog, brave and snappish in defense of its flock. Selective breeding toward the end of the eighteenth century left it strong and resistant to bad weather, but made it gentler in its contacts with people.

**Description**  Average height: 28 inches (70 cm.). Weight: from 66 to 77 pounds (30–35 kg.). Depending on the variety, its coat may be black, gray, fawn, or reddish-black. As a rule, the tips of its ears are docked. The Beauceron is also known as "red stockings" because of the socklike red markings on its feet. It has dark, intelligent eyes, a muscular neck without dewlap, and very straight limbs. It is known almost exclusively in France.

**Personality**  It has been said of the Beauceron that it looks kindly only upon its master. However, in reality, selective breeding has produced a dog that is obedient, intelligent, and steady. In light of its aggressive ancestry, however, thorough training is advisable. The Beauceron, which is gentle with its family, will not always be so submissive with strangers, and it should most certainly have a firm master. Because it needs long walks and runs, it should have at least a yard available to it.

**Uses**  Like the Doberman, it is used as a guard in open areas.

## 6 BRIARD

**Origin** The breed has been known for some centuries (Charlemagne had Briards). However, it became popular only after the Paris dog show of 1863, in large part due to the improvement in its looks achieved by crosses with the Beauceron and the barbet.

**Description** Its hair is from 2 to 3 inches (5–7 cm.) long, giving the dog an attractive bushy coat. Admissible colors are black, gray, and fawn. Height: dogs, 24 to 27 inches (62–68 cm.); bitches, 22 to 25 inches (56–64 cm.). Average weight: 75 pounds (35 kg.). Eyes: dark, with an intelligent expression. Ears: docked round (not obligatory). Gait: elegant.

**Personality** The Briard is a peasant by birth, but it is a sensitive and obedient dog. It was used as a sentry dog during World War I because of its fine hearing. It is kind and good-natured and adaptable to living with children. It prefers to live outside.

**Uses** Some Briards have retained their ancient shepherding and guarding instincts, but others, bred as companions, are timid with strangers. In general, the Briard is a very beautiful, decorative, and good-natured dog. It has been said that "it returns tenfold any affection given to it."

## 7 SMOOTH-MUZZLED PYRENEES SHEEPDOG

**Origin** The smooth-muzzled Pyrenees sheepdog has the same ancient origin as the long-haired Pyrenees sheepdog.

**Description** The same as the long-haired Pyrenees sheepdog except, as its name implies, it has short hair on its muzzle. This does not detract from the beauty of its face. Indeed, its eyes, which are clearly visible, are brilliant and full of interest.

**Personality** Jaunty, bold, intelligent; more cheerful than its long-haired brother.

**Uses** For centuries accustomed to living day and night out in the open, it has developed a formidable resistance to cold weather and sickness. It is highly esteemed as a herd dog and a companion dog.

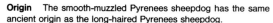

## 8 PYRENEES SHEEPDOG

**Origin** The Pyrenees sheepdog is thought to be the oldest of the French sheepdogs. The breed took shape and developed in the Pyrenees area. It was shown for the first time in 1921.

**Description** The Pyrenees sheepdog is a medium-sized dog. Height: from 16 to 20 inches (40–50 cm.). Weight: around 44 pounds (20 kg.). Its head is like that of a brown bear, with black nose, chestnut eyes, black-ringed eyelids, and upright ears. It has a lively, cheerful face. It has nervous limbs, muscular thighs, and very flat oval feet. Its long, coarse coat is thick and woolly, especially on its back. Its color may be various shades of gray, gray-silver, white, or yellow. There is a variety of Pyrenees sheepdog with short hair on its muzzle.

**Personality** Bold, audacious, cheerful, intelligent.

**Uses** The Pyrenees sheepdog has the reputation of being a dog that never falls ill. It is resistant not only to bad weather but also to illnesses such as distemper. Furthermore, it can go without food for several days, eating only grass. During the war, Pyrenees sheepdogs were used to help find the wounded. Today they are excellent sheepdogs and faithful, lively, and honest house pets.

---

## 9 PICARDY SHEEPDOG

**Origin** The Picardy sheepdog has been known since the Middle Ages and is widespread throughout northern France; however, its exact history is unknown.

**Description** The Picardy is an energetic, likable, sturdy-looking dog of medium size. It has a lively face similar to the griffon's. Height: around 24 to 26 inches (60–65 cm.). Weight: 60 to 70 pounds (27–32 kg.). It has a large head and a strong muzzle. Eyes: dark, with a merry expression. Ears: carried erect, wide at the base. Tail: curved at the end. It has muscular thighs and bony legs. Its coat is semilong, rough, and straight. Colors: all shades of gray, gray-blue, and gray-fawn.

**Personality** It is not a viciously aggressive dog, but it stands up to its enemies courageously, snarling ferociously and showing its powerful teeth.

**Uses** The Picardy is a classic sheepdog with all the qualifications of a persevering and careful herder and an excellent guard dog. It is resistant to all sorts of bad weather due to its thick coat, which no water can penetrate.

## 10 CATALAN SHEEPDOG
### Perro de pastor catalan

**Origin** The Catalan sheepdog is physically similar to the sheep-dogs of the Pyrenees. It is therefore thought that these dogs migrated to Spain along with cowherders and then later developed the specific characteristics and personality of the breed.

**Description** The height of the dog varies from 18 to 20 inches (45–50 cm); that of the bitch, from 17 to 19 inches (43–48 cm.). Weight: dogs, about 40 pounds (18 kg.); bitches, about 35 pounds (16 kg.). Muzzle: straight, with the shape of a truncated cone. Teeth: extremely strong. Eyes: expressive, amber-colored. Ears: pointed. Tail: long, short, or docked. The coat is long and wavy. Its gray-black hairs are cream-colored at the tips.

**Personality** Intelligent, obedient, active, a good worker, and easily trained. It is energetic when around other animals but gentle and companionable with people.

**Uses** The Catalan sheepdog has been outstandingly successful in various areas of activity. In herding it earns the respect of both horses and herd. It can be trained for police work and defense of property; and, finally, it is an excellent companion dog.

**Note** It likes the environment of Catalonia, with its rocky terrain, its large herds, and its people, who appreciate the dog's uncommon intelligence.

---

## 11 DUTCH SHEEPDOG

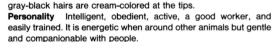

**Origin** The Dutch sheepdog was derived from the Belgian sheepdog.

**Description** Height: dogs, from 23 to 25 inches (58–63 cm); bitches, 10% less. Weight: about 66 pounds (30 kg.). Body: muscular and symmetrical. Muzzle: long. Teeth: strong and regular. Eyes: dark, slightly oblique. Ears: upright. Tail: slightly curved. There are three varieties of Dutch sheepdog: one with short hair (very widespread in Holland), one with rough hair (less common), and a long-haired variety that is very rare. Colors: yellow-red, brown with golden or silvery streaks.

**Personality** The Dutch sheepdog is obedient, docile, always alert, attached to its territory, and an enthusiastic worker. It needs little care and can withstand fatigue and bad weather.

**Uses** Almost unknown outside Holland, the Dutch sheepdog is valued there for its ability as a herder and for its quick reflexes.

**Note** Puppies with short tails and white markings are frequently born in sheepdog litters. These defects are not acceptable at dog shows.

## 12  KOMONDOR

**Origin**  Descended from Tibetan dogs, the Komondor was brought to Hungary a thousand years ago by nomadic Magyars. Its spread throughout the rest of the world began in 1920 when the breed began to be presented at dog shows.

**Description**  The Komondor is a massive dog with a proud gait. Height: 25½ inches (65 cm.) and upward. Weight: dogs, up to 125 pounds (59 kg.); bitches, 10% less. Its body is totally covered with an extraordinary felted and corded coat, which is 8 to 11 inches (20–27 cm.) long, always white. This must never be brushed or combed. The hair is divided into cords and trimmed. Eyes: dark brown. Ears: pendent and U-shaped. It has a large head and a generally massive bone structure, a hanging tail, and a very strong scissors bite.

**Personality**  Obedient and respectful of its master, but implacable against wolves and bears that would attack the flock with which it is entrusted. In a few minutes, the Komondor can get the better of even the strongest enemy.

**Uses**  Typical sheepdog for large flocks (or herds) in isolated places. It is especially alert at night. It has also been used with outstanding results as a police dog in snowy regions. Recently, breeders have softened its personality and it has become appreciated as a companion dog.

## 13  KUVASZ

**Origin**  Some authors claim that the kuvasz has been known since the age of the Huns. Others describe it as a sheepdog that accompanied the Turkish refugees and their flocks fleeing the Mongols into Hungary in 1200. Its name in Turkish means "safe-keeper." The kuvasz had its great moment of splendor in the fifteenth century in the court of King Mátyás I, who claimed to trust only his kuvasz dogs and not people. At the death of the king, the kuvasz returned to being a sheepdog throughout the medieval period.

**Description**  The kuvasz is a robust, well-proportioned dog. Height: up to 26 inches (75 cm.). Weight: around 110 pounds (50 kg.). It has a very beautiful head with a well-curved stop and a long nose, narrowing nobly toward the muzzle. Eyes: oblique, dark brown. Ears: folded and close to the head. The tail, which is carried low, is raised when the dog is excited. Coat: white or ivory. The hair is short on the head and feet, but on the body and legs it is wavy and can be as much as 4 to 6 inches (10–15 cm.) long.

**Personality**  Bold, but obedient and gentle.

**Uses**  It is outstanding as a herder and as a defender of the flock against wolves. Thanks to its beauty and gentleness, it is today also esteemed as a companion dog.

## 14  MUDI

**Origin**  The breed formed spontaneously and is only about one hundred years old. It is still not widespread.

**Description**  Height: medium, from 14 to 19 inches (35–47 cm.). Weight: from 18 to 29 pounds (8–13 kg.). Head: elongated, with a pointed nose, muscular jaw, and scissors bite. Its skull is convex with a well-marked stop. Eyes: oval, dark brown. Ears: erect, in the shape of upside-down V's. It has a deep thorax; a short, straight back; and a short or docked tail. The hair on its muzzle is short, becoming bristly toward the ears. Its coat is about 2 inches (5 cm.) long on its body. Colors: shiny black, white, or brindle.

**Personality**  Extremely vigorous and courageous, the mudi is afraid of nothing, not even wild boar, which it can overpower quickly.

**Uses**  It is noted in Hungary for the multiplicity of its uses: sheepdog (also cow herder), guard dog, hunter of wild animals, killer of mice and weasels. It is very gentle in the family and has therefore gained appreciation as a companion dog that, if the need arises, will defend both property and person.

## 15  PULI

**Origin**  The puli was brought into Hungary by Oriental nomads around the year 1000. It is very similar to the Tibetan terrier.

**Description**  The puli is the smallest of the Hungarian sheep-dogs. It is like a smaller version of the Komondor, but the coat is black or gray instead of white. Ideal height: about 17 inches (44 cm.). Weight: 29 to 33 pounds (13–15 kg.). It has a square, muscular body and a round head. Eyes: coffee-colored, with a lively expression. Ears: pendent. Tail: curved, not showy. The hair, which covers its entire body, is felted and tufted.

**Personality**  The puli is a dynamic sheepdog and cheerful and kindly with its family. It is a protective dog and may become aggressive if someone touches something belonging to its master. It has a tendency toward wandering. It does not enjoy strangers or small children.

**Uses**  In Hungary it is widely used as a leader of flocks, in which capacity it is energetic, attentive, untiring, and curious. It loves the water, and it is likely that in past centuries it was used for hunting in marshy areas.

## 16  PUMI

**Origin**   The breed was developed in 1700 by crossing pulis with French and German sheepdogs. The blood of ancient terriers probably also flows in its veins.

**Description**   The pumi is a medium-sized dog, from 13 to 17 inches (33–44 cm.) high, weighing from 18 to 29 pounds (8–13 kg.). It has a large head in proportion to its muzzle. Nose: black and pointed. Eyes: coffee-colored. Ears: like upside-down V's. Tail: docked to two-thirds its length. Its square body is covered with tangled but not matted hair of medium length which may be slate gray, silver-gray, clear gray, matte black, white, or reddish-brown, but always all of one color.

**Personality**   Aggressive, a barker, watchful, with a tendency to wander. It is very affectionate with its master but does not make friends with strangers.

**Uses**   The pumi is a vigorous and sturdy sheepdog, and it can also be used successfully as a guard dog and a hunting dog. Its probable terrier heritage has given it a great interest in the lairs of wild animals such as foxes and hares. Ready to spring at the slightest noise, the pumi is an ideal guardian for isolated houses or for factories.

## 17  ANATOLIAN SHEPHERD DOG

**Origin**   This is an ancient breed native to Asia Minor. It is also known as the Turkish guard dog. It was introduced into the United States in 1968.

**Description**   Dogs are 28 to 30 inches (71–76 cm.) high; bitches, 26 to 28 inches (66–71 cm.). Weight: dogs, 100 to 150 pounds (45–68 kg.); bitches, 90 to 130 pounds (41–59 kg.). The Anatolian shepherd dog is very similar to the Great Pyrenees and the kuvasz, but it is more slender and agile. It has straight, hard, thick hair in either white or chamois. The ears and muzzle are often black.

**Personality**   Intelligent, easy to train, patient with children, sensitive to reprimands, desirous of affection, possessive with respect to its home and property. It is very suspicious of strangers, and it is therefore necessary to provide a secure, fenced yard.

**Uses**   For centuries it was used as a combat dog in war and for hunting. It was particularly valued for the victorious battles it could fight with wolves. As a sheepdog, it was bothered by neither fatigue nor bad weather. Today it is still used as a sheepdog as well as a guard dog.

## 18 BERGAMASCO

**Origin** More than two thousand years ago Phoenician merchants brought into Europe some hairy sheepdogs. These were first centered in Tuscany, where the Maremma sheepdog developed, and then in the north of Italy, where the development of the Bergamasco began. The name of the breed comes from the valleys of the province of Bergamo. From here, the Phoenician sheepdogs spread into France and Spain where they provided the foundation for many excellent breeds.

**Description** The Bergamasco is a medium-sized countrified dog about 24 inches (60 cm.) high and weighing between 71 and 84 pounds (32–38 kg.). The bitch measures between 22 and 23 inches (56–58 cm.) and weighs around 66 pounds (30 kg.). The length of the head should be two-fifths the dog's height at the withers and should be equally divided between muzzle and skull. It has a large, wet black nose with open nostrils, a well-developed jaw, and a scissors bite. Its eyes are chestnut, varying in shade according to the color of its coat. Its ears are triangular and pendent. Tail: low and thick, narrowing toward the tip. It has strong, muscular limbs and oval feet with well-curved black nails. The Bergamasco's coat should be abundant; the hair, long, strong, rough, and wavy. It parts in the middle of the dog's back, hanging down on either side of its body. The hair on its face is less harsh in texture and falls down, covering its eyes completely. Colors: all shades of mottled gray or uniformly black. An all-white coat is considered a defect.

**Personality** The Bergamasco is a dog of excellent character: respectful, loyal, intelligent, courageous, a good worker, and possessed of a long memory. It is adaptable to the simplest living conditions and modest feeding. Its natural stubbornness can be overcome by an energetic and effective master.

**Uses** Its constitution and character make it a sheepdog par excellence. It loves the flock and is an energetic herder, impervious to all sorts of bad weather. However, with a minimum of training the Bergamasco can be used as a guard dog (especially for factories and work yards), a bodyguard, or an aid to firemen in dramatic situations such as conflagration or earthquake. As a companion dog, it is distinguished for its sweet, affectionate manner with its master. It is not, however, adapted to apartment life.

**Note** Its coat is coarse and tangled, making it impervious to rain and cold. It is necessary to wash it thoroughly a couple of times a year, but one should be careful not to disturb the knots, which are its most beautiful feature.

## 19  MAREMMA SHEEPDOG
### Pastore Maremmano-Abruzzese

**Origin**   These dogs have existed for as long as man has kept sheep and needed a guardian to defend them.

**Description**   At one time there were two separate breeds: the Abruzzese was more of a mountaineer and had a longer body, while the Maremmano had a slightly shorter coat. In 1950, the two were officially established as a single breed with a hyphenated name. The Maremma is a massive dog: dogs from 26 to 29 inches (65–73 cm.) high; bitches from 24 to 27 inches (60–68 cm.). Weight: dogs, 77 to 99 pounds (35–45 kg.); bitches, 66 to 88 pounds (30–40 kg.). It is a majestic, distinctive-looking dog with a large bearlike head, strong jaws, and a scissors bite. Its eyes are not large, but have a lively, intelligent look. It has a straight nasal canal ending in a brown nose which does not protrude. Its ears are triangular and hang flat by the side of its head. But its majestic look is mainly due to its beautiful rough white coat, which clings tightly to its body. A slight waviness of the hair is admissible.

**Uses**   The Maremma is a marvelous sheepdog and loves its work. It is a terrible enemy to the wolf, but tame with man. It is held in high esteem by shepherds, especially in the mountains, where it thrives in the snow, resistant to both cold and brambles. For several decades, it has also achieved success as a companion dog. This is due to the fact that English breeders have developed dogs of excellent character. As a family dog, it will defend both house and master and is particularly vigilant with children. It is not, however, well suited to apartment life. Accustomed for centuries to wide-open spaces, it needs at least a yard.

**Note**   The Maremma suffers from the heat. It should never be shorn, but in summer it should have a place in the shade, and it should always have a large bowl of water available.

## 20  VALÉE SHEEPDOG
### Polski owczarek nizinny

**Origin**  The Valée sheepdog belongs to the group of sheepdogs descended by way of the Bergamasco from sheepdogs originally imported by the Phoenicians.

**Description**  The Valée sheepdog is a strong, muscular, medium-sized dog. Height: 17 to 20 inches (43–52 cm.) for dogs; 16 to 18 inches (40–46 cm.) for bitches. Weight: under 66 pounds (30 kg.). It has a well-proportioned head with hair falling over its eyes and cheeks, a large black nose, and strong muzzle and teeth. Its ears are heart-shaped, wide, and pendent. Tail: rudimentary either by birth or docking. It has a thick coat over its entire body. All colors and markings are admissible, but a curly coat is considered a defect.

**Personality**  It has a prodigious memory, remembering a slight or a caress given years before. It is kind, tranquil, clean, and adapted to living with children.

**Uses**  It was originally a herd dog. Today, due to its merry, good-natured temperament, it is valued as a companion that will, if necessary, defend both person and property with all the authority of a guard dog.

**Note**  Unlike the Bergamasco, its coat can be combed, making it decidedly more attractive.

---

## 21  TATRA SHEEPDOG
### Owczarek podlhalanski

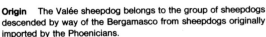

**Origin**  Like the Valée sheepdog, the Tatra sheepdog belongs to the group of dogs descended via the Bergamasco from dogs originally brought to Europe by the Phoenicians.

**Description**  Dogs must not be under 26 inches (65 cm.) high; bitches, not under 24 inches (60 cm.). Weight: 66 to 77 pounds (30–35 kg.). It has a rectangular body; well-proportioned head; short, pointed muzzle; and pincers bite. Eyes: dark, slightly oblique. Ears: triangular, pendent. Tail: carried low. Colors: white or light cream. The hair on its head and muzzle is short and lies close to the skin, but that on its neck, body, and thighs is long.

**Personality**  Intelligent, courageous, wise, cheerful, and not given to nervousness. An irritable nature is sufficient to disqualify a Tatra sheepdog in a dog show.

**Uses**  The Tatra is an outstanding sheepdog in mountainous terrain. It can withstand long, cold winters without falling ill. In the last decades, tourism has grown in the Polish region of Tatra, and pasturing has taken second place. Therefore, the Tatra sheepdog is now used for personal protection and as a guard dog in houses and factories.

## 22 NORSK BUHUND

**Origin** According to historians of dog breeding, the Norsk buhund was already widespread in the early Middle Ages. Norwegian colonists brought the dogs to Iceland in 874, and these dogs are the ancestors of the local Icelandic breeds. The name buhund means simply cattle dog (*bu*) dog (*hund*).

**Description** It has a short, compact body. Height: 17 to 18 inches (42–45 cm.). Weight: around 55 pounds (25 kg.). Head: large, narrowing considerably toward the stop. Eyes: dark, with an energetic expression. Ears: pointed and moving. Tail: short, thick, and tightly rolled. Legs: strong. Feet: small and oval. The Norsk buhund has a thick, coarse coat, short on its head and longer over the rest of its body. Colors: wheat, black, medium red, sand, wolf, always unicolored or with symmetrical markings.

**Personality** Courageous, energetic, obedient, loyal; an excellent worker.

**Uses** The buhund is adapted to many jobs, from guarding the flock to defense of people and animals to hunting wild animals. It has exceptional vision, hearing, and sense of smell. It never ceases to be active, even during the long months of darkness of the Norwegian winter. Outside of Norway, it is widespread in England and Australia.

## 23 SWEDISH SHEPHERD
### Västgötaspets

**Origin** According to the official Swedish Kennel Club, which recognized the breed on October 20, 1948, the Swedish shepherd originated and developed naturally. Despite its similarities to the Welsh corgi, it should not be confused with similar breeds from other countries.

**Description** The bold, energetic Swedish shepherd is a muscular dog with short legs. Height: 13 to 16 inches (33–40 cm.). Weight: 20 to 31 pounds (9–14 kg.). It has a flat head with a pointed muzzle and black nose. Eyes: oval, very dark. Ears: erect, pointed. Tail: not longer than 4 inches (10 cm.), carried horizontally. Its coat is of medium length, thick, and hard with a tight undercoat. Ideal color: gray, darker on the back, nape, and shoulders.

**Personality** Courageous, active, loyal, independent. When brought in from the country to live in the city, it may have trouble adapting and be subject to nervousness.

**Uses** Its true métier is guarding the flock. It is tireless day and night and capable of exerting its authority even over cows. Due to its amusing appearance and its warm and spirited expression, it has become a companion dog much loved by small children.

## 24 ILLYRIAN SHEEPDOG
### Charplaninatz, Sar Planina

**Origin** Like the majority of herd dogs, the Illyrian sheepdog comes from the ancient Orient and became autochthonous through acclimatization and selective breeding. The breed was officially recognized in 1930.

**Description** It is a dog of medium size with a strong bone structure. Height: dogs, 22 to 24 inches (55–60 cm.); bitches, 20 to 22 inches (50–55 cm.). Weight for both sexes: from 55 to 77 pounds (25–35 kg.). It looks a little like a rustic collie with a roundish skull, well-developed black nose, and strong jaws and teeth. Eyes: dark, almond-shaped, with a melancholy expression. Ears: pendent along the head. Tail: curved in repose; raised onto the back when the dog is in motion. Its coat should be at least 4 inches long with a good undercoat. Colors: either light or dark iron gray, sometimes with white patches on the paws.

**Personality** Bold, attentive, energetic. Normally, the Illyrian sheepdog is obedient to only one master. Everyone else is the enemy.

**Uses** It is an excellent sheepdog, much used on the Adriatic coast of Yugoslavia (ancient Illyria). It can fight as an equal with wolves, which it spies out even at night.

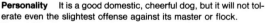

## 25 KARST SHEEPDOG
### Kraški ovčar

**Origin** Like the majority of sheepdogs, the Karst came originally from the Orient.

**Description** It is a robust dog of medium size. Height: from 22 to 24 inches (55–60 cm.). Weight: dogs, 66 to 88 pounds (30–40 kg.); bitches, 10% less. Head: large, with very well developed teeth, almond-shaped eyes (chestnut or dark brown in color), and pendent ears. Tail: saber-shaped, reaching the hocks. Abundant coat and undercoat about 6 inches (14 cm.) long. Color: iron gray with dark shadings.

**Personality** It is a good domestic, cheerful dog, but it will not tolerate even the slightest offense against its master or flock.

**Uses** The Karst is valued as a shepherd because of its ability and energy in guiding and defending the flock and for its resistance to the most severe weather. Round feet with hard leathery pads enable it to walk tirelessly over nearly impassable terrain (Kras is a rocky region). The Karst is also delightful as a companion dog, in contrast to its less friendly cousin the Illyrian sheepdog.

## 26 BEARDED COLLIE

**Origin** At the time of the Roman invasions, the bearded collie was already popular in Scotland. By 1500 it was celebrated by shepherd and nobility and in the songs of poets. It is in all likelihood related to the bobtail.

**Description** The bearded collie is robust without being massive-looking. Height: from 21 to 22 inches (53–56 cm.). Average weight: 66 pounds (30 kg.). Head: large, with an elongated muzzle. Teeth: large and white. Eyes: wide-set and harmonious in color with its coat; set high on its head and pendent. Tail: carried low in repose, but carried high when the dog is excited. Its coat is dense and strong with a thick, soft undercoat. Colors: slate, reddish-tan, all shades of gray, black, or sandy with lighter markings.

**Personality** Joyous and affectionate.

**Uses** For centuries, the bearded collie has been used as a herder. It is resistant to the hardest winters and is extremely attentive to its work. Because of its pleasing personality and its lovable looks, the bearded collie has become an outstanding companion dog. It prefers sleeping outside. The breed is not widespread.

## 27 SMOOTH COLLIE

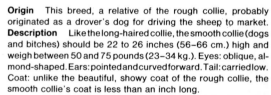

**Origin** This breed, a relative of the rough collie, probably originated as a drover's dog for driving the sheep to market.

**Description** Like the long-haired collie, the smooth collie (dogs and bitches) should be 22 to 26 inches (56–66 cm.) high and weigh between 50 and 75 pounds (23–34 kg.). Eyes: oblique, almond-shaped. Ears: pointed and curved forward. Tail: carried low. Coat: unlike the beautiful, showy coat of the rough collie, the smooth collie's coat is less than an inch long.

**Personality** Intelligent, mild, obedient, especially devoted to the family.

**Uses** The smooth collie is known almost exclusively in Great Britain, where it is considered an outstanding companion dog, suited to apartment life. However, the long-haired collie, with its aristocratic beauty, has always outstripped the smooth collie in popularity.

## 28 COLLIE
## Rough Collie

**Origin**  For centuries, the collie has been an outstanding sheepdog. The standard was fixed and the breed was presented at dog shows in 1860. The name collie probably comes from Colley, the black-faced, black-footed Scottish sheep that collies guarded.

**Description**  Height: dogs, from 24 to 26 inches (61–66 cm.); bitches, 22 to 24 inches (56–61 cm.). Weight: dogs, 60 to 75 pounds (27–34 kg.); bitches, 50 to 65 pounds (23–29 kg.). The collie should give the impression of beauty and harmony combined with robustness and agility. The head, which is extremely important in evaluating the breed, should be flat between the ears with a straight, elongated muzzle and a black nose. Ears: rather small, carried toward the back of the head, two-thirds erect with the top third folded forward. Its body is rather long in comparison with its height. Its tail, which should reach its hocks, is carried low with a slight lift at its end. Its coat is thick and dense, especially at the collar, although the hair is short on its head and muzzle and at the ends of its ears. It may be any shade of tan, from sand-colored to mahogany; tricolored (tan, black, and white); or blue merle.

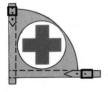

**Personality**  Its temperament displays contrasting aspects. It is fundamentally kindly and sensitive; but at the same time, it is stubborn and indolent. It has a fairly well developed sense of protectiveness for its master, especially for children. It is aristocratic, intelligent, loyal, and not aggressive, though it tends to be suspicious of people it does not like.

The collie must be trained with sensitivity and gentle persuasion. Otherwise it will refuse to learn even the simplest things.

**Uses**  The collie is a robust, vigorous, active dog and is still used as a sheepdog. Due to its intelligence, however, it is also known as a guard dog, a rescue dog (especially in water or fire), and as a guide dog for blind children. Because of its beauty it has become primarily a companion dog.

**Note**  Frequent brushing is required to maintain the beauty of its coat. The collie should be bathed occasionally. In summer, it suffers from the heat and should always have access to a shady spot.

## 29   BORDER COLLIE

**Origin**   The border collie is descended from reindeer herding dogs brought to Scotland by the Viking invaders. These dogs were later crossed with the Valée sheepdog.

**Description**   Height: dogs, 20 to 22 inches (50–56 cm.); bitches, 19 to 21 inches (48–53 cm.). Weight: 40 to 50 pounds (18–23 kg.) for dogs; 35 to 45 pounds (6–8 kg.) for bitches. There are two varieties of border collie: one with coarse hair (thick, straight, about 3 inches [7.6 cm.] long) and one with sleek hair (about 1 inch [2.5 cm.] long). Colors: black and white; black, white, and tan; gray and black; red and white; and solid black.

**Personality**   Intelligent, steady, willing, attentive, trainable. A highly sensitive breed, easy to train, it thrives on praise.

**Uses**   This is a hardy, agile, untiring sheepdog, capable of mastering any type of herd. It is said that the border collie has an eye that can hypnotize cattle.

## 30   OLD ENGLISH SHEEPDOG
### Bobtail

**Origin**   The Old English sheepdog's origin is uncertain. Three major views prevail: One, that the breed is descended from a hairy Russian dog called the owtchar that was brought to Great Britain on ships from the Baltic. Two, that the breed is a close relative of the Briard and the Bergamasco. And three, that it is related to the barbone and the deerhound.

**Description**   It is a stocky, muscular dog with an elastic gait. Height: 22 inches (56 cm.) or more (slightly less for bitches). Weight: around 66 pounds (30 kg.). Head: large, square. Eyes: dark. Ears: small, carried flat to the head. Coat: thick, any shade of gray, grizzle, or blue with or without white markings. Tail: as bobtail implies, it is a dog without a tail. In earlier times, drovers' dogs were exempt from taxation, and their tails were docked to indicate their occupation. Some pups are born tailless, but if there is a tail, it should be docked to the first joint.

**Uses**   It is an outstanding herd dog. It is also used as a guard dog, sled dog, retriever, and companion dog. It is particularly good with children.

**Note**   Frequent brushing is necessary to avoid snarls and mats in its coat.

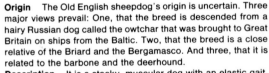

## 31   SHETLAND SHEEPDOG

**Origin**   The Shetland is probably descended from collies brought to the Scottish island of Shetland and crossed with the yakkin, a small island dog now no longer recognized, brought over in the boats of fishermen. By 1700, the breed was completely developed.

**Description**   It has been described as "an excellent collie seen through reversed binoculars," which is to say that it is almost a perfect copy in miniature of the long-haired collie. Height: 13 to 16 inches (33–41 cm.). Weight: from 14 to 16 pounds (6–7 kg.). Under- or oversized dogs are disqualified. Head: conical. Nose: black. Eyes: almond-shaped, with a kind expression. Ears: semierect with the tips folded. Tail: reaching the hocks in repose. Its coat is rough with a soft undercoat; it is abundant, especially at the neck. Colors: tricolor (black, bright chestnut, and white), fawn, blue merle, black and white.

**Personality**   Very lively, suspicious with strangers, affectionate with its family, especially with children, stubborn.

**Uses**   It is above all an intelligent herder, capable both of commanding large cattle and holding small sheep in check. Because of its beauty and kindliness, it has become an outstanding companion dog.

## 32   WELSH CORGI

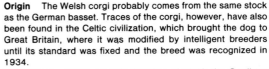

**Origin**   The Welsh corgi probably comes from the same stock as the German basset. Traces of the corgi, however, have also been found in the Celtic civilization, which brought the dog to Great Britain, where it was modified by intelligent breeders until its standard was fixed and the breed was recognized in 1934.

**Description**   There are two varieties of corgi: the Cardigan and the Pembroke. Both should have a foxlike look and a height of between 10 and 12 inches (25–30 cm.). Weight for dogs should be less than 30 pounds (13.5 kg.); for bitches, less than 28 pounds (12.6 kg.). Low in stature, the corgi moves agilely on its short legs. Skull: large and flat. Eyes: hazel, harmonizing with the color of its coat. Ears: erect. The Cardigan has a long tail, while the Pembroke has almost no tail. The Cardigan has short, stiff hair in various colors, but without any white. The Pembroke has a uniformly reddish, sand-colored, fawn, or black coat of medium length with areas of bright tan; white markings on its paws, chest, and neck.

**Personality**   Lively, affectionate, spirited, intelligent, easy to train.

**Uses**   The corgi is an agile and energetic sheepdog. For centuries it was used to guard flocks. It is also an extremely pleasant and winning companion dog.

## 33 RAFEIRO DO ALENTEJO

**Origin** This indigenous breed has taken the name of the famous Portuguese historic region of Alentejo, bordering on Spain. This is a region of climatic extremes: very hot summers and very cold winters.

**Description** The Rafeiro is a sturdy and powerful dog, up to 30 inches (75 cm.) high and weighing 110 pounds (50 kg.) (10% less for bitches). It has a body like a St. Bernard and a bearlike head. Jaws: muscular. Teeth: strong. Eyes: dark and kindly. Ears: hanging, almost immobile. Short neck with a medium dewlap. Tail: long and curved at the end. Its coat, which may be short or medium in length, is dense and sleek over its entire body. Colors: black, fawn, yellow, wolf-colored, brindled, or tiger mixed with white.

**Personality** Although the Rafeiro appears stolid, dreamy, and even tired, it is a good worker and a strong walker.

**Uses** A most attentive guard dog, the Rafeiro do Alentejo is relentless against predatory animals and would-be human attackers. It can be successfully trained to guard either property or persons. It is resistant to bad weather conditions, and if necessary can go without food for several days.

## 34 LAPPONIAN HERDER
### Lapinporokoira

**Origin** The Lapponian herder is indigenous to the Lapponian tundra, where it developed.

**Description** Height: dogs, 19 to 22 inches (49–55 cm.); bitches, 17 to 19 inches (43–49 cm.). Weight: not more than 66 pounds (30 kg.). Musculature: strong. Muzzle: short and wide. Ears: erect and turned forward. Lean, strong neck. Sturdy back and retracted abdomen. Tail: long, rolled up. Coat: stiff and coarse, of medium length, with a thick soft undercoat. Ideal color: black with a reddish cast. White markings on the throat, chest, and paws are allowed.

**Personality** Energetic, obedient, hardworking, with a tendency toward barking.

**Uses** Due to its great courage in the face of wolves, its speed over snow, its resistance to arctic climates, and its herding instincts, it has become a valued and irreplaceable colleague of those who raise reindeer. There is also a variety with long hair, but the herders prefer the agile short-haired variety.

## 35  LAPPHUND
### Lapplandska spetz

**Origin**  Widespread throughout Sweden for centuries, the breed was only recognized officially in 1944.

**Description**  The Lapphund is a medium-sized dog. Maximum height: 20 inches (50 cm.). Weight: around 44 pounds (20 kg.). It has a conical head and an extremely black nose. Scissors bite. Eyes: large, dark chestnut in color. Ears: short, erect, either pointed or slightly folded. The dog's tail is naturally rolled up on its back; but in dog shows, dogs without tails (either from birth or through docking) are also admitted. Coat: thick, stiff, long except on the head, muzzle, and legs, where it is short. Coloring: dark chestnut, black, chestnut and white. White patches on the feet, chest, and neck are also accepted.

**Personality**  Disciplined, affectionate, patient with children, alert. It is distrustful of strangers.

**Uses**  The Lapphund is a born sheepdog; but due to its excellent psychological and physical qualities, it is also used as a guard dog for houses, for personal protection, for hunting, and as a companion dog.

**Note**  When working in cold areas, it should be especially well fed on a diet that includes meat and fish.

## 36  SLOVAK TCHOUVATCH
### Slovensky čuvač

**Origin**  This breed developed over the centuries in the mountains of Czechoslovakia. Thanks to the Veterinarian School of Brno, its characteristics have been fixed, and a precise standard was established and approved in 1964.

**Description**  The Tchouvatch is an animal of imposing stature. Dogs may be as much as 28 inches (70 cm.) tall; bitches, at the most, 26 inches (65 cm.). Weight in dogs ranges from 77 to 99 pounds (35–45 kg.) and from 66 to 88 pounds (30–40 kg.) in bitches. It has a large head, half of which is taken up by the nasal canal. Strong jaws; scissors bite. Eyes: oval, dark, lively. Ears: long and hanging, carried at the sides of the head. Tail: thickly furred, hangs down when the dog is at rest. Coat: completely white; the hair can be as much as 4 inches long (10 cm.).

**Personality**  Courageous, extremely alert both day and night, wonderful with its master. A fearful adversary of wolves or bears.

**Uses**  These dogs are used for defending herds and flocks as well as property. They are especially prized in the mountain regions of Tatra and the Carpathians, where they have proved themselves to be resistant to all sorts of inclement weather.

**Note**  This breed is very similar in appearance to the Hungarian kuvasz.

## 37 CROATIAN SHEEPDOG
## Hrvatški ovčar

**Origin**   Originally from the Orient, over the centuries the Croatian sheepdog became native to Yugoslavia.

**Description**   Height for both dogs and bitches: from 16 to 20 inches (40–50 cm.). Weight: 31 to 44 pounds (14–20 kg.). Head: somewhat delicate; conical in shape; about 8 inches (20 cm.) long. Eyes: almond-shaped; either chestnut or black; lively. Ears: triangular, erect. Tail: mounted high but carried low; docking to about 2 1/2 inches (4 cm.) is allowed. Its hair, which reaches a length of 3 to 6 inches (7–14 cm.) on its back, is very short on the cheeks and around the ears. Color: totally black. Some white markings are acceptable.

**Personality**   Watchful, pugnacious, with aggressive instincts to protect its flock at all costs. Obedient and amenable to training.

**Uses**   The Croatian sheepdog is used almost exclusively for guarding flocks or property.

## 38 ICELAND DOG

**Origin**   The breed is directly descended from dogs that accompanied the colonists who settled in Iceland. Practically destroyed by an epidemic of distemper, the Iceland dog was "reconstructed" by Icelandic and English breeders.

**Description**   The Iceland dog belongs to the spitz family. Dogs are 13 to 16 inches (33–41 cm.) high; bitches, 12 to 15 inches (30–38 cm.). Weight: dogs, 25 to 30 pounds (11–14 kg.); bitches, 20 to 25 pounds (9–11 kg.). It has an elongated muzzle, a black nose, muscular limbs, and carries its tail on its back. Its hair is of medium length, thick and tight to the body with a good undercoat. Colors: chestnut, fawn, gray, dirty white, black with white markings, or solid black.

**Personality**   Lively, affectionate, active, intelligent, pleasant. Its character continues to develop into maturity at about eighteen months, but it needs close contact with its master.

**Uses**   The Iceland dog is an all-around dog that performs a variety of tasks well. It may be used as a sheepdog, watchdog, or companion. It will gladly live in a stable with horses.

**Note**   Due to its Icelandic origins, it is a rather temperate eater and is fond of fish.

## 39 AUSTRALIAN KELPIE

**Origin** Probably descended from the border collie and the dingo, the breed has been known since 1870.

**Description** This is a beautiful dog with a foxlike look. It is vigorous and agile with a lively and intelligent expression. Dogs are 18 to 20 inches (46–51 cm.) high; bitches, 17 to 19 inches (43–48 cm.) high. Their respective weights are 25 to 30 pounds (11–14 kg.) and 20 to 25 pounds (9–11 kg.). It has crinkly, thick, short hair. Colors: black, black and chestnut, red, red and chestnut, tan, dark chestnut, or bluish-gray.

**Personality** Trainable, intelligent, steady, obedient, an enthusiastic worker.

**Uses** This is a marvelous herd dog, hardy, very fast, ready to respond immediately to any signal given by its master, even from a great distance. It is used to open spaces and cannot live in an apartment.

## 40 AUSTRALIAN SHEPHERD

**Origin** Developed by crossings among Australian and New Zealand sheepdogs, the Australian sheepdog was brought to California in the mid 1800's.

**Description** It is a medium-sized dog, robust and rustic. Height: 18 to 23 inches (46–58 cm.) for dogs; 17 to 21 inches (43–53 cm.) for bitches. Weight: 30 to 45 pounds (14–20 kg.) for dogs; 27 to 40 pounds (12–18 kg.) for bitches. It has a very prominent head, pendent ears, and a semierect tail. Its eyes are almost always blue. Coat: rather abundant. Colors: black, red, or white with chestnut markings.

**Personality** Loyal, affectionate, courageous, playful, adaptable to family life.

**Uses** The Australian shepherd is a very active sheepdog that can herd almost any farm animal into a pen. Smaller dogs are most sought after because they are able to dodge more quickly the hooves of cattle. When necessary, it makes a sound somewhere between a bark and a howl.

## 41  BOUVIER DES ARDENNES

**Origin**  The Bouvier des Ardennes is an indigenous breed. It probably developed around 1700 through crossings of local dogs.

**Description**  It is a rustic-looking dog. Height: around 24 inches (60 cm.). Weight: around 55 pounds (25 kg.). Bitches, 10% less. It has a large head with a short muzzle, beard and mustache, and powerful jaws. Eyes: dark. Ears: upright or slightly folded forward. Short, thick neck; deep thorax; rounded rib cage. Its front legs are straight; rear legs, angled. Normally, the Bouvier des Ardennes is born without a tail. If not, the tail must be docked. Its coat is about 2 inches (5 cm.) long and bushy. In winter it has a thick undercoat that protects it from bad weather. All colors are admissible.

**Personality**  The Bouvier des Ardennes is gruff both in looks and temperament. It is hostile to strangers but very affectionate and obedient to its master. It is extremely intelligent.

**Uses**  It is a typical country sheepdog, able to live outdoors the year around. Although not a common breed even in its country of origin, it is held in high regard for its tirelessness and the reliable way it takes care of flocks of sheep or herds of cows.

## 42  CÃO DA SERRA DE AIRES

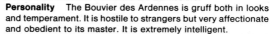

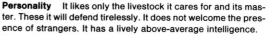

**Origin**  The breed is about a hundred years old. It developed in the Serra de Aires region of Portugal, probably with the augmentation of Briard blood. Because of its peculiar-looking muzzle, the Cão da Serra de Aires has been nicknamed "monkey dog."

**Description**  It is a medium-sized dog, from 17 to 19 inches (42–48 cm.) high, weighing from 26 to 40 pounds (12–18 kg.). It has a wide, sturdy head with a prominent nose, and strong jaws and teeth. Eyes: round, dark, with a gentle expression. Ears: triangular, pendent. Prominent chest. Tail: pointed, reaching the dog's hocks. Its coat is long or slightly wavy. It has a beard and mustache and thick eyebrows. Colors: yellow-red, chestnut, gray, fawn, wolf, or black.

**Personality**  It likes only the livestock it cares for and its master. These it will defend tirelessly. It does not welcome the presence of strangers. It has a lively above-average intelligence.

**Uses**  It is an all-purpose shepherd and has proved outstanding in both guarding and herding sheep, cows, horses, and pigs. It is extremely able in tracking down strays.

## 43   BOUVIER DES FLANDRES

**Origin** There is no real agreement concerning the origin of this Franco-Belgian breed. Probably it was formed by crossing the griffon and the Beauceron, but during World War I it was almost totally destroyed in the bloody fighting in Flanders. Only in 1923, gathering the few remaining Bouviers from here and there, were breeders able to "reconstruct" the breed.

**Description** Similar to the giant schnauzer, the Bouvier des Flandres is about 26 inches (68 cm.) high and weighs about 88 pounds (40 kg.). It has a large, heavy head with beard and mustache, an elongated nose, and a wide, powerful muzzle. Eyes: dark, with an affectionate but lively expression. Ears: triangular, erect, docked. Front legs: muscular and perfectly straight. Its body is short and powerful. Its tail should be docked. It has steel-wool hair in black, fawn, gray, or brindle. The AKC allows a white marking on the chest.

**Personality** The Bouvier des Flandres is an extremely good-natured dog and is thus adapted to being a family dog.

**Uses** Its true mission is herding cows, but due to its powerful physique and its intelligence, it has been used as a guard dog and for rescuing the wounded in battle.

---

## 44   APPENZELL MOUNTAIN DOG

**Origin** There are two theories concerning the origin of the Appenzell mountain dog. One, that it is a native breed dating back to the Bronze Age; the other, that it is descended from the Molossus brought into Switzerland by the Romans.

**Description** It is a muscular but not massive dog, from 19 to 23 inches (48–58 cm.) high, weighing from 49 to 55 pounds (22–25 kg.). It has a wide, flat head with a muzzle that narrows toward a black nose. Eyes: small and dark. Ears: pendent. Tail: carried rolled up on its back. Straight, nervous limbs. Its hair is short, thick, and glossy, shading from yellow to fawn with symmetrical white markings. Markings over the eyes are obligatory.

**Personality** The Appenzell is a noisy, extroverted dog. It is winsome and affectionate, but it loves the freedom of open spaces and thus is not adapted to living indoors.

**Uses** It is an outstanding herd dog. It is tireless and surefooted in the mountains. It is also adaptable to pulling a cart and is used to bring milk and cheese from the valleys to the merchants in town. It doesn't have a lazy bone in its body. When it is not working with the herd, it will guard its master's property.

## 45 BERNESE MOUNTAIN DOG
### Berner Sennenhund

**Origin**   The breed arrived in Switzerland along with the ancient Roman soldiers.

**Description**   The Bernese mountain dog is a strong, muscular dog. It is from 23 to 27 1/2 inches (58–70 cm.) high and weighs about 88 pounds (40 kg.). It has a short, massive head with dark lively eyes. Ears: V-shaped, pendent. Tail: long-haired, not rolled up. Coat: thick, brilliant black with patches of light brown on upper legs and above eyes; white chest blaze edged with light brown. Feet, tail tip, and mask may be white also.

**Personality**   Energetic, attentive, impetuous, but not given to biting. It attaches its affections to one person (its master) and is suspicious of strangers.

**Uses**   The ancient Romans used Bernese mountain dogs as fighting dogs and sent them into battle armed with heavy iron-studded collars. Subsequently the breed became excellent guardians of the herds, especially in the hilly regions of Switzerland. They are untiring, often unruly, resistant to the coldest winters, and excellent defenders of stable or home. Because of their amenability to training, they have also been used by the police. They are intelligent, loyal, and beautiful. Breeding by enthusiastic dog lovers has developed this herd dog into a companion dog.

**Note**   The breed is not suited for hot climates.

---

## 46 GREAT SWISS MOUNTAIN DOG
### Grosser Schweize Sennenhund

**Origin**   The breed was well known toward the end of the Middle Ages, when, as a bodyguard and attack dog, it accompanied its Swiss masters into battle.

**Description**   The great Swiss mountain dog is a large dog, about 28 inches (70 cm.) high, weighing around 130 pounds (59 kg.). It is a robust, lively dog with a strong scissors bite, heavy thighs, and short, round feet. The color of its eyes may vary from hazel to chestnut; their expression is attentive and intelligent. Its ears are triangular and pendent. Its tail is carried down, never rolled up. Its coat is made up of stiff hairs not more than 2 inches (5 cm.) long. It is black or bronze with symmetrical markings of rust and white. Its nose and lips must always be black.

**Personality**   Loyal, courageous, intelligent, wise, friendly with children.

**Uses**   Its specific work is as herd dog and stable guard. But it has been used very successfully as a bodyguard and for pulling a cart. It is reputed to be a dog that never sleeps, and, in fact, it is attentive day and night, ready to leap to its feet at the slightest noise. Because of its good temper, its patience, and the ease with which it can be trained, the great Swiss mountain dog has become popular as a companion dog. It is, however, used to lots of open space and is not adaptable to city life.

## 47 ENTLEBUCHER SENNENHUND

**Origin** Probably descended from the Roman Molossus, this breed is considered to be native to the region of Entlebuch in the Canton of Lucerne in Switzerland.

**Description** It is a medium-sized dog, not more than 20 inches (50 cm.) high. Weight: around 55 to 66 pounds (25–30 kg.). It has powerful jaws, small but lively chestnut eyes, and V-shaped pendent ears. Its tail is docked at birth and should not be more than 4 to 6 inches (10–15 cm.) long. It has short, thick, close-fitting hair that is hard and glossy. Color: black with shadings from yellow to fawn. The markings must be symmetrical.

**Personality** It is adaptable to a variety of jobs and environments, and is tireless and attentive in its work. It is extremely strict with cows, but extraordinarily gentle with children.

**Uses** The Entlebucher is highly regarded as a strict guardian of the herd, especially in mountainous regions. It is an energetic defender of stable, hut, and house. It is one of a group of herd dogs known as "milkmen", since even today they are used to transport cans of milk and mountain cheese from stables to shops. In the house, the dog is very gentle, cheerful, amusing, and friendly, inclined above all to playing with children, and, if necessary, defending them.

## 48 AUSTRALIAN CATTLE DOG

**Origin** The breed was obtained principally by crosses between the collie and the dingo.

**Description** This is a small to medium-sized dog. Height: dogs, 17 to 19 inches (43–48 cm.); bitches, 16 to 18 inches (41–46 cm.). Weight: dogs, 40 to 50 pounds (18–23 kg.); bitches, 35 to 45 pounds (16–20 kg.). It has straight, hard, moderately short hair. Colors: blue, blue with black or chestnut markings, or red with black spots on the head.

**Personality** Astute, intelligent, obedient.

**Uses** For years this dog has been an indispensable aid on Australian farms both as a hardy and agile herd dog and as a guard dog. It is more accustomed to working in huge spaces and covering longer distances than most other breeds.

**Note** It has an atavistic habit of biting at the heels of cows (and people).

## 49 CATAHOULA LEOPARD DOG

**Origin**   The breed was developed in Louisiana by the first colonists. Its name comes from the fact that it was especially popular in the parish of Catahoula and its coat is marked like that of a leopard.

**Description**   Height: dogs, 22 to 25 inches (56–64 cm.); bitches, 20 to 23 inches (51–58 cm.). Weight: dogs, 60 to 80 pounds (27–36 kg.); bitches, 50 to 70 pounds (23–32 kg.). It has thick, compact, dense, short hair. The color of its coat is usually blue-gray with black speckles or markings; or its markings may be red or yellow. Dogs with turquoise-blue eyes are particularly prized.

**Personality**   It is an affectionate, devoted, trainable dog, very loving toward its master but an aggressive guard dog.

**Uses**   It is still used today as a herd dog, capable of keeping order among sheep, cattle, or hogs even over vast territories. It has also been used successfully for hunting raccoons and squirrels.

## 50 STANDARD SCHNAUZER

**Origin**   The breed comes from Bavaria, but the date of its origin is not known. The name comes from the German word *Schnauze,* muzzle.

**Description**   The standard schnauzer is a medium-sized dog. Height for dogs: between 18½ and 19½ inches (47–50 cm.). Weight: around 33 pounds (15 kg.). It is a squarely built dog, more robust than slender. It has a powerful elongated head with an accentuated stop, black nose, and a scissors bite. Eyes: oval and dark. Ears: docked to a point. Tail: docked at the fourth vertebra. Its front legs must appear straight from every angle, while its rear legs and thighs are oblique and very muscular. Coat: coarse, hard, strong, thick. Its beard and mustache are stiff and its eyebrows appear spiky. Silky or wavy hair is a defect. The color of its coat should be salt-and-pepper or pure black. Grooming (stripping) is necessary.

**Personality**   Very lively, but not restless. It is courageous and affectionate, bold and devoted.

**Uses**   The schnauzer in the eighteenth century was a carriage dog and a watchdog in stables. Since it has some terrier blood, it was also used as a hunter of rodents. Today, it is esteemed as a watchdog and bodyguard, but above all, as a very lovable, spirited, loyal, intelligent companion.

**Note**   Among the schnauzer's good qualities, two are noteworthy: its longevity (schnauzers usually live about fifteen years) and its lack of a doggy smell.

**GREAT DANE**
**Deutsche Dogge**

**Origin** Incised on some Greek money dating back to 36 B.C. is the image of a dog very similar to the Great Dane of today. If you are of the opinion that its origin is Greek, therefore, you understand why the Great Dane is known as the "Apollo of dogs." However, we have more precise, incontrovertible information regarding this breed from a period several centuries later. In 407 A.D. German Gaul and part of Italy and Spain were invaded by an Asiatic people——the Alans——who brought with them powerful mastifflike dogs. In Germany especially, where these magnificent animals, capable of overcoming bears and wild boars, were much admired, a process of selective breeding was begun. The dogs were crossed with Irish greyhounds, and the issue was the beautiful, large, thin, agile dog known today as the Great Dane. Despite the fact that they are called Danes in English, these dogs have nothing to do with Denmark.

**Description** The Great Dane is a giant dog that combines nobility with robustness, power with elegance. The minimum height for the dogs is 30 inches (76 cm.); for bitches, 28 inches (72 cm.). Dogs of even larger size, however, are more prized. Weight: about 132 pounds (60 kg.). It has a long, narrow head with an accentuated frontal stop and rather large nasal canal. Its neck is long and muscular. Its front legs are perfectly straight. It has muscular thighs and round feet with short, dark nails. Tail: medium length, reaching to the point of the hock. Eyes: round, usually dark, with a lively, intelligent expression. Ears: docked rather long and pointed, carried erect. Its well-developed white teeth must close in a scissors bite. All Danes have short, thick, shiny, close-fitting hair. The color of the coat indicates the variety. Black Danes must have glossy black coats and dark eyes, while blue Danes may have lighter eyes.

**Personality** The Great Dane is by nature a steady dog and becomes aggressive only when the circumstances require it. Fundamentally, it is sweet, affectionate, and patient.

**Uses** In its long history, the Great Dane has been a battle dog, a hunting dog, a cart dog, a watchdog, and a bodyguard. Today it is still used as a watchdog, but due to its beauty and good nature, it is sought after above all as a decorative companion.

## 52 TAWNY GREAT DANE

**Origin** The origin of the tawny Great Dane is the same as the black Dane; that is, a perfect crossing of ancient mastiffs and Irish greyhounds.

**Description** The physical appearance and characteristics of the Great Dane are the same for all varieties. The color of the coat naturally changes. For the tawny Great Dane, it is a light to bright golden yellow with a black mask.

**Personality** There is a connection between the color of the Great Dane's coat and its personality. The tawny Dane is thinner and more agile than the black Great Dane; therefore, its temperament is more lively.

**Uses** Once a wild-boar hunter and a bodyguard, it is used today as a watchdog in open areas where it can get the exercise it needs to stay in good physical shape.

**Note** It needs frequent brushing with a stiff brush. The place where it sleeps must be protected from the cold and damp.

## 53 BRINDLE GREAT DANE

**Origin** Same as black Great Dane.

**Description** It has the same characteristics as the other varieties of Great Dane, except that like the tawny Dane it has a slightly thinner build. Its coat is light or bright gold with continuous transverse black streaks. The deeper the base color, the more marked is the brindle. White spots on the paws and light eyes are considered defects.

**Personality** Together with the tawny Dane, it is considered to be the liveliest of the Danes. It is basically good-natured, patient with children, affectionate with its master and others with whom it is familiar, and not aggressive with strangers.

**Uses** It is a good watchdog, but above all a loyal and decorative companion.

**Note** It is important that all Great Danes be well trained to obey immediately in order to avoid their frightening strangers or knocking someone down in a headlong rush.

## 54 HARLEQUIN GREAT DANE

**Origin** The result of crossing mastifflike dogs with Irish grey-hounds. Although German, the dog is known as a Dane in English-speaking countries (see Great Dane).

**Description** It is the most imposing of all the Danes and sometimes is as much as 3 feet (1 meter) tall. The base color should be pure white, if possible without speckles. It has irregular black markings over its entire body. Dogs with very large black markings or with black coats interrupted by white areas at the neck, on the limbs, and at the end of the tail are considered to be black Great Danes.

**Personality** Heavier than the other varieties of Great Dane, the harlequin is equally good-natured and intelligent, but it is somewhat more phlegmatic and not as quick in responding to orders.

**Uses** It is used for guarding isolated open areas, but it is also considered the most unusual and decorative of the Great Danes because of its markings.

## 55 HOVAWART

**Origin** The Hovawart was famous in the Middle Ages as a watchdog, but with the vicissitudes of history, it dropped from view. Some sixty years ago, it again captured the attention of dog lovers, and from drawings and texts of the thirteenth century, it was "reconstructed," bred from watchdogs from the Black Forest area.

**Description** The Hovawart is a robust but not heavy dog, with a strong, sonorous bark. It is resistant to all sorts of weather. Height: dogs, 24 to 28 inches (60–70 cm.); bitches, 22 to 26 inches (55–65 cm.). Weight: dogs, 66 to 88 pounds (30–40 kg.); bitches, 55 to 77 pounds (25–35 kg.). It has a sturdy head with a wide convex forehead and a scissors bite. Ears: triangular, pendent. Tail: long-haired, reaching the hocks. Its coat is long, thick, and slightly wavy in colors of black, dark blond, or black with areas of bright tan. The color of its eyes, nose, and nails harmonizes with its coat.

**Personality** Intelligent, determined, obedient, and affectionate, especially toward its master. It is resistant to training at an early age since it tends to retain its lively, good-natured puppy instincts for a long time.

**Uses** It is an outstanding watchdog, especially adaptable to stables, fields, and country houses. It has the ability to run easily over difficult terrain.

## 56 NEAPOLITAN MASTIFF
### Mastino Napoletano

**Origin** All European mastiffs are descended from the Tibetan mastiff, the most ancient member of the canine species. The first Asian mastiffs were probably brought to Greece from India by Alexander the Great around 300 B.C. The Greeks introduced the dogs to the Romans, who adopted them enthusiastically and used them in circus combats. The word "mastiff" derives from the Latin *massivus*, meaning massive. English experts, however, have another theory. They contend that the mastiff was brought to Britain by the Phoenicians in about 500 B.C. and spread from there to the rest of Europe.

In any case, the Neapolitan mastiff is a direct descendant of the Roman Molossus. While the breed became extinct throughout the rest of Europe, it continued to survive in Campania despite the perils of weather and war. One can therefore say that the Neapolitan mastiff has existed in Campania for two thousand years, even though it was not officially recognized until 1946, and its standard was not set until 1949.

**Description** Height: dogs, 26 to 30 inches (65–75 cm.); bitches, 24 to 28 inches (60–70 cm.). Mastiffs may weigh up to 155 pounds (70 kg.). They are serious, powerful-looking dogs. Head: very large with pronounced dewlaps falling in great folds to its neck. Coat: short, thick, even, and shiny in colors of black lead, gray, tiger, or fawn, sometimes with white markings on the toes and paws. Eyes: color varies in accordance with color of coat. According to tradition established when the dogs were used in combat, the ears should be docked short, and the tail should be docked by a third.

**Personality** Despite the churlishness or even ferocity of its appearance, the Neapolitan mastiff is a peaceful, steady dog, sweet and affectionate with its master and with friends of the family. It is a very brave animal and will endure physical pain stoically.

**Uses** In the course of history, the Neapolitan mastiff and its ancestors have been used in war, as fighting dogs in the circus, as collaborators to criminals and aides to the police, as draft animals, companions, and bodyguards. Today, a trained mastiff makes an excellent guard for both person and property.

**Note** The Neapolitan mastiff needs a great deal of exercise. It is adaptable to living in a house with a garden, or even in an apartment so long as there is a strong person willing to take it on long walks twice a day.

## 57 FRENCH MASTIFF
## Dogue de Bordeaux

**Origin** There are numerous hypotheses about the origin of this breed. It may be descended from the Greek and Roman Molossus, from mastiffs brought to Europe by the Alans, from the dogs of Aquitaine, or from Spanish dogs from Burgos.

**Description** Its height is between 24 and 27 inches (60–80 cm.); 10% less for bitches. Minimum weight: 110 pounds (50 kg.). It has a very large head with a powerful muzzle and dewlaps. Chest: wide. Ears: pendent and slightly rounded. Eyes: oval. Its coat is made up of fine, short, soft hair in all shades of blackened fawn.

**Personality** Careful breeding has succeeded in softening the French mastiff's aggressive nature until today it is a tolerant, affectionate, loyal dog.

**Uses** In the past, it has been employed in wild boar and bear hunts and in circus combat with bulls. Because of its power and courage, it has been trained by the police in the pursuit of criminals. In this role, however, it has shown itself to be excessively ferocious.

## 58 MASTIFF
## Old English Mastiff

**Origin** The breed is descended from the Tibetan mastiff, which was introduced into Europe by the Phoenicians. It quickly became native to Great Britain, where it is highly valued.

**Description** The mastiff is a massive, vigorous, well-built dog. Minimum height: dogs, 30 inches (75 cm.); bitches, 27½ inches (70 cm.). Weight: from 175 to 190 pounds (79–86 kg.). It has a wide, heavy, rectangular head with well-developed, slightly pendent lips. Eyes: small, dark hazel. Nose: large and black. Ears: set high, rounded, pendent. Tail: reaching the hocks. Its coat is made up of short, thick hair in colors of golden fawn, light fawn, silver, and tiger. In the eighteenth century, it was described as follows: "As a lion is to a cat, so is the mastiff compared to a dog."

**Personality** Careful breeders have eliminated its ancient ferocity. Today it is a steady, gentle animal, eager for affection, and especially good with children. If trained, it will attack malefactors with extraordinary pugnacity.

**Uses** In the past it was a particularly bloodthirsty fighting dog used in spectacles. Thereafter, it was used to guard flocks and isolated factories. Today, it is still used as a watchdog and bodyguard as well as a companion.

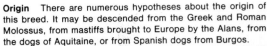

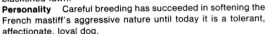

## 59 BULLMASTIFF

**Origin** This is a 1924 breed obtained by crossing mastiffs with bulldogs.

**Description** It is a powerfully built but not cumbersome dog. Dogs should measure 25 to 27 inches (63.5–68.5 cm.) at the withers and weigh 110 to 130 pounds (50–58 kg.). Bitches are from 24 to 26 inches (61–66 cm.) high and weigh 100 to 120 pounds (45–54 kg.). It has a wide, square, wrinkled head with wide-open nostrils, and strong, regular teeth. Eyes: dark hazel with a furrow between them. Ears: V-shaped, carried backward. Tail: straight or curved, reaching the hocks. Its coat is made up of short, stiff hair in all shades of fawn, red, and tiger.

**Personality** Its temperament is a combination of gaiety, fearlessness, seriousness, obedience, and affection, but the bull mastiff must be under the command of an energetic master.

**Uses** It has been prized as a hunting guard, as an aid in army and police work, and is used as a watchdog by the Diamond Society of South Africa. It is mainly used today as a most frightening watchdog and bodyguard. It enjoys living with the family, with whom it comports itself well. In order that it does not get fat, it needs a balanced diet and frequent walks.

## 60 ROTTWEILER

**Origin** The Rottweiler is probably descended from the Italian mastiff. During the Middle Ages, it was used as a herd dog. It was bred in the German town of Rottweil in Wurttemberg. Practically extinct in 1800, the breed became popular in the early twentieth century due to enthusiastic breeders centered in Stuttgart.

**Description** It has a massive, powerful body. Height for males: from 23¾ to 27 inches (60–68 cm.). Weight: around 110 pounds (50 kg.). Bitches are slightly smaller. It has a globular head, very wide between the ears. Muzzle: well developed, with a scissors bite. Eyes: dark brown, with an expression of good will and loyalty. Ears: triangular, carried forward. If the tail is too long, it may be docked. Coat: short, hard, and thick. It is black with markings on the cheeks, muzzle, paws, and legs.

**Personality** Balanced, tranquil, obedient, brave, easily trained. It becomes vicious only when its master is attacked.

**Uses** It has been used as a herd dog and in police work, but above all as a watchdog and bodyguard. It is also esteemed as a companion dog and is particularly affectionate with children.

**Note** Litters of twelve puppies are not unusual.

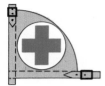

# 61  BOXER

**Origin**  The first picture of a boxer appears in a seventeenth-century Flemish tapestry, but it must have been a product of the artist's imagination, since the boxer did not exist at that time. The breed was developed in 1850 in Munich by crossing the Bullenbeisser mastiff and the bulldog. The first of these breeds was used in bear hunting; the second, to fight bulls; so it was only to be expected that the boxer would inherit the ferocious instincts of its forebears. In fact, however, the intelligent breeders made a point of eliminating the ferocity and of softening the dog's looks into something a bit more reassuring. The perfection of the lines and character of the breed was accomplished in 1896, the year the first boxer club was founded.

**Description**  The boxer has been described as "a dog of most beautiful ugliness." Its head should be in proportion to its body, lean and unwrinkled. Its lower jaw extends beyond its upper one, curving upward. Neither teeth nor tongue are to show when the mouth is closed. The nose is large and black with very open nostrils. Ears: set high, docked to a point. Eyes: dark. Neck: round, strong, and muscular, without dewlap. The body must be square. Tail: short and carried high. Its front legs should be straight and parallel. Height at the withers: dogs, 22½ to 25 inches (57–63 cm.); bitches, 21 to 23½ inches (53.2–58.4 cm.). Weight: dogs, 66 to 71 pounds (30–32 kg.); bitches, 53 to 55 pounds (24–25 kg.).

**Personality**  The boxer is a very good-natured and loyal dog. It doesn't bear grudges and is particularly affectionate with children. Easily trained.

**Uses**  The boxer has been used in police work, as a watchdog and bodyguard, and as a guide dog for the blind. Above all, however, it is prized as an amiable and lively companion. It is a tolerant, playful dog, but somewhat suspicious of strangers. It likes exercise and must be taken for long walks often.

**Note**  The boxer is not a long-lived dog. It often does not reach ten years of age. It is subject to rheumatism and should therefore be dried carefully when brought in from walks in the rain. Its teeth need frequent veterinary care.

## 62 BRINDLE BOXER

**Origin** The breed was developed in Munich in 1850 by crossing the Bullenbeisser mastiff and the bulldog.

**Description** The basic color of the brindle boxer is the same as that of the fawn boxer, but it is covered with dark or black streaks that run transversely around its body in the direction of the ribs. The contrast between the base color and the color of the streaks should be marked, but the streaks must be neither too narrow nor too wide. White markings are not considered a defect and are even preferred as long as they cover in total less than a third of the dog. Displeasing white areas, such as a white head or one white side, black dogs, or dogs in colors other than fawn, brindle, or yellow are not admissible in shows. The coat must be short, shiny, and tightly adhered to the body. The black mask must be limited to the muzzle. (For Personality and Uses, see Boxer.)

## 63 TAWNY BOXER

**Origin** The breed was developed in Munich in 1850 by crossing the Bullenbeisser mastiff with the Bulldog.

**Description** Its coat varies from a deer red to light yellow. Most sought after are dogs of a shade intermediate between the two. Its black mask should cover only the muzzle to avoid giving the dog a fierce look. White markings on the tawny or brindle boxer are not considered defects, but they may cover only less than a third of the dog. Its hair must be short, shiny, and tight to its body. The standard of this variety is the same for that of the brindle. (For Personality and Uses, see Boxer.)

**Origin** This is a breed of relatively recent origin. It was developed in Germany in 1860, presumably by crossings among Great Danes, German shepherds, Rottweilers, and pinschers, with possibly some blood of the Beauceron and the English greyhound. The creator of this mixture was a German tax collector named Louis Dobermann. Dobermann had to travel frequently through bandit-infested areas, and he decided to "construct" a watchdog and bodyguard capable of handling any situation that might arise. Bearing the name of its originator (shortened by one *n*), the Doberman was first presented in a dog show in 1876. It was immediately a big success.

**Description** The Doberman is a muscular and extremely elegant dog. Height: dogs, from 26 to 28 inches (66–71 cm.); bitches, 24 to 26 inches (61–66 cm.). Weight: from 66 to 88 pounds (30–40 kg.). It has a long, narrow head with a flat skull and an accentuated stop. Its teeth are strong and close in a scissors bite. Eyes: dark, with a lively, intelligent expression. Ears: docked, carried upright. Tail: docked short. Legs: perfectly straight. Its hair is short, thick, hard, and tight to its body. Colors: black, dark brown, or blue with limited patches of rust. White markings are not admitted. The Doberman's gait must be elastic, elegant, and cover a lot of ground.

**Personality** Males and females have different temperaments. The bitch is tranquil, sensitive, affectionate with the family, but suspicious of strangers. The dog is extremely intelligent, but impetuous, often aggressive, and must be ruled by an energetic master. It has been said that there are no bad Dobermans, just bad owners.

**Uses** Bred as a watchdog and bodyguard, the Doberman has continued to serve these functions during the hundred-some-odd years of its existence. It has been used by the police, the military (the Marines used Dobermans to rout out snipers), and for guarding all sorts of industrial property. The bitch is more adaptable to apartment life than the dog, but both need a daily outlet for their nervous energy.

**Note** The personality of the Doberman is still developing even after it is two years old; however, firm training should begin when the dog is ten to twelve months old. It is a rather long-lived dog and may reach fifteen or even twenty years of age.

## 65 GIANT SCHNAUZER
### Riesenschnauzer

**Origin** The giant schnauzer has the same Bavarian origins as the standard schnauzer, probably with the addition of Great Dane and Bouvier des Flandres blood.

**Description** It is the larger, stronger image of the standard schnauzer. Height for dogs: from 25½ to 27½ inches (65–70 cm.). Weight: around 77 pounds (35 kg.). Ten percent less for bitches. It has a long, powerful head and a muscular jaw. Eyes: oval and dark. Ears: docked, set high. Neck: very thick, with a healthy nape. Its front legs should be perpendicular. Tail: docked at the third vertebra. Coat: hard and bristly with a woolly undercoat. The most usual color is black, but there are salt-and-pepper individuals.

**Personality** Tranquil, steady, trainable, a patient friend even with children.

**Uses** In the 1700's it was used to guard the beer halls and butcher shops of Munich. Later, it was used in police work and by the military. Because its size and its looks command respect, it is still esteemed as a watchdog and a bodyguard. It is an excellent companion dog but is not adapted to apartment living.

**Note** Needs stripping twice a year. Ear cropping is optional.

---

## 66 LEONBERGER

**Origin** The breed was established in 1846 in Leonberg in the region of Wurttemberg by the German breeder Heinrich Essing from a crossing of the Newfoundland, the St. Bernard, and the Great Pyrenees. The official standard was set in 1949.

**Description** The Leonberger is a large, muscular, elegant dog. Height: from 30 to 31 inches (76–80 cm.). Weight: more than 88 pounds (40 kg.). It has a medium-sized head with a black nose and should not·have pendent lips or drool. Eyes: of medium size, chestnut in color. Ears: wide and round. Tail: bushy, carried partially raised. Its coat is rough but not shaggy, long, and crested at the neck and paws. Colors: light yellow, golden yellow, reddish-brown (dogs in these colors sometimes have a black mask), sand, silver-gray. White is not admissible.

**Personality** The Leonberger has a lively nature and is steady, affectionate and alert. It has a sweet expression.

**Uses** This is an outstanding water rescue dog. Only a short period of training is needed to augment its natural instincts. Not only does it have a waterproof coat, but nature has furnished it with webs between its toes which facilitate swimming.

## 67 LONG-HAIRED ST. BERNARD
### Langhaariger St. Bernhardshund

**Origin**   The St. Bernard has a very ancient origin. It is descended from the Tibetan mastiff and therefore must have originated with the mastiffs brought to the Alps by the Romans some two thousand years ago. As a St. Bernard, it appeared around the year 1000 in the Hospice of St. Bernard de Menthon near the Great St. Bernard Pass. The monks probably crossed the ancient mastiff with the Great Dane and the Great Pyrenees. Their attentive and continuous breeding produced a stupendous dog whose image first appeared on a Swiss coat of arms in 1350. Its use and popularity as a rescue dog began in the middle of the seventeenth century.

**Description**   The St. Bernard is a colossal dog, robust and muscular, with a powerful head. Minimum height: dogs, 27½ inches (70 cm.); bitches, 25½ inches (65 cm.). Weight around 110 to 121 pounds (50–55 kg.). It has a wide, slightly convex skull, the skin of which is distinctly wrinkled; a straight nasal canal; and a pronounced stop. The muzzle is high rather than long. The upper lip hangs. Dentition is full and powerful. Eyes: dark brown, medium-sized, and slightly sunken, placed rather more toward the front than the sides of the head. Ears: medium-sized, falling sideways. Strong neck with dewlap. Coat: medium length, shiny, and slightly wavy but neither curly nor crinkly. Colors: red with white markings or white with red markings. The red may be of any shade. Males are often black.

**Personality**   The St. Bernard is very good with people. It is obedient, extremely loyal, tranquil, and reflective, but it often dislikes small dogs. It seems to have the uncanny ability to predict avalanches.

**Uses**   As is well known, it was used in the past to rescue lost travelers and Alpinists in trouble in the snowy passes near the Hospice of St. Bernard. Today, it is almost exclusively a companion dog. It is not suited to apartment life. Some dogs are still trained for rescue work in cases of avalanche.

**Note**   The long-haired St. Bernard's coat needs frequent grooming with a wide-toothed comb and a stiff brush. Even if it lives in a yard, it needs long walks daily.

## 68 SHORT-HAIRED ST. BERNARD

**Origin** Same as for the long-haired St. Bernard.

**Description** It has very thick, short, shiny hair that lies close to its body. Its thighs appear slightly pantalooned. The hair on its tail is long and thick at the base, thinning out toward the point. It is bushy, but should have no fringe or pennant. In all other respects, the standard for the short-haired St. Bernard is the same as for the long-haired St. Bernard.

**Personality** Good, loyal, tranquil, obedient.

**Uses** The short-haired St. Bernard can withstand very cold temperatures and is the variety most sought after in the mountains. The long-haired St. Bernard has the problem of collecting snow on its coat. This forms icicles, which can obstruct its movement. The short-haired St. Bernard continues to be trained for avalanche rescue with excellent results. Because of its size, minimum height 27½ inches (70 cm.), this dog is not suitable for apartment life. Nonetheless, it is well loved the world over.

---

## 69 GREAT PYRENEES
### Chien des Pyrénées

**Origin** Descended from the Hungarian kuvasz and the Maremmano-Abruzzese, the Great Pyrenees is considered the aristocratic relative of the St. Bernard and the Newfoundland.

**Description** It is a very large, strong, muscular, but elegant dog. Average height: dogs, 27 to 32 inches (69–81 cm.); bitches, 25 to 29 inches (64–74 cm.). Some dogs are as much as 40 inches (1 meter) high. Weight: 90 to 125 pounds (41–57 kg.), depending on its size. Its head is large and bearlike. Muzzle: wide and slightly pointed. Nose: black. Lips: not pendent. Eyes: brown, set obliquely, with a sweet expression. Ears: small, triangular, pendent. Tail: rolled up when the dog is excited. Coat: white (sometimes with light-tan, badger, or gray markings). At the court of the Sun King, the dog was known as the "gentleman with the white fur."

**Personality** Obedient, hardworking, affectionate, loyal, patient.

**Uses** It was born to live in the mountains. With a minimum of training it can be used for guarding sheep, as a guide through heavy snows, a rescue dog for avalanche victims, and a guardian of person and property. It needs space, but is well adapted to family life.

**Origin** There are conflicting hypotheses about the origin of the Newfoundland. There are those who claim the breed derives from Nordic dogs brought to Newfoundland in 1600. Others feel the breed has British origins and date its development from the year 1700, when the island of Newfoundland became a British possession. According to this theory, the British brought Tibetan mastiffs to Newfoundland, and the Newfoundland dog was the result of a long period of breeding between these mastiffs and local dogs. The third hypothesis is that the Newfoundland is a close relative of the Labrador. This theory is based on the similarities between the two breeds and the fact that the coasts of Newfoundland and Labrador are very close to each other. It is possible that the Labrador, which is an excellent swimmer, was able to swim the Strait of Belle Isle or cross on foot when the water was frozen.

**Description** The Newfoundland is a large dog. It is strong, elegant, harmonious, agile, and hardy. Average height: dogs, 28 inches (70 cm.); bitches, 26 inches (65 cm.); however, many dogs are even larger. Average weight: 120 to 150 pounds (54–68 kg.). It has a massive head with a short, square muzzle. Eyes: small and dark; the conjunctiva should not show as it does in the St. Bernard. Ears: flat to the head. Tail: medium length, pendent. The Newfoundland has flat, slightly wavy, long hair; it is coarse to the touch and a bit oily. The undercoat is also oily, to keep water from reaching the skin. Dogs that live indoors, however, tend to lose their undercoats. Main colors: black with blue highlights, black, bronze.

**Personality** It is a dog with an outstanding temperament: good, courageous, generous, intelligent, human. Lord Byron wrote of one of this breed: ''. . . Courage without ferocity, And all the virtues of man without his vices.'' It is also a patient dog, mild with guests and not obsequious with its master.

**Uses** The Newfoundland is an instinctive water rescue dog. Many owe their lives to members of the breed. In 1919, a gold medal was awarded to a Newfoundland that pulled to safety in a lifeboat some twenty shipwrecked people. It has been called the St. Bernard of the water. Today, safer ships and improved communications have limited the dog's professional activities, but its appeal has not diminished due to the fact that it is considered a handsome, devoted, delightful companion.

## 71 LANDSEER

**Origin** A variety of Newfoundland named after Sir Edwin Landseer, the famous nineteenth-century animal painter. In the 1920's, the breed nearly disappeared, but German dog lovers "reconstructed" it by crossing St. Bernards and Great Pyrenees.

**Description** It is a large, strong, extremely elegantly built dog, slightly longer-legged than the Newfoundland, with a lithe, elegant gait. It is about 31 inches (78–80 cm.) high and weighs from 132 to 155 pounds (60–70 kg.). Bitches are about 10% smaller. It has long, thick hair that is soft to the touch. Eyes: dark brown, with a friendly expression. Ears: flat to the sides of the head. Tail: hanging when the dog is at rest. Color: white with markings on the chest and back and a black head.

**Personality** Affectionate, courageous, intelligent, friendly to children.

**Uses** It is at home in the water. Therefore, it is excellent in fishing with its master, in retrieving game in marshy areas, and in lifesaving. From puppyhood it is a strong swimmer and an amusing swimming companion.

## 72 ALASKAN MALAMUTE

**Origin** The Malamute is a Nordic dog, descended from the Arctic wolf. Its name comes from Mahlemuts, an Alaskan tribe that raised and cared for these beautiful snow dogs.

**Description** It is a ponderous dog, well built, with a solid body, a wide head, and a proud expression. Ears: upright. Eyes: small, almond-shaped, like those of a wolf, but with a sweet expression. Its coat is thick but not long, stiff, with a soft, woolly undercoat. Colors vary from light gray to black with all shades in between. The legs and muzzle are almost always white. Its tail is long-haired and waves over its back. Height: dogs, 25 inches (64 cm.); bitches, 23 inches (58 cm.). Weight: dogs, 85 pounds (38 kg.); bitches, 75 pounds (34 kg.).

**Personality** Extremely loyal and intelligent, sweet, most affectionate toward its master, an aggressive fighter among dogs. Firm handling and training are necessary. It is a clean, odorless dog which does not bark.

**Uses** The Malamute is a sled dog. Packs of Malamutes have participated in many polar expeditions, for which they were particularly well adapted due to their tenacity, sense of direction, and excellent sense of smell. They have appeared as unforgettable characters in the stories of Jack London and Rudyard Kipling. In the last decades, they have become accustomed to being family pets and have proved themselves to be civilized and good-natured in this role.

## 73 ESKIMO DOG

**Origin** The Eskimo dog is native to eastern Siberia. In the nineteenth century, it was introduced into Alaska and Greenland where it found an ideal environment.

**Description** A very large dog with a wolflike expression. Dogs weigh from 66 to 110 pounds (30–50 kg.); bitches, from 55 to 88 pounds (25–48 kg.); height of dogs from 16 to 18 inches (40–45 cm.). The Eskimo dog has a large, conical head, a muzzle of medium length, and powerful jaws. Eyes: deep-set and oblique, with an ardent expression. Ears: small, triangular. Tail: bushy, curved over the dog's back. Its coat is about 6 inches (15 cm.) long with an extremely thick undercoat that is naturally oily to prevent dampness from reaching the dog's skin. It can bear temperatures as low as −76° to −94° F. (−60° to −70° C.). Its coat may be any color.

**Personality** Docile, loyal, affectionate, untiring, but a bit timid. If treated harshly, it tends to become diffident.

**Uses** Typical arctic draft dog. A team of twenty Eskimo dogs can pull a sled carrying a two-ton load for 25 miles (40 km.) without stopping. The Eskimo does not bark, but howls like a wolf. It is not adapted to family life.

## 74 GREENLAND
## Grünlandshund

**Origin** The Greenland is descended from the Arctic wolf.

**Description** It is an extremely robust dog. Height: 24 inches (60 cm.) and over for dogs; 22 inches (55 cm.) or more for bitches. Weight: about 66 pounds (30 kg.). It has a muscular, big-boned body, broad chest, perfectly straight limbs, and large, round feet with strong soles. Muzzle: cone-shaped. Nose: black, but can become flesh-colored in summer. Teeth: extremely strong. Eyes: dark, slightly oblique, with an honest expression. Ears: small, triangular, carried erect. Thick tail carried rolled up on the back. Coat: straight, coarse, rather long, with a heavy undercoat. All colors and combinations are admissible except albino.

**Personality** Like all Nordic dogs, it has a fundamentally good, loyal, lively, and affectionate temperament. Since the dogs usually work in teams, they seldom have the opportunity to develop an affectionate relationship with one master.

**Uses** Due to its exceptional hardiness and resistance to cold, the Greenland is ideally adapted to pulling a sled. It is not suited to living in an apartment.

## 75 SAMOYED

**Origin** Since ancient times there has lived in Siberia a population of hunters and fishermen known as Samoyeds. For centuries, they have used a beautiful, robust white dog to pull their sleds. This dog has become known by their name. In 1889, the explorer Robert Scott brought several of the dogs to England, where the breed was developed and spread throughout the world.

**Description** The Samoyed is a strong, dynamic, active dog. Height: dogs, 21 to 23½ inches (53–60 cm.); bitches, 19 to 21 inches (48–53 cm.). Weight: 50 to 65 pounds (23–30 kg.). It has a powerful wedge-shaped head with a black or brown nose and strong jaws. Eyes: dark, oblique, deep. Ears: medium-sized, slightly rounded at the point, and carried erect. Tail: long, full-haired, carried rolled on the back. Its legs are solid and muscular; its feet, flat and covered with hair. Its coat is thick and harsh, not wavy, with a thick, soft undercoat, which protects it against the arctic cold. The color preferred is pure white, but off-white, yellow, and white and yellow are accepted.

**Personality** It is a calm, gentle, dignified, obedient, loyal, affectionate dog. Since it is used to working in teams, its outstanding qualities often do not have the opportunity to be expressed. However, when it becomes attached to a single master, it proves itself an outstandingly good-natured, lively, and sociable dog. It never seeks trouble but can handle an adversary if necessary.

**Uses** Classic sled dog, able to pull heavy loads long distances. It has also been used successfully in hunting walruses, guarding herds, and as a bodyguard. It has proved itself an excellent companion and watchdog. Its beauty and gentleness continue to win it friends throughout the world. It is absolutely not vicious, plays gladly with children, and is clean. Its only defect is that it tends to be a frequent and lively barker. It also may be hard to housebreak.

**Note** Among its good qualities is the fact that its coat will remain white naturally, without the need of periodic baths. It is necessary, however, to brush it daily, especially in summer when parasites begin their invasion.

## 76 SIBERIAN HUSKY

**Origin** Native to Siberia, the husky was brought to Alaska in 1909.

**Description** It is a medium-sized dog, robust, lively, pleasant, agile in movement. Height: dogs, 21 to 23½ inches (53–60 cm.); bitches, 20 to 22 inches (51–56 cm.). Weight: dogs, from 45 to 60 pounds (20.5–27 kg.); bitches, from 35 to 50 pounds (16–22.5 kg.). It has brown or light-blue eyes set obliquely, with a friendly expression. Ears: set high, erect. Tail: wolflike, rolled on its back. The Siberian husky has a thick, woolly undercoat and a soft outer coat. It is able to withstand temperatures as low as −58° to −76° F. (−50° to −60° C.). All colors are admissible, from wolf-gray to silver-gray; from light sand to black with white markings.

**Personality** Sociable, affectionate, good company, extremely stubborn, and easily bored.

**Uses** Due to its light weight, which allows it to run quite fast, the husky is used in sled races. These are particularly popular in Canada and the northern U.S.

## 77 CANAAN DOG

**Origin** This breed is indigenous to Israel, dating back many centuries. Formerly known only in the Middle East, it has in recent years also found favor in Europe and the United States.

**Description** The Canaan is a lively, elegant, medium-sized dog. Height: 20 to 24 inches (50–60 cm.). Weight: 40 to 55 pounds (18–25 kg.). It has a well-proportioned head, a deep muzzle, and a dark nose. Eyes: almond-shaped. Ears: erect. Tail: medium length, slight plume. Front legs: perfectly straight with a light bone structure. Body: robust but not massive. Its coat is of medium length, coarse, with a good undercoat. Colors: all brown tones, black, white with red, brown, or black markings.

**Personality** Pugnacious, devoted, gentle, home-loving.

**Uses** It is primarily used as a watchdog for herds or houses, as a guide dog for the blind, and as a test dog in mines. During the conflicts in Israel, it was used to carry messages over the rocky desert and to find the wounded. It has an extremely high capacity for learning, and it is therefore likely that other uses will be found for it in the future. It is also an outstanding companion dog.

## 78 PORTUGUESE WATER DOG
### Cão de Agua

**Origin**   Unknown.

**Description**   The Portuguese water dog is a hardy, muscular, medium-sized dog. Height: dogs, 20 to 22 inches (50–57 cm.); bitches, 17 to 20 inches (43–52 cm.). Weight: dogs, from 42 to 55 pounds (19–25 kg.); bitches, 35 to 49 pounds (16–22 kg.). It has a well-proportioned head with a muzzle narrowing toward the end and strong jaws with very well developed canines. Eyes: slightly oblique, chestnut or black. Ears: heart-shaped, close to the head. Limbs: straight and muscular. Its coat is thick and strong, either wavy or curly, without undercoat. Colors: black, white, chestnut, and mixtures thereof. The back parts and the muzzle should be shorn entirely.

**Personality**   Lively, impetuous, pugnacious, pleasing, affectionate, good company. Equally happy in a country place or a city apartment; physically hardy, protective of children, water-loving, most adaptable.

**Uses**   For centuries, members of the breed have lived on the boats of Portuguese fishermen. They are able swimmers and can be taught to catch in their mouths and bring back fish escaping from the net. They are also useful at catching ropes and other objects thrown from boats toward the shore. They are also used as guard and companion dogs. But because they spend so much time in the water, they may become prematurely deaf.

---

## 79 FILA BRASILEIRO

**Origin**   Probably descended from bulldogs, mastiffs, and bloodhounds brought to Brazil by Portuguese and Spanish conquistadores in the seventeenth century.

**Description**   The Fila Brasileiro has a strong musculature and bone structure and a well-proportioned body. Average height: 26 inches (65 cm.). Weight: about 110 pounds (50 kg.). It has a large, square head; strong muzzle; wide, dark nose; and scissors bite. Eyes: slightly almond-shaped, with a pensive look. Its coat is short and soft. All colors are admissible.

**Personality**   Courageous, attentive, impetuous, devoted to its master, but suspicious of strangers.

**Uses**   Because it has an acute sense of smell, it was used in the past to find fugitive slaves in the forest. Later, it proved to be an excellent herd dog and guard dog. Although it has a good disposition, it is not suited to city life, since its vigorous body must work off energy in the freedom of the country. Its gait is measured and elastic, like that of a cat, and this fascinating carriage has earned it great success in dog shows.

## 80 PYRENEES MASTIFF
### Mastín de los Pirineos

**Origin**   The Pyrenees mastiff is indigenous to the southern slopes of the Pyrenees. It is also known as the mastiff of Navarre and the mastiff of León. It is not to be confused with the Great Pyrenees, which is of French origin.

**Description**   It is a strong, symmetrical, powerful dog of elegant beauty. It may be as high as 31 inches (80 cm.) and weigh as much as 155 pounds (70 kg.). However, the Pyrenees mastiff has a step so light that it hardly leaves footprints. It has a large head with a long muzzle, black nose, and very pointed teeth. Eyes: small and dark. Ears: pointed and pendent. Tail: fringed, carried low. Its coat is thick, coarse, not long. Colors: white with two golden or gray markings on the sides of the head and at the beginning of the neck. The dog may also have markings on its posterior. Least prized are black-and-white dogs.

**Personality**   Silent, friendly, bright. It eats sparingly.

**Uses**   The Pyrenees mastiff is adapted to all sorts of uses: guard dog, hunter of wild game, bodyguard, cart dog. But it is above all an excellent sheepdog, resistant to cold weather, and capable of combating wolves.

---

## 81 SPANISH MASTIFF
### Mastín Español

**Origin**   This breed is native to the region of Estremadura in Spain. It is, in fact, also known by the names mastiff of Estremadura and mastiff of La Mancha.

**Description**   It is a stocky, robust, rustic-looking dog. Height: from 26 to 28 inches (65–70 cm.). Weight: from 110 to 132 pounds (50–60 kg.). Bitches are somewhat smaller. It has a well-proportioned head with a long muzzle, strong jaws, and full lips. Eyes: small, with an intelligent expression. Ears: pointed, pendent. Tail: fringed, carried low. Its coat is abundant but not long. The most common colors are reddish, wolf color, fawn, black and white, white and gold, white and gray, and brindle.

**Personality**   Vivacious, obedient, affectionate with its master, but suspicious of strangers, trainable.

**Uses**   It is a typical guard dog, used especially in the country, in factories, or in work yards. But it is also excellent at other jobs: shepherd (it is ferocious against wolves), hunting dog for wild boar and other large game, and cart dog over the roughest trails. It has been used by the military for guarding munitions.

## 82 AUSTRIAN SHORT-HAIRED PINSCHER
### Österreichischer Kurzhaariger Pinscher

**Origin** The origin of this breed is not known. It is also called the Austrian short-haired terrier, but it is not to be confused with the German terrier, the Zwergpinscher, which is a small companion dog.

**Description** It is a shortish, well-built dog of medium bulk. Height: from 14 to 20 inches (35–50 cm.). Weight: from 26 to 40 pounds (12–18 kg.). Its standard demands that it have a pear-shaped head with a thick nose, ears like a bat, a barrel-shaped chest, and that it appear from the front to be wider than it is long. Its tail is carried rolled on its back. It has short hair in light yellow, fawn, stag red, reddish-black, or tiger, almost always with white markings.

**Personality** Courageous, tenacious, vigilant. It is a barker and has quick reflexes. Very likable.

**Uses** It is considered an outstanding watchdog, ready to give the alarm at the slightest suspicion, decisive in its assault against malefactors, and vigilant the entire night. In the field, however, it shows the qualities of a terrier: it tends to dig holes, to enlarge lairs, and to launch itself furiously against foxes and rabbits. Because of its liveliness and need for space, it is more adapted to country than to city life.

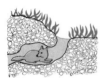

---

## 83 KYŪSHŪ

**Origin** The Kyūshū comes from the region of Hokkaido in Japan, an area rich with mountains, volcanoes, forests, rivers, and rural areas. It is an ancient breed.

**Description** The Kyūshū is well built and muscular. Height: dogs, from 19 to 21 inches (48.5–54.2 cm.); bitches, 17 to 19 inches (42.4–48.5 cm.). Weight: under 66 pounds (30 kg.). It has a pointed muzzle and a dark nose. Its teeth are solid and must not be undershot. Eyes: brown, Oriental in shape. Ears: short and pointed. Tail: rolled on the back. Coat: short, rather coarse hair, gray-white in color.

**Personality** It is a very patient dog, intelligent, trainable, silent, docile, affectionate.

**Uses** Its intelligence allows it to pick up quickly whatever it is taught. Thus it can be a hunter, shepherd, watchdog, companion, or fisherman's helper. It has been accustomed for centuries to working on rocky terrain. It can withstand the cold, and it eats sparingly.

**Note** It is an extremely clean animal both in its body and its habits, and is thus well adapted to living in the home.

## 84 NORRBOTTENSPETS

**Origin** The Norrbottenspets is a Nordic dog of unknown origin.

**Description** It is a small dog. Average height: 16 inches (40 cm.). Weight: 26 to 33 pounds (12–15 kg.). It is compact and light with a pleasing carriage and an attentive expression. It has a wedge-shaped head, a pointed muzzle with a distinct stop, a black nose, thin lips, and a scissors bite. Its eyes are medium-sized and dark and give the impression that the dog is "always on the lookout." Its ears are erect and mobile. Neck: muscular. Body: square. Tail: curved, carried to the side with the tip touching its thighs. It has thick, coarse, medium-length hair with a soft undercoat. All colors are permissible, but most highly valued are white dogs with hard-edged red or yellow markings.

**Personality** Affectionate, loyal, vigilant.

**Uses** It is used to draw little carts and for guarding property. However, because of its elegant carriage and because of its irresistible liveliness, it has become a companion dog. It is clean, attached to the family, and useful against robbers.

## 85 HOKKAIDOKEN

**Origin** The ancient Ainus who settled in Japan ten centuries before Christ brought with them a robust dog for pulling sleds. The Hokkaidoken of today is descended from these dogs and is the most important breed in Japan.

**Description** It is a thin, muscular, sturdy-looking dog. It is impetuous and fast and has a light gait. The height of dogs is not over 20 inches (50 cm.), and their weight is about 55 pounds (25 kg.). Bitches are about 10% smaller. Head: square, with a straight nose and healthy, solid, nonprotruding teeth. Eyes: triangular, with black pupils and an intelligent expression. Ears: erect, pointed. Neck: thick, with slight dewlap. Tail: sickle-shaped, clearly fringed. Its coat is hard and straight with a soft, thick undercoat. Colors: red, white, black, pepper and salt, brown.

**Personality** Stubborn, courageous, obedient, loyal, home-loving.

**Uses** The Hokkaidoken has always distinguished itself in big-game hunting (especially bears), in guarding property, and as a draft animal. It has an innate sense of direction and can, therefore, return to its master no matter how great the distance.

## 86  TOSA

**Origin**  This is a modern breed developed in the period between 1868 and 1912 by crossing the Kōchi (a local Japanese breed), the bull-terrier, the bulldog, the Great Dane, and the St. Bernard.

**Description**  The Tosa is a sturdy, solid dog. Height: around 24 inches (60 cm.). Weight: over 83 pounds (37.5 kg.). Its muzzle is of medium length with powerful jaws and very solid teeth. Eyes: reddish-brown, small, but with a penetrating expression. Ears: thin, falling along its cheeks. Neck: muscular, with dewlaps. Tail: reaching the hocks. Its coat is made up of very short, strong, dense hair. The usual color is red; however, white with red markings or red markings on other background colors are acceptable.

**Personality**  Aggressive, courageous, sometimes threatening, but nonetheless, wise, obedient, ready to accept good training.

**Uses**  The Tosa began its career as a combat dog, and proceeded to the duties of watchdog and bodyguard. Pugnacious but patient, it has also achieved success as a companion dog, friendly with the family, but suspicious of strangers.

## 87  AKITA INU

**Origin**  The breed is native to the island of Honshu in the region of Akita in Japan, where it has remained unchanged for centuries.

**Description**  Powerful, solid, well-proportioned, distinctive-looking. Height: from 25 to 28 inches (63.6–71 cm.) for dogs; from 23 to 26 inches (57.5–66 cm.) for bitches. Weight: from 77 to 88 pounds (35–40 kg.). It has a powerful, short, pointed muzzle and solid teeth that should not be undershot. Eyes: dark, slightly triangular. Ears: erect, tilted slightly forward. Tail: thick and strong, reaching the hocks, but carried rolled in a ring on the dog's back. Stiff, moderate-length hair with a fine undercoat. Colors: all colors are acceptable, including white, pinto, and brindle. The undercoat may be of a different color than the outer coat, and the dog may or may not have a mask.

**Personality**  Docile but occasionally impetuous, careful, affectionate, intelligent, courageous.

**Uses**  For centuries the Akita was used as a fighting dog, and for this reason the breed became nearly extinct. However, the Japanese government, unwilling to lose this national treasure, prohibited its use in bloody spectacles. It was also used in big-game hunting, but today it is practically exclusively a companion dog with fans in the United States and Europe.

## 88 SANSHU

**Origin** This is a modern breed, developed in 1912 by crossing the ancient Japanese dog the Aichi and the Chinese chow chow.

**Description** The Sanshu is a very hardy dog, able to withstand the worst climates. Seen from the side, its body appears square. Height: dogs, from 20 to 22 inches (50–55 cm.); bitches, 18 to 20 inches (45–50 cm.). Weight: from 44 to 55 pounds (20–25 kg.). It has a robust, wedge-shaped muzzle; a black nose; dark, almond-shaped eyes; small, triangular ears; and a thick, strong neck. Its skull is slightly flat on top. Its hair is strong, not particularly short, in colors varying from reddish to gray. There is also a smaller variety of Sanshu, similar to the above but about 4 inches (10 cm.) shorter.

**Personality** Sensitive to its master's orders, affectionate, extremely clean in its habits.

**Uses** Its ancestor the Aichi was always used as a hunting dog and a guard dog. The Sanshu, for its part, is an excellent guard dog, but is able to combine this gift with that of being a companion dog, in which role it is esteemed and sought after even outside Japan.

---

## 89 AÏDI

**Origin** The Aïdi's origin is uncertain. It is probably native to some place in the Moroccan Sahara.

**Description** It is a robust, sturdy dog, bearing a vague resemblance to the Airedale. Height: dogs, from 20 to 24 inches (52–62 cm.); bitches, 18 to 20 inches (45–50 cm.). Weight: around 66 pounds (30 kg.). Muzzle: short, wedge-shaped, bearlike. Extremely strong teeth. Eyes: dark, of a hue corresponding to the color of its coat. Ears: carried semierect. Neck: muscular, without dewlap. Tail: reaching the hocks, beautifully plumed. Its hair is strong, about 2 inches (6 cm.) long, in a variety of colors: sand, fawn, white, blackened fawn, tricolor, etc.

**Personality** Curious, nervous, good company, extremely amenable to training.

**Uses** Little known outside Morocco, it is used as a sheepdog, a guard dog, a bodyguard, a hunter of jackals, and to warn of the presence of venomous snakes. It has a thick coat with a mane at the neck which protects it from the strong rays of the sun and from the nocturnal cold in mountainous regions. It is particularly prized by nomads and hunters.

## 90 CÃO DA SERRA DA ESTRÊLA

**Origin** This is one of the oldest breeds on the Iberian peninsula. Presumably, it is indigenous to the Estrêla Mountains in Portugal, from which it takes its name.

**Description** It is a sturdy dog with extremely strong shoulders and a massive head. It measures about 31 inches (80 cm.) around the chest. Its limbs are straight and solidly muscled. Height: dogs, from 26 to 28 inches (65–72 cm.); less for bitches. Weight: from 88 to 110 pounds (40–50 kg.). It has dark, wide-open oval eyes, with an intelligent and serene expression. Its ears are small, thin, and pendent. Its tail is thick and sickle-shaped. It has strong, coarse, but not hard hair, somewhat like that of a goat, with a fine, thick undercoat. The only admissible colors are fawn, wolf, and yellow, either unicolored or with markings.

**Personality** Extremely docile with its master, but very ferocious toward strangers; intelligent, trainable, combative.

**Uses** It has been trained to defend flocks and herds, for hunting, for pulling small carts of milk and cheese over mountain roads, for guarding houses, and for attacking wolves. It does not, however, have a good reputation as a companion dog.

## 91 CÃO DE CASTRO LABOREIRO

**Origin** This is an extremely ancient Portuguese breed that bears the name of the village of Castro Laboreiro, where it is particularly popular.

**Description** It is vigorous, sturdy, and stern, but nonetheless agile and of noble carriage. Height: dogs, from 22 to 24 inches (56–60 cm.); bitches, from 20 to 22 inches (52–57 cm.). Weight: from 66 to 88 pounds (30–40 kg.) for dogs; from 44 to 66 pounds (20–30 kg.) for bitches. It has a light, narrow head; flared black nostrils; a solid jaw with strong white teeth; a wide, deep chest; and a retracted abdomen. Its tail is long and hairy. Eyes: brown, almond-shaped. Ears: triangular with rounded tips. Its hair is coarse and strong and evenly distributed. Colors: various shades of wolf.

**Personality** Very courageous, docile, loyal, affectionate. It has a unique bark that begins in a deep baritone and rises to a ringing tenor.

**Uses** It is a wonderful guardian of flocks and herds and is particularly ferocious against wolves. Since it is resistant to all sorts of bad weather and difficult terrain, it is also useful as a guard for isolated houses. In the family, it is a peaceful companion, but it tends to be somewhat suspicious of strangers.

**TIBETAN MASTIFF**

**Origin** The Tibetan Mastiff is descended from the famous Tibetan dogs that were the source of the majority of Molossuses and mastiffs throughout the world. The English have perfected the breed, which has virtually disappeared in the Orient.

**Description** The Tibetan mastiff is a vigorous dog with a sturdy bone structure. It may reach a height of 31 inches (80 cm.) and a weight of nearly 220 pounds (100 kg.). Marco Polo described it as "tall as a donkey with a voice as powerful as that of a lion." It has a wide, massive head; a muzzle that is lighter than that of the English mastiff; and an extremely strong jaw. Eyes: brown, medium-sized. Ears: heart-shaped, pendent. Neck: powerful. Tail: curled over its back. Its coat is long, heavy, thick, black with areas of bright tan or gold.

**Personality** The few individuals that remain in Tibet are ferocious and aggressive, unpredictable in their behavior, and very difficult to train. But the dogs bred by the English are obedient and attached to their masters.

**Uses** The Tibetan mastiff is an outstanding sheepdog, ferocious against wolves or leopards that try to approach its flock. It is also an excellent guard both of entire villages and of isolated houses. For it to live in civilization, it must have at least a yard.

---

**93** **KEESHOND**

**Origin** The Keeshond has an arctic origin. In its veins runs the blood of the Samoyed, chow chow, elkhound, and Pomeranian. At the beginning of the French Revolution it became the symbol of the common and middle-class Dutchmen who were led by the patriot Kees de Gyselaer. The breed then suffered a long period of neglect and did not become popular again until 1920.

**Description** This is a medium-sized dog. Dogs are from 17 to 19 inches (44–48 cm.) high; bitches, 10% less. Average weight: from 55 to 66 pounds (25–30 kg.). In looks, it is reminiscent of its ancestor the Samoyed, with oblique chestnut eyes, erect triangular ears, and its medium-length tail rolled on its back. It has a singular and magnificent coat of thick stiff hair and an ample undercoat. It always appears to have just been washed and combed. Color: a mixture of gray and black.

**Personality** Vivacious, lively, intelligent, lovable, impertinent, and always alert.

**Uses** The Keeshond is a good swimmer and for years it was the dog-of-all-jobs on Dutch boats. Today, it is used as a companion dog, adapted to living in the city, and as a watchdog because of its notable gift for warning of danger.

TERRIERS

**Origin** The history of terrierlike dogs dates back to ancient times. Pliny the Elder, in his *Natural History*, wrote that when the Romans invaded Britain in 55 B.C., they were surprised to find small dogs that followed their prey into its den or lair. Similarly, Marco Polo reported that of all the hunting dogs of the Great Khan, the most prized were the little terriers. The first true terrier was described in 1570 by the English physician John Caius of Cambridge. From that time on, canine history has been filled with stories of the terrier: stories of its deeds, its magnificent temperament, and the beautiful varieties that have proliferated throughout the world.

In developing the terriers we know today, breeders crossed ancient dachshunds, the English hound, and later the foxhound and the beagle. The first standard for the smooth fox terrier was established in 1876.

**Description** The fox terrier is blessed with many weapons of attack: strong jaws, well-developed teeth, vehemence, physical strength, and, above all, courage. It is a well-built, elegant dog, concentrating a lot of strength in a little space. It should not be more than 16 inches (40 cm.) high and should weigh around 18 pounds (8 kg.). Bitches are a bit smaller. It has a flat, narrow skull with a muzzle that narrows gradually to a black nose. Eyes: dark, small, deep-set, extremely lively. Ears: V-shaped, folded forward. Neck: thin and muscular. Tail: carried high, normally docked to one-fourth its length. Coat: shiny, abundant. The background color is always white with small black or brown markings.

**Personality** As one can tell from its looks, the fox terrier is a lively, active, lovable dog. It has a tendency to fight with other dogs, but it is enthusiastically playful, especially with children. It is extremely affectionate with members of its family and does not hide its jealousy.

**Uses** The fox terrier was originally bred as a hunting dog capable of following small game into its lair and fighting as an equal against foxes. Its name, fox terrier, tells the whole story. While even today its hunting instincts remain evident, it is considered a companion dog. It is intelligent, curious, and pugnacious. Disdaining soft cushions, it takes part in all the family's activities. It is a barker, and is therefore considered a good watchdog in apartments and automobiles.

**Note** The fox terrier is a very dynamic dog and uses up a lot of energy. Its diet, therefore, should be especially nourishing.

## 95    WIREHAIRED FOX TERRIER

**Origin**    The same as for the smooth fox terrier.

**Description**    The wirehaired fox terrier has been called the well-dressed brother of the smooth fox terrier. Strictly speaking, however, they are considered two different breeds. The wirehaired fox terrier should not be more than 15½ inches (39.37 cm.) high, and its weight should not exceed 18 pounds (8 kg.). While all other standards are the same as for the smooth fox terrier, the wirehaired fox terrier has a coat that should be dense, shaggy, and compact without excessive curling, like the fibers on a coconut shell. The background color is white with black or brown markings. The wirehaired fox terrier needs periodic stripping and its tail should be docked, two procedures that tend to give it the look of a stuffed animal.

**Personality**    The same as the smooth fox terrier's.

**Uses**    Although born to hunt animals in lairs, today, mainly due to its good looks, the breed is considered only as a companion dog. It has been described as an animal that "brings joy into the world." It is also useful as a watchdog in apartments and cars.

## 96    AIREDALE TERRIER

**Origin**    The breed was developed about a hundred years ago in the county of York by crossing the ancient working terrier and the otterhound. Its name comes form the river Aire in Yorkshire.

**Description**    Like a giant rough terrier, the Airedale has a brown coat with large black or grizzle markings. Its hair is bristly and resistant to dampness, but it needs stripping. Height: approximately 23 inches (59 cm.). Weight: around 44 pounds (20 kg.). Eyes: small, dark, lively. Ears: V-shaped, semierect. Tail: docked, carried high.

**Personality**    At one time the Airedale was used for hunting bears and wolves, but over the years, breeding has made it a true gentleman of a dog. It is patient, lively, pleasant. It needs to feel loved and respected.

**Uses**    Unlike smaller terriers, it is not suited to searching out the lairs of small animals, but it is good at hunting otter in the marsh and at stag and wild-boar hunting. In time of war it has distinguished itself as a carrier of messages, a sentry, in sounding an alarm, in assault, and as a mouser. It has been trained as a police dog and a bodyguard. Today, however, perhaps mistakenly, it is considered only as an excellent companion dog.

## 97 BEDLINGTON TERRIER

**Origin** The Bedlington was developed around 1825 by English miners who wanted a dog that would exterminate the rats in mines. The breed, which takes its name from a small town in England, was obtained by crossings among the Dandie Dinmont, the otterhound, and the whippet.

**Description** It has been described as a dog with "the heart of a lion; the appearance of a lamb." In fact, it does look very much like a sheep. It has a pear-shaped head, a long jaw, and robust teeth that meet in a scissors or pincers bite. Eyes: small, deep-set. Ears: set low on the head and hanging along the cheeks. Pointed tail; straight front legs; harelike feet. Its coat is dense and cottony and must be trimmed. Colors: blue, reddish-blue, sand, liver. Height: 18½ inches (42 cm.). Weight: 17 to 23 pounds (7.7–10.5 kg.).

**Personality** Despite its lamblike looks, the Bedlington is by nature snarly and aggressive, and is a great ratcatcher. Breeding has softened its personality, however, and today it is considered affectionate, devoted, and intelligent.

**Uses** Originally developed for the hunting of rats and small game in lairs or on open ground (talents it has certainly not forgotten), the Bedlington is today an apartment dog. It is also an attentive and barking watchdog.

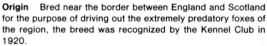

## 98 BORDER TERRIER

**Origin** Bred near the border between England and Scotland for the purpose of driving out the extremely predatory foxes of the region, the breed was recognized by the Kennel Club in 1920.

**Description** It is the smallest and least flashy of the terriers. Its height is about 10 inches (25 cm.) and it weighs from 13 to 15 pounds (6–7 kg.). It has an otterlike head with a short, sturdy muzzle and scissors bite. Eyes: dark, with a lively expression. Ears: small, V-shaped, falling forward. Tail: thick but not long, carried cheerfully. Its limbs are not heavy-boned. Coat: thick and dense, with a thick undercoat. Colors: red, wheat, pepper-and-salt, reddish-blue.

**Personality** Bold, very lively, implacable in the hunt but amiable in the home. It is especially affectionate with children.

**Uses** This is a typical terrier, resistant to illness, nimble, and robust. For decades it was used exclusively for hunting foxes and martens. As with most terriers, the border terrier gradually began to be taken into the home, and today it is highly prized as a companion dog because of its temperament and adaptability. Despite its great hatred of foxes, it manages to get along well with domestic animals.

## 99  BULLTERRIER

**Origin**  In 1830, when combats between bulldogs and bulls were at their height, lovers of this "sport" decided to create a dog that would attack even more agilely. By crossing the bulldog with the Old English terrier and adding a bit of Spanish pointer blood, they came up with the bullterrier. In 1850 the white-coated variety was obtained.

**Description**  It has a very elongated oval head without stop, powerful jawbones, and strong, healthy, regular teeth. Eyes: dark, small, almond-shaped. Shoulders: robust and muscular. Body: full and rounded. Tail: carried horizontally. Its coat is made up of short, hard, shiny hair. Colors: solid white, white with black markings or tigered on its head, tiger, tan, black, or tricolor. Height is 21 to 22 inches (53–56 cm.); its weight should be between 52 and 62 pounds (23.5–28 kg.).

**Personality**  At one time, the bullterrier was an extremely ferocious dog. However, it has been gentled considerably by modern breeders, and today it is a good, loyal, polite, and obedient dog.

**Uses**  Born to be a bloody and courageous gladiator, it was later used as a guardian of flocks, mouse hunter, companion dog, and bodyguard/watchdog.

**Note**  For show purposes there are two classes: white and colored.

## 100  CAIRN TERRIER

**Origin**  This dog, known since 1500, was first publicly presented in 1909 and became popular after 1930. In Scotland, it is an ancient practice to pile up small mounds of stones to indicate property boundaries or to mark graves. Small animals often made homes in these stone monuments, or cairns. For this reason, it was decided to develop a small dog capable of getting through the small openings and catching the intruders.

**Description**  The cairn terrier has a foxlike expression. It has a powerful but not heavy muzzle, a scissors bite, and a wide, robust skull. Eyes: deep-set, dark hazel. Ears: pointed, carried erect. Tail: carried merrily. Legs: short but with good bone structure. Maximum height: 12 inches (30 cm.). Ideal weight: 14 pounds (6.3 kg.). Its coat is abundant and hard and its undercoat is thick and furry. Colors: red, sand, gray, pepper-and-salt, almost black.

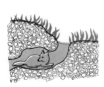

**Personality**  Lively cheerful, affectionate, lovable, can be trained to do tricks.

**Uses**  A den burrower, it was used for centuries in the hunting of foxes, badgers, rabbits, and otter. Despite so many years of country living, the cairn adapted easily to apartment life and has become an excellent companion dog. It puts up with a leash better than any other terrier.

## 101    DANDIE DINMONT TERRIER

**Origin** This is an old breed formed by crossings among the Scottish and the Skye terriers and raised mainly by gypsies. Its popularity, however, dates from the early 1800's, when such a dog appeared in a novel by Walter Scott. From that time on, this lovable terrier became known by the name of the protagonist of the novel, Dandie Dinmont. Thus, the dog entered history bearing the name of its master.

**Description** Height: from 8 to 10 inches (20–25 cm.). Weight: about 18 pounds (8 kg.). It has a large, solid head with a black nose. Its eyes are brilliant and lively, but not protruding. Its ears are pendent. It has a long, flexible body with short but very muscular legs and well developed thighs. Its tail is from 8 to 10 inches (20–25 cm.) long. Its hair is about 2 inches (5 cm.) long and is mixed hard and soft. Colors: dark pepper, silver-pepper, mustard brown, or light mustard tan.

**Personality** The Dandie Dinmont is playful and affectionate, a most pleasant companion.

**Uses** By instinct it has always been a great mouse catcher, and it has lost none of this talent today. It is also an enemy of martens, weasels, and skunks. An amusing-looking dog (long body, very short legs, toupee on its head), it has become a most sought-after companion dog.

## 102    IRISH TERRIER

**Origin** The breed is two thousand years old, but the earliest image we have of it is in a painting of the 1700's.

**Description** It is very similar to the wirehaired fox terrier, to which it is obviously a close relation. It is about 18 inches (46 cm.) high and ideally weighs 27 pounds (12.3 kg.). It has a flat skull, narrow between the ears; an elongated muzzle; muscular jaws; and a scissors bite. Eyes: small and dark. Ears: V-shaped, falling forward. Tail: docked, carried erect. Its front legs are very straight, strongly boned and muscled. Its hair is hard and coarse and slightly wavy. It is red, as is traditional for Irish breeds. More specifically, it may be bright red, wheat red, or yellowish-red. Light stripping is necessary.

**Personality** Once known as a "little daredevil" because of its exceptional courage, it is now a kind, affectionate, trainable, dignified dog.

**Uses** It has been used to penetrate the dens of small animals, as a retriever, as a hunter in water of otter and water rats, and as a messenger in times of war. A medal was conferred on the breed in 1918 for, among other things, "its boldness and complete scorn for danger." Today, the Irish terrier is much appreciated as a companion dog. It lives well in the city and in any climate.

## 103   JACK RUSSELL TERRIER

**Origin**   This breed was developed in the last century by an English clergyman, Parson Jack Russell, a great breeder and well-known dog lover.

**Description**   The breed has not been recognized by the American Kennel Club, and there is no precise standard. It is a dog similar to the fox terrier, with shorter legs, about 9 inches high (22 cm.), weighing 10 pounds (9 kg.), with dark deep-set eyes, folded-down ears carried wide, and "steel-wool" hair. Colors: white with reddish markings on its muzzle and body. There are two varieties: smooth-haired and wirehaired.

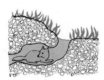

**Personality**   Courageous, merry, devoted, obedient.

**Uses**   Like all small terriers, it has been used for hunting small game in its lair. It was especially appreciated for the ability and rapidity with which it could burrow into even small holes. A rather rare terrier, it has passed into the ranks of the companion dog.

**Note**   After a period of notoriety in the mid-nineteenth century, and the death of Parson Jack Russell, the breed did not find great acceptance among dog lovers and has been in decline. Nonetheless, there still exist in England dogs of as perfectly pure breeding as their creator could have wished.

---

## 104   KERRY BLUE TERRIER
Irish Blue Terrier

**Origin**   The Kerry blue was developed in the 1700's by Irish shepherds of County Kerry. It is mainly the result of crossing the Irish terrier and the Dandie Dinmont. Its standard was fixed at the end of World War I. Together with the shamrock, the Kerry blue has become a symbol of Ireland.

**Description**   Height: from 18 to 19 inches (46–48 cm.) for dogs; a bit less for bitches. Weight: from 33 to 38 pounds (15–17 kg.). It is a powerful, compact, graceful dog with a long, narrow head; strong muzzle; and slightly marked stop. Eyes: very dark. Ears: V-shaped, carried forward. Neck: strong and long. Tail: upright, docked. Limbs: straight, with a powerful bone structure. Its coat is soft and silky and wavy in every shade of blue from silver to steel.

**Personality**   Pugnacious, but trainable and affectionate. It is a good friend to the family, but a bit stubborn.

**Uses**   It is a commendable hunter that chases its prey into its den. It is also a retriever of fowl, a guardian of flocks and herds, a house guard, a mouser, and an aide to the police.

**Note**   Must be trimmed for exhibitions.

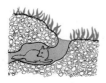

## 105  LAKELAND TERRIER

**Origin**  The breed was developed in the nineteenth century, probably by crossings between the Bedlington and an Old English wirehaired terrier. It was recognized in 1921.

**Description**  The Lakeland is an elegant dog with a beautiful, elongated head and straight, strongly boned legs. Height: not above 14½ inches (36.8 cm.). Weight: 17 pounds (7.7 kg.) for dogs; 15 pounds (6.8 kg.) for bitches. It has powerful jaws, dark nor hazel eyes, and small V-shaped ears. Its tail is carried cheerfully, but not curved over its back. Its hair is thick, hard, and resistant to bad weather; has a good undercoat. Colors: reddened black; reddened blue; reddish; wheat; pepper, salt, and red; liver; blue; or black. White markings on the feet and chest are not considered defects. The coat needs stripping.

**Personality**  Affectionate, cheerful, spirited, emotional, stubborn, active, and tenacious.

**Uses**  Originally from the Lake District of England (Lakeland), it has been successfully used for otter hunting in water and for fox and badger hunting in their dens, especially on rocky and uneven terrain. Due to its beauty and good character, the Lakeland is today esteemed as a fine and luxurious companion dog.

## 106  MANCHESTER TERRIER

**Origin**  The breed was developed in Manchester in the nineteenth century by crossings between the black-and-tan terrier and the small Italian greyhound.

**Description**  Average height: 16 inches (40 cm.). Weight: 18 pounds (8 kg.) for dogs; 17 pounds (7.7 kg.) for bitches. It is an elegant, compact dog with a long, wedge-shaped head, thin jaws, and a scissors bite. Ears: V-shaped. Eyes: small and oblong. Tail: short but not docked. It has a thick, sleek, shiny coat that does not need any special grooming. Color: black with mahogany-red shadings of the head and chest.

**Personality**  Intelligent, extremely lively, loyal.

**Uses**  Its nickname is "rat terrier," since it was for a long time the best dog for hunting rodents of all sizes. It was used thus in the countryside, in the basements of old English houses, and in general stores. Because of its small size and pleasantness, it is today appreciated as a companion dog. Nonetheless, its popularity has somewhat diminished, even in its native city.

**Note**  In 1879, the year the Manchester Terrier Club was founded, the breed was divided into two varieties: a large variety (the rat hunter described above) and a smaller one (an apartment dog). The latter is the progenitor of the black-and-tan toy terrier.

## 107 NORFOLK TERRIER

**Origin**   Originally from the county of Norfolk, the breed has only recently been recognized.

**Description**   One of the smallest terriers. Height: 10 inches (25 cm.). Weight: 10 to 12 pounds (4.5–5.4 kg.). It has short legs but is a solid dog with strong bones. Its muzzle is strong, with a robust jaw and frightening teeth. Eyes: dark, with a very lively expression. Ears: hanging, tight to the cheeks. Tail: docked by half. Front legs: straight and strong. Back legs: very muscular. Its hair is hard, coarse, and straight and lies flat to its body. Colors: all shades of red, red wheaten, black and tan or grizzle.

**Personality**   Active, courageous, affectionate, balanced, without any nervousness or quarrelsomeness.

**Uses**   Created to attack wild game, it proved very successful in entering the narrowest lairs and dens and overcoming foxes, otter, and rabbits. It thrives also as an apartment dog but is still not widespread.

---

## 108 NORWICH TERRIER

**Origin**   Norfolk and Norwich terriers were originally classed as one breed but are now separated. The Norfolk has dropped ears and the Norwich pricked ears.

**Description**   Its ideal height is 10 inches (25 cm.), which makes it one of the smallest terriers. Weight: 10 to 14 pounds (4.5 kg.). It has short, strongly boned legs, and a foxlike muzzle with large, solid teeth. Eyes: dark and expressive. Ears: upright. Body: compact. Tail: docked by half. Its coat is hard, coarse, and straight, and lies flat to its body, but it is short and shiny on its head and muzzle. Colors: red, red-wheat, shaded black, salt-and-pepper.

**Uses**   Originally a hunter of prey in its lair, the Norwich has joined the ranks of the companion dog. It is adapted to living with young, sporty people and is the mascot of the students at Cambridge Univesity.

**Note**   The bitch has a very protective and exclusive attitude about her pups.

# 109 SCOTTISH TERRIER

**Origin** This breed was developed in Scotland in 1700, but the dog with the size and shape we know today dates from 1890. Until that date, it was known as the Aberdeen terrier, after the town in which it was raised.

**Description** It is a vigorous compact, robust dog with short legs and has been described as "a large dog in a small package." Its ideal size is 10 to 11 inches (25–28 cm.) high with a weight of 19 to 23 pounds (8.5–10.5 kg.). Its head is long but proportionate to its body. It has a large nose and large teeth. And there is a stop between its skull and its muzzle. Eyes: almond-shaped, dark brown. Ears: pointed and carried erect. Neck: muscular. Tail: of medium length, carried straight or slightly curved. Its coat is compact, coarse, hard as bristles, with a soft undercoat that protects it thoroughly from bad weather. Colors: black, brindle, wheat.

**Personality** Lively, ardent, proud, independent, intelligent, dignified. It pins its affections almost exclusively on members of the family with which it lives, remaining indifferent to strangers. It has been described as "a dog that can go anywhere and do anything." It is very sensitive to criticism and praise and therefore should be trained gently.

**Uses** Courageous and undaunted in the face of danger, merciless against its prey, it was used for a long time for hunting animals in their dens. It specializes in foxes, badgers, otter, and rabbits. Due, however, to its singular good looks (its large, spirited head and romantic beard), the Scottish terrier has become a unique and well-loved companion dog. It is especially appreciated because it plays well with children, barks little, and has a watchful nature in regard to the house. Its attractive image has been used for advertising Scotch whiskey, on greeting cards, toys, and talismans.

**Note** For the sake of its health, it should be taken for long walks frequently. It needs stripping at least twice a year and frequent brushing for its good looks to be fully appreciated.

## 110 SEALYHAM TERRIER

**Origin** The Sealyham was developed in the middle of the nineteenth century by Captain John Edwards by crossing hounds, the Dandie Dinmont, the basset of Flanders, the corgi, the West Highland terrier, and the wirehaired fox terrier. It was officially recognized in 1910.

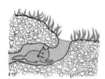

**Description** Height: not more than 12 inches (30 cm.). Maximum weight: 20 pounds (9 kg.) for dogs; 18 pounds (8.1 kg.) for bitches. It has a dome-shaped skull, a large nose, and powerful jaws with sturdy teeth and very long canines. Its eyes are round and dark. Its ears are wide, carried against its cheeks. Neck: long and muscular. Tail: docked, carried upright. Front legs: short and straight. Hind legs: powerful and muscular. Hair: long, coarse, and bristly; must be stripped. Colors: white, yellowish-white.

**Personality** Spirited, combative, affectionate, and aristocratic, it has been described as "the most beautiful union between cheerfulness and courage."

**Uses** For years it was an excellent hunter in dens and lairs, capturer of foxes, otter, badgers, and skunks. Beautiful and amusing as this dog is, with its humorous beard and cheerful temperament, it has, like so many other terriers, become appreciated mainly as a companion dog.

---

## 111 SKYE TERRIER

**Origin** The origin of the Skye terrier is connected with a shipwreck. In the early 1600's a Spanish ship came to grief against the rocks of the island of Skye in the Scottish Hebrides. Among the survivors were Maltese dogs that mated with local terriers and produced this new extremely pleasing and unique breed.

**Description** Its length should be twice its height. Average height is 10 inches (25.5 cm.). Its weight should be about 25 pounds (11.5 kg.); 10% less for bitches. It has a powerful muzzle, black nose, dark-brown eyes, and either upright or falling ears. Its tail is pendent, never curled. Its undercoat is soft, but its outer hair is long, hard, and straight, free of any rippling. Colors: gray-blue, dove, or cream, always with black ears.

**Personality** Very good-natured, polite, and affectionate. In Edinburgh there is a plaque commemorating a Skye that lived for ten years by the grave of its master.

**Uses** Like all short-legged terriers, the Skye is used for hunting in dens and lairs. However, the particular beauty of its coat, which covers it from head to foot, makes the Skye a handsome companion dog.

## 112 SOFT-COATED WHEATEN TERRIER

**Origin** This is the youngest representative of the vast family of terriers. Its first public presentation was in 1933. It is not well known outside County Kerry in Ireland.

**Description** It is a strong dog that moves gracefully. Height: about 18 inches (45 cm.). Ideal weight: 35 pounds (15.8 kg.). It has a rather short muzzle, jaws that are able to seize and grip prey well, and large teeth. Eyes: dark hazel. Ears: small, folded forward. Tail: docked, carried cheerfully, but not over its back. Legs: perfectly straight; the back legs are strongly muscled. Its coat is thick and soft (as its name indicates), and is wavy or curly. Color: wheat.

**Personality** Courageous, active, enterprising, versatile. It is resistant to fatigue and bad weather.

**Uses** The Irish consider this dog to be adaptable to many uses: guarding, defense, leading flocks, hunting in the lair. It is also a good dog for an apartment or yard.

## 113 STAFFORDSHIRE BULLTERRIER

**Origin** This breed was developed in the region of Staffordshire, England, during the nineteenth century. It was obtained by crossing the bulldog with various terriers. After a long period of oblivion, it returned to the show ring in 1935.

**Description** It is a strong and muscular dog, which is at the same time active and agile. Height: 14 to 16 inches (35–40 cm.). Weight: dogs, 28 to 38 pounds (12.5–17 kg.); bitches, 24 to 33 pounds (10.8–15 kg.). It has a short, deep head with a wide skull, muscular cheeks, clearly defined stop, and upper and lower teeth that meet exactly. Eyes: round and dark. Ears: semierect. Neck: short and muscular. Chest: deep. Tail: medium length, set low, never curled. Limbs: straight and far apart. Its coat is composed of short, sleek, soft hair that lies tight to its body. Colors: red, beige, white, black, blue, or any of these colors with white.

**Personality** Combative but steady, obedient, tolerant of children, devoted to the point of giving its life for its master.

**Uses** Originally used for dog fighting, it later suffered several decades of decline. Returning to vogue in the twentieth century, it caught the interest of American dog enthusiasts. In the U.S. it is now well bred in a size slightly larger than that called for in the European standard.

## 114    WELSH TERRIER

**Origin**   The breed was first presented in 1885, but in fact it had existed for some time as the old reddish-black wirehaired terrier.

**Description**   Aesthetically it is a miniature of the Airedale, from which it is descended through crossings with other terriers. Maximum height allowed: 15 inches (39 cm.). Weight: from 20 to 21 pounds (9–9.5 kg.). It has a black nose, strong teeth with a scissors bite, and a muzzle somewhat deeper than that of the fox terrier. Eyes: dark and small. Ears: V-shaped, carried forward. Tail: docked, carried high. Limbs: straight and muscular. Feet: small, round, catlike. Its coat is rough, hard, thick, and full. Ideal colors: reddened black or reddened gray-black.

**Personality**   Lively, independent, gay, affectionate, obedient, courageous.

**Uses**   Created to be a hunter in dens and lairs, it has also worked in packs together with hounds. Today it is exclusively a companion dog, well adapted to live in an apartment and useful also as a watchdog. It is very attached to its master but a bit timid with strangers. It needs frequent brushing, and stripping two or three times a year.

## 115    WEST HIGHLAND WHITE TERRIER

**Origin**   In the middle of the nineteenth century it happened that a breeder of cairn terriers in the county of Argyll in England got some white pups in his litters. These dogs were selected and bred to obtain the West Highland white terrier, which is simply a white cairn.

**Description**   This is a small terrier of hardy construction from its deep chest to its muscular limbs. Height: about 12 inches (28 cm.). Weight: from 15 to 22 pounds (7–10 kg.). It has short, closely fitted jaws with a scissors bite, a pronounced stop, and a slightly convex skull. Eyes: dark, deep-set, with a penetrating gaze. Ears: small, erect. Tail: not docked, about 5 to 6 inches (12.5–15 cm.) long. Its coat is always pure white and is composed of a soft, dense undercoat and an uncurled outer coat about 2 inches (5 cm.) long.

**Personality**   Ardent, agitated, self-assured.

**Uses**   Originally, like so many terriers, this dog was bred for the hunting of game in the lair, and in this role it always proved itself tenacious and threatening. But now, this sympathetic and spirited little dog has become an appreciated and sought-after family friend. It will gladly live in an apartment, but it also loves its freedom and should have available a terrace or a small yard.

## 116 GLEN OF IMAAL TERRIER

**Origin** The Glen of Imaal terrier was first presented publicly at an Irish dog show in 1933. It was imported into the U.S. in 1968.

**Description** It resembles the Welsh corgi, but its hair is hard. Height: dogs, 14 inches (36 cm.); bitches, 13 inches (33 cm.). Weight: dogs, 30 to 35 pounds (14–16 kg.); bitches, about 30 pounds (14 kg.). This is a small, compact dog with a beautiful head, short legs, a cheerfully carried tail, and chestnut eyes. Its coat is wheat-colored or blue-gray.

**Personality** Pugnacious and tenacious like all terriers, it is most affectionate with the family, but mordant with other animals. It is a most intelligent pet with a cocky fighting Irish spirit.

**Uses** It is a companion dog that, should the opportunity arise, makes itself useful as a hunter of mice. With brief training it can still be used successfully for hunting foxes and badgers.

## 117 GERMAN HUNTING TERRIER

**Origin** This breed was developed during the last century by crossings among various English den or lair hunting dogs.

**Description** Its height must be under 16 inches (40 cm.). Weight between 20 and 22 pounds (9–10 kg.) for dogs; 17 to 19 pounds (7.5–8.5 kg.) for bitches. It has a powerful muzzle with pronounced cheeks, a robust jaw, very strong teeth, and a flat skull that is wide between the ears. Eyes: small, dark, deep-set, with a lively expression. Ears: V-shaped, falling. Front legs: straight, ready to sprint. Tail: carried horizontally. There are two varieties of this German terrier: a wirehaired and a smooth-haired. Its predominant color is black mixed with gray or lighter shadings.

**Personality** Courageous, aggressive, stubborn, obedient only to its master.

**Uses** It is one of the few terriers that has remained solely a hunting dog. It is used to follow game into its den or lair and for the discovery of game and the retrieval of game in water. It does not hesitate to attack any kind of wild game, even the dangerous wild boar. It is also an outstanding guard dog for house or automobile. It will not tolerate friendly advances from anyone other than its master.

## 118 BOHEMIAN TERRIER
### Český Terrier

**Origin** This breed was developed by the Bohemian (Czechoslovakian) breeder Franta Horàk. It was officially recognized in 1963.

**Description** Short-legged but agile and robust. It has a long head with a well-developed nose (black or liver) and a robust jaw. Eyes: deep-set, with a cordial expression. Ears: pendent, close to the cheeks. Shoulders: muscular. Limbs: sturdy. Tail: 7 to 8 inches (18–20 cm.) long, carried horizontally when the dog is excited. Height: 11 to 14 inches (27–35 cm.) high. Weight: 13 to 20 pounds (6–9 kg.). Its coat is gray-blue or light coffee-colored and must be trimmed. It has a thick beard and eyebrows.

**Personality** Good, obedient, loyal, patient, courageous.

**Uses** Born to hunt small prey in its den, it has shown itself to be a particular enemy of rats and mice. It gets along well, however, with domestic animals, is playful and trainable, and pleasant-looking. It is an excellent companion dog capable of playing with children, but at the same time being an attentive and threatening house guard.

## 119 AMERICAN STAFFORDSHIRE TERRIER
### American Pit Bullterrier

**Origin** In the nineteenth century in the English region of Staffordshire, the muscular, active, combative Staffordshire bullterrier was developed by crossings among the bulldog and various terriers. Brought to the United States, the breed was perfected by American breeders who increased its weight and gave it a more powerful head.

**Description** Height: from 17 to 18 inches (44–46 cm.) for dogs; 10% less for bitches. Weight: from 38 to 44 pounds (17–20 kg.). It has a strong, muscular body but is, at the same time, very agile. Eyes: round, preferably black. Ears: erect, docked slightly. Tail: short, carried horizontally. Its coat is made up of thick, short, shiny hair. All colors are admissible, but dogs must not be more than 80% white. Classed by AKC as American Staffordshire terrier. By UKC as American pit bullterrier.

**Personality** It is an extremely courageous dog (offspring of ancient fighting dogs) and very full of vitality; it will fight an enemy to the death. However, a minimum of training will produce a tranquil, good, obedient dog with the ability to distinguish immediately the good or evil intentions of strangers.

**Uses** It has given outstanding results as a guard of property, but is at the same time esteemed as a companion dog.

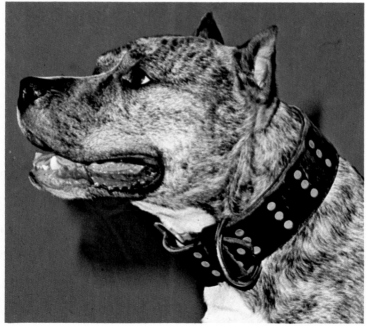

## 120 BOSTON TERRIER

**Origin** This breed was developed through long breeding of the bulldog, the French bulldog, the bullterrier, and the boxer. It was first shown in Boston in 1870. It is thus an American dog with French and English blood.

**Description** Height: 15 to 17 inches (38.1–43 cm.). Its weight varies from 15 to 25 pounds (6.75–11.3 kg.). It has a broad, flat head without wrinkles and a short, square muzzle leading to an ample black nose. Eyes: dark, large, round, with a sweet and intelligent expression. Ears: small and fine, carried erect. Neck: slightly arched. Chest: broad. Limbs: straight and muscular. Hair: short, brilliant, of a fine texture; does not shed. Colors: Brindle with white markings on its head, chest, and tail.

**Personality** Most affectionate with its master, patient with children, very intelligent, and alert.

**Uses** The Boston terrier is a perfect companion dog that behaves wherever it may be taken. Its gifts as a guardian of the house are also noteworthy. It is very popular in the U.S. due, above all, to its excellent character.

## 121 TIBETAN TERRIER

**Origin** This is an ancient breed that has contributed to the development of all the other Tibetan breeds, from the Shih-Tzû to the Lhasa Apso to the Tibetan spaniel.

**Description** The Tibetan terrier looks like a miniature bobtail. It is 12 to 16 inches (30–40 cm.) high and weighs 18 to 30 pounds (8.2–13.6 kg.). It has a medium-length skull and head with thick hair that falls over its eyes, a scissors bite, a marked stop, large dark eyes, and pendent heavily fringed ears. Its body is compact and vigorous with a feathered tail that is curled on its back. Hair: abundant, not silky, white, golden, smoke gray, black, bicolor, or tricolor. All colors are acceptable except chocolate.

**Personality** Lively, affectionate, mild, intelligent, reserved with strangers.

**Uses** It is considered a companion dog. Its deep bark, rising like a siren, makes the Tibetan a fine watchdog.

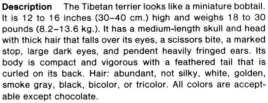

# HUNTING DOGS

## 122 SHORT-HAIRED DACHSHUND
### Teckel

**Origin** The dachshund was perfected at the end of the nineteenth century, but the first images of the breed appear in the tomb of a pharaoh that dates back five thousand years. This ancient ancestor was known as the *Teckel,* and the Germans have retained the ancient Egyptian name.

**Description** There are three varieties of dachshund: the short-haired, the wirehaired, and the long-haired. Within each of these three varieties, there are three sizes: normal, weighing about 20 pounds (9 kg.); miniature, weighing about 9 pounds (4 kg.); and toy, weighing 8 pounds (3.5 kg.). Heights range from 5 to 9 inches (12–22 cm.). The dachshund is an elongated, vigorous, muscular dog with short legs. It carries itself proudly and has an intelligent expression. It has an elongated head, a slightly convex skull, arched and protruding eyebrows, a long muzzle, robust jaws with nonpendent lips, and pincers or scissors bite with extremely strong canine teeth (dachshunds usually have 42 teeth). Its eyes are oval, dark red or brown-black, with an energetic and friendly expression. Its ears are mobile and hang along its cheeks. Its body should have a strongly protruding sternum and a moderately retracted abdomen. Its tail is carried in line with its back. The short-haired dachshund's coat should be shiny, sleek, and uniform. Colors: solid-colored dachshunds may be tan or yellow; bicolors may be deep black, brown, or gray with areas of bright chestnut. There are also speckled, streaked, or harlequin varieties.

**Personality** Courageous, tenacious, cheerful, affectionate, proud, without complexes.

**Uses** Born a den-hunting dog, the dachshund is still used in Great Britain, Germany, and Switzerland for sport hunting. However, the majority of breeders aim above all to produce intelligent, spirited companion dogs.

**Note** The dachshund is a good barker and often proves useful as a watchdog.

## 123    LONG-HAIRED DACHSHUND

**Origin**    Most probably the breed was developed by crossing the short-haired dachshund with some sort of spaniel.

**Description**    It differs from the short-haired variety only in its coat. This is soft, sleek, and shiny and is long enough over the lower part of its body, its ears, and its paws to form a rich fringe. The longest and thickest hair is on its tail. Colors: the same as the short-haired variety.

**Personality**    It is more tranquil and docile and less of a barker than the short-haired variety, possibly because it carries spaniel blood and the spaniel is known for its good temperament.

**Uses**    Because of its beauty it is almost exclusively used as a companion dog.

**Note**    The thickness of its coat protects it well from cold climates. It needs daily brushing.

## 124    WIREHAIRED DACHSHUND

**Origin**    This variety is about one hundred years old and was obtained by crossings among the short-haired dachshund, the schnauzer, and the Dandie Dinmont.

**Description**    In general, its looks are like those of the short-haired dachshund. Its body, however, is uniformly covered with a coarse, dense coat with an undercoat. It also has a goatee and bushy eyebrows. All colors are admissible, but white markings are not desirable. It must undergo stripping twice a year.

**Personality**    Tranquil, affectionate, sensitive, charming; it is always an alert watchdog.

**Uses**    Because of its courage and tirelessness, it continues to be trained to hunt down game in its lair, even in difficult terrain. However, it is also highly recommended as an apartment dog. Since this is originally a sporting breed, it needs long walks and occasional free runs outside.

## 125 HANOVER HOUND
### Hannoverischer Schweisshund

**Origin** The breed was developed in the nineteenth century by gamekeepers in the city of Hanover in Saxony by crossing German hounds known since the fifth century with the Harz hound, a breed that is no longer raised.

**Description** It is a medium-sized dog, low, but with a robust body. Height: dogs, 22 inches (57 cm.); bitches, 20 inches (52 cm.). Weight: from 84 to 99 pounds (38–45 kg.). It has a sympathetic, melancholy expression due in large part to the wrinkles that crowd its forehead. It has a medium-sized head with a wide skull, a very large nose (black, brown, or pink), and pendent lips. Eyes: brown, deep-set, with an energetic expression. Ears: long, wide, rounded, tight to the head. Tail: long, low, lightly curved. The hair is short, thick, and shiny. Its colors may be gray-brown with a dark-brown mask, red-brown, yellow-red, yellow-ocher, dark yellow, or blackened brown.

**Personality** Obedient, tenacious, affectionate.

**Uses** The Hanover hound's specialty is searching out game. It senses the animal's presence, unearths it, picks up its trail and chases it, while calling for the aid of the hunter. These dogs were once used in packs over vast territories, but today they work equally well in pairs or alone.

---

## 126 BLOODHOUND
### St. Hubert Hound

**Origin** This breed is more than one thousand years old. It was perfected, if not created, by the monks of St. Hubert in Belgium. Later, the dogs were brought by the Normans into England.

**Description** Massive, powerful, slow, it is the tracker par excellence. Dogs are 26 inches (67 cm.) high; bitches, 24 inches (60 cm.). Its weight varies from 88 to 105 pounds (40–48 kg.). It has a very long head, a black nose, and pendent lips. The skin over its forehead and cheeks is extremely wrinkled. It has been defined as "a dog walking behind a nose." Eyes: dark hazel-brown, kindly. Ears: very long, set low, hanging. Tail: elegantly curved. Hair: short, hard on the body and silky on the head and ears. Colors: black with tan shadings or solid bright fiery red.

**Personality** Meek, silent, timid, good-natured, polite, lovable.

**Uses** The bloodhound is gifted with the finest sense of smell. Besides unearthing small game (a job it performs faultlessly), it is used by police the world over for searching for people. It is capable of picking out a trail several days old. It has been very successful in finding lost children, buried miners, and buried treasure. It is also a commendable companion dog, but due to its good nature, it cannot be trained as a guard dog.

## 127 KARELIAN BEAR DOG
### Karjalankarhukoira

**Origin**   This is a breed that was developed several centuries ago by the Finns but perfected by the Russians, who introduced into its makeup the blood of the Utchak sheepdog.

**Description**   The Karelian bear dog is a medium-sized dog, from 21 to 24 inches (54–60 cm.) high, and weighs 44 to 49 pounds (20–22 kg.). It is a robust animal, slightly longer than it is high. It has a conical head, a straight black nose, and thin lips. Eyes: small and brown, with a lively expression. Ears: medium-sized, upright but turned slightly outward. It has vigorous limbs and muscular shoulders, an ample chest, and a tail that forms a full arch. Its hair is straight and stiff, with a soft undercoat. Colors: black with white markings on its head, throat, chest, and feet.

**Personality**   Extremely courageous, aggressive, obedient to its master.

**Uses**   Originally an elk hunter, the Karelian bear dog was bred to a more robust size so that it could be used for bear hunting. It will put a bear to flight or attack it with great pugnacity.

## 128 GRAND BLEU DE GASCOGNE

**Origin**   Brought to Europe by the Phoenicians, this hound found a new home in Gaul. Over the course of centuries and with the infusion of bloodhound blood, the Grand Bleu was perfected. It is known as "the most noble and powerful of all hounds both in France and the rest of the world."

**Description**   Height: from 25 to 28 inches (63–70 cm.). Weight: 71 to 77 pounds (32–35 kg.). It has a strong, elongated head with skin forming wrinkles on its cheeks, pendent lips, and a convex skull. Its eyes are dark chestnut, sad and sweet. Its ears are very long, thin, and conical. It has a thick, long tail carried with a sickle curve. Its coat is thick and should not be too short. It has black markings on a white background which is in turn speckled with black. Two black markings cover its ears and circle its eyes. Some dogs are simply white, speckled with black. Its name comes from the fact that from a distance its coat looks to be a beautiful bright blue.

**Personality**   Audacious and tenacious in its work, it is affectionate and aristocratic away from the hunt.

**Uses**   It is used for wolf hunting and for finding wild rabbits. It is truly one of the best tracking dogs. Besides having an exceptional sense of smell, it has a modulated bark that can indicate from a great distance the progress of the hunt.

## 129 GRAND GASCON SAINTONGEOIS
Virelade

**Origin** The breed was developed by the Baron de Virelade by crossings among the best of the French hunting dogs: the Saintongeois, the Gascon Bleu, and the Ariégeois. In remembrance of its original breeder, the Grand Gascon Saintongeois is also known as the Virelade.

**Description** Height: dogs, 25 to 28 inches (63–70.5 cm.); bitches, 24 to 26 inches (60–65 cm.). Weight: 66 to 71 pounds (30–32 kg.). It has a lean, elongated head, a well-developed black nose, and pendent lips. Eyes: dark chestnut. Ears: long and conical. It has a deep chest, a strong back, and an elegant saber tail. Its coat is composed of very short fine hair, white speckled with black or irregularly marked with black. Some markings begin on the sides of the head, curve around the eyes, and end on the cheeks.

**Personality** Audacious, resistant, aristocratic, very affectionate off the field of the hunt.

**Uses** Gifted with an ultrasensitive sense of smell and a beautiful reaching gallop, it is used not only for hunting small game but also for deer and wolves. It is an excellent hound, but is today quite rare.

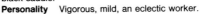

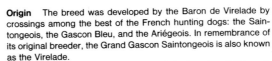

## 130 POITEVIN

**Origin** The breed was originated in 1692 by the Marquis François de Larrye, who crossed various hounds and the foxhound. It disappeared during the French Revolution but has been successfully re-created.

**Description** This is a dog that unites strength and elegance. It is from 24 to 28 inches (60–70 cm.) high and weighs 66 pounds (30 kg.). It has an elongated head, a pointed muzzle, and a wide, prominent nose. Eyes: large, brown, bordered in black. Ears: thin, slightly conical. Neck: long, without dewlap. Tail: thin with a slight curve. Its chest is deep and its back muscular. Its limbs are straight and lean. Its hair is short and shining. Color: tricolor with black saddle.

**Personality** Vigorous, mild, an eclectic worker.

**Uses** This is an outstanding hound be it in bogs and marshes, on high plateaus, or on the plains. It is always staunch and elegant. French hunters have described it as "the best dog in the world for hunting wolves; capable of following its prey from sunrise to sunrise."

## 131 BILLY

**Origin** The Billy was obtained by crossing several excellent breeds of hunting dog that have since passed into oblivion: Céris (a white-and-orange dog used for hunting hare and wolves); Montaimboeuf (a robust and fast hunter of wild boar); and Larrye (a hound with a great sense of smell).

**Description** This is an aesthetically well-balanced dog, distinguished and noble, strong and light. Height: from 24 to 26 inches (61–66 cm.) for dogs; 23 to 24 inches (58–62 cm.) for bitches. Weight: 55 to 66 pounds (25–30 kg.). It has a fine, lean head with a rather square muzzle, a marked stop, and a very well-developed nose. Eyes: lively, wide-open, dark. Ears: flat and slightly curled. Tail: long and strong. Its coat is composed of very short, hard hair in colors of white, off-white, or white with orange or lemon markings. Black markings are a disqualification in shows.

**Personality** Proud, courageous, obedient; an untiring worker. Away from the hunt field, however, it tends to be a bit quarrelsome.

**Uses** It is considered a master deer hunter. It has a very pleasing voice that it sends out through the valleys, expressing by differences in tone the importance of the game it has sighted.

## 132 CHIEN FRANÇAIS

**Origin** The Chien Français is descended from Gascons and the Saintongeois crossed with the English foxhound. Official recognition of the breed took place in 1957.

**Description** This is an elegant, muscular, well-balanced dog. Height: from 26 to 28 inches (65–72 cm.). Weight: 62 to 66 pounds (28–30 kg.). It has a convex skull, an elongated head, and an open nose. Eyes: dark, with a friendly, intelligent expression. Ears: long, curled. Tail: thick at the base, carried with elegance. Legs: strong, with lean, sturdy feet. There are three varieties of this beautiful dog: the black and white, the tricolor, and the black and orange. In shows they are judged by the same standard, except for minor details, and of course the color of their coats.

**Personality** Bold, courageous, and ferocious in the hunt, but affectionate, tranquil, silent, and obedient in the home.

**Uses** This is a "professional" hunting dog, interested in every type of game but specializes in deer.

**Note** Of the three varieties of Chien Français, the most widespread is the black and white, followed by the tricolor, and then the black and orange.

## 133 SWEDISH ELKHOUND
### Jämthund

**Origin** The Swedish elkhound is probably the first dog to appear by man's side in the Stone Age.

**Description** It is a large foxlike dog, measuring 23 to 25 inches (58–63 cm.) and weighing around 66 pounds (30 kg.). It has an elongated, narrow head; a straight muzzle; and a wide nose. Eyes: small, dark, with a lively but serene expression. Ears: erect, pointed, mobile. Neck: long and robust. Tail: tightly rolled on the back. Limbs: straight and agile. Its coat is long and hard, with a soft, woolly undercoat. Colors: light or dark gray.

**Personality** Balanced, proud, obedient.

**Uses** At one time it was used for hunting elk and bear, but it later proved to be excellent in rousing smaller game such as marten, ermine, and grouse. Its method is to slither over the snow until it manages to reach the game, cut off its path, and maneuver it into the gunsights of the hunter. The Swedish elkhound has also been used as a shepherd, a guardian of the home, a sled dog, and in the army.

**Note** In warm countries, this dog may be subject to eczema.

---

## 134 ENGLISH FOXHOUND

**Origin** The foxhound was developed by an intelligent mixing of various hounds, subsequently carefully bred with the greyhound, the bulldog, and the fox terrier. From these latter breeds the foxhound inherited respectively its sudden spurts of speed during the chase, its force and authority, and its passion for the hunt.

**Description** This is a vigorous, tenacious dog of elegant lines. The height of dogs should be between 22 and 25 inches (56–63 cm.); that of bitches, between 21 and 24 inches (53–61 cm.). Weight is 65 to 70 pounds (60–63 kg.). It has a wide skull and a long neck. Eyes: large, with a sweet expression. Ears: lying flat to the head. Tail: carried semierect. Limbs: well boned, with muscular thighs. Coat: very short and hard. Colors: tricolor (black, white, and tan) or bicolor with a white background.

**Personality** Courageous, energetic, pugnacious, untiring, good and obedient with its master.

**Uses** It is considered the nonpareil of hounds, used especially in foxhunting in combination with mounted hunters. It can trot along through brambles, marshes, and sunny countryside for five or six hours without stopping.

**Note** Since the foxhound uses up a great deal of energy in its youth, covering thousands of miles without respite, it is ready to be retired at the age of about seven or eight.

## 135     AMERICAN FOXHOUND

**Origin** This marvelous foxhound is directly descended from English hounds brought to America in 1650 and bred over a century later to a French hound sent as a gift by Lafayette to George Washington. The two breeds, French and English, in combination have produced the American foxhound.

**Description** While similar to its English cousin, the American foxhound has been developed by its breeders to be lighter, to have a keener sense of smell, and to be even faster in the chase. Height: dogs, 22 to 25 inches (56–63 cm.); bitches, 21 to 24 inches (53–61 cm.). Weight: 65 to 70 pounds (56–63 kg.). It has a large skull. Its eyes are large and wide-set, either brown or hazel, with a sweet, imploring expression. Ears: wide, flat to the head. Tail: carried cheerfully with a slight curve. Its coat is hard, a typical hound's coat. All colors are admissible.

**Personality** A warrior in the hunt field, it is sweet and affectionate when not at work.

**Uses** In the seventeenth century, these dogs were used for seeking out Indians. Later, however, they became efficient and untiring hunters of wild animals. The American foxhound can run around a square-mile (200 sq. km.) farm from early morning to late at night and return home still enthusiastic and eager to run.

**Note** This dog has a melodious bark, so much so, in fact, that its tones have been used in popular songs.

## 136     TRIGG HOUND

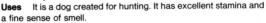

**Origin** This is a breed developed in Kentucky by Colonel Hayden Trigg using the Walker hound and Irish hounds.

**Description** The Trigg is a beautiful hound, thin and with noble lines, robust and fast. Height: dogs, 23 to 24 inches (58–61 cm.); bitches, 20 to 22 inches (51–56 cm.). Weight: dogs, 45 to 55 pounds (20–25 kg.); bitches, 35 to 45 pounds (16–20 kg.). It has an elongated muzzle; pendent ears; long, straight legs; and soft, fine, dense hair. All colors are permissible.

**Personality** Tenacious, attentive to orders.

**Uses** It is a dog created for hunting. It has excellent stamina and a fine sense of smell.

## 137 PLOTT HOUND

**Origin** The German ancestors of the Plott hound were able wild-boar hunters. Brought to the United States in 1750 by Jonathan Plott, the breed has been carefully developed to be stronger and more tenacious.

**Description** This is a heavy, muscular dog with large ears and a long tail. Height: dogs, 22 to 25 inches (56–64 cm.); bitches, 21 to 24 inches (53–61 cm.). Weight: dogs, 50 to 65 pounds (23–29 kg.); bitches, 40 to 55 pounds (18–25 kg.). Its coat is soft, fine, sleek, and gleaming; tiger with a black saddle.

**Personality** Decisive, courageous, proud.

**Uses** The Plott hound is exclusively adapted to hunting. It is most efficient in the search for coyotes, wolves, stags, or wildcats. It is extremely hardy and has superior hunting instincts.

**Note** The descendants of Jonathan Plott have only rarely put these dogs on the market; so while the breed was officially recognized in 1946, it is still little known.

## 138 DACHSBRACKE

**Origin** Known since the end of the eighteenth century, this breed was officially recognized in 1896.

**Description** There are two types of Dachsbracke: the Westphalian basset (stature: 12 to 14 inches [30–35 cm.]; weight: 33 to 40 pounds [15–18 kg.]) and the Montano-Alpine (stature: 13 to 17 inches [34–42 cm.] and a slightly heavier build; weight: about 22 pounds [10 kg.]). It has a slightly convex skull, a pincers bite with well-developed canine teeth, and thin lips. Eyes: chestnut (light or dark, depending on the color of its coat). Ears: wide, flat, pendent. Back: solid and long. Chest: round, with a noticeably protruding sternum. Limbs: strong and muscular. Tail: pendent, with a slight curve. Its coat is short, thick, and tight to its body. Colors: black with lighter shadings, chestnut with lighter streaks, stag red, blackened red, golden red. The Westphalian basset is often white with reddish markings.

**Personality** Headstrong and pugnacious in the hunt; warm and affectionate when not at work.

**Uses** The breed is adapted to hunting hare, fox, deer, and wild boar. It can also be used for retrieving fowl. It works well over difficult terrain; is agile and tireless in the mountains. It has a keen sense of smell that allows it to pick out game at a great distance.

## 139 GERMAN SPANIEL
### Wachtelhund

**Origin** The German spaniel was developed in the early 1900's by the German breeder Frederick Roberth. He crossed small and medium-sized long-haired dogs that had a proven passion for hunting, but the "recipe" has always remained a secret.

**Description** Height for dogs and bitches: 16 to 20 inches (40–50 cm.). Weight: 44 pounds (20 kg.). It has a wide, robust muzzle and a very well-developed chestnut-colored nose. Bite: scissors or pincers. Lips: thin, never drooling. Eyes: dark brown, very expressive. Ears: wide, flat, pendent. Tail: carried upright, but never raised over the back, docked slightly. Coat: made up of long, sturdy hair in colors of black with areas of light tan, chestnut, or stag red; thick and wavy, but not silky.

**Personality** Affectionate and obedient with its master, but violent and inflexible in the hunt field. It will go for the throat of its prey.

**Uses** The German spaniel is used over the most difficult terrain (over snow, slush, and wet areas), particularly in fox and hare hunting. In typical spaniel fashion, it will stop in the presence of game and alert the hunter by its "set." It is a particularly courageous and hardy dog.

## 140 TYROLEAN HOUND
### Tiroler Bracke

**Origin** Descended from ancient Austrian hounds, the Tyrolean hound was bred specifically for hunting over the snows and under the sun of the mountainous Tyrol.

**Description** Height: 16 to 19 inches (40–48 cm.). Weight: 33 to 49 pounds (15–22 kg.). There is also a smaller variety 12 to 15 inches (30–39 cm.) in height. It has an elongated head with a light bone structure, a slightly rounded forehead, marked stop, and strong teeth. Eyes: large, dark, lively. Ears: wide, thin, and flat. Tail: long and straight. Coat: thick, bristly, in hues of black, red, yellow-red, or tricolor. Gait: regular, broad, rapid.

**Personality** Lively, courageous, pleasant, obedient.

**Uses** Muscular, extremely fast, with the finest sense of smell, the Tyrolean hound fits perfectly into its milieu. It can be used either for tracking or for hunting. Due to its moderate size, it is easily transportable to the hunting site.

## 141 WIREHAIRED STYRIAN MOUNTAIN HOUND

**Origin** The wirehaired Styrian mountain hound was obtained by crossings between the Hanover hound and the wirehaired Istrian hound.

**Description** It is a medium-sized dog with a serious, intelligent face and a strong musculature. Height: from 16 to 20 inches (40–50 cm.). Weight: 33 to 40 pounds (15–18 kg.). It has strong teeth, a black nose, limpid eyes that may vary in color from chestnut to yellow, and flat ears. Neck: slightly arched. Tail: of medium length, never rolled. Limbs: straight, muscular. Its coat is heavy and coarse and curly, red and yellowish, sometimes with white markings on its chest. The hair on its ears is less coarse than that over the rest of its body.

**Personality** Obstinate and rough during the hunt, this dog is good and affectionate with its master. It is a cheerful, clean dog.

**Uses** Styria is a region of Austria with an Alpine climate and hard winters, but this well-muscled, tireless hound is resistant to cold and adapted to rocky terrain. It fits perfectly into the mountainous geography and difficult weather of its native land. Because of its uncommon intelligence and sensitivity and its wonderful sense of smell, it is also prized by German and Yugoslavian hunters. It is particularly adapted for seeking out small game.

---

## 142 FINNISH SPITZ
### Suomenpystykorva

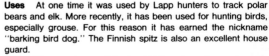

**Origin** This breed has been raised for centuries in Finland. Its standard was set in 1812. It is also mentioned in several heroic national songs.

**Description** The Finnish spitz is an aesthetically pleasing dog with a proud carriage. With its pointed muzzle, erect ears, and reddish coat, it appears something like a cross between a fox and a chow chow. Its height is between 17 and 20 inches (44–50 cm.); 10% less for bitches. Weight: 25 to 30 pounds (23–27 kg.). It has a short, muscular neck, a deep chest, and a retracted abdomen. Eyes: lively, preferably dark. Tail: curved on its back. Its coat is short and smooth with a lighter undercoat. Colors: brownish-red or yellowish-red with white markings on its chest and feet.

**Personality** Loyal, friendly, courageous.

**Uses** At one time it was used by Lapp hunters to track polar bears and elk. More recently, it has been used for hunting birds, especially grouse. For this reason it has earned the nickname "barking bird dog." The Finnish spitz is also an excellent house guard.

**Note** The puppies are delicate at birth and require much care.

## 143 FINNISH HOUND
### Suomenajokoira

**Origin** Known since 1700, the breed became widespread throughout Finland at the end of the nineteenth century.

**Description** This is a medium-sized hound. Height: from 22 to 24 inches (55–61 cm.) for dogs; 20 to 23 inches (52–58 cm.) for bitches. Weight: 55 pounds (25 kg.). It is longer than it is high; robust, but at the same time nimble, with a narrow, noble head and a prominent nose with wide, flaring nostrils. Its good looks are in large part due to its singular ears, which are attached high and stick out from its cheeks like ailerons. Its standard also prescribes strong jaws; a straight, thin neck; a deep chest; retracted abdomen; strong muscular limbs; resilient footpads; and a rather long tail, which, in repose, reaches the dog's hocks. Its coat is dense and coarse to the touch. Color: black with bright markings on the head, abdomen, thighs, and limbs. There are white areas on the muzzle, neck, chest, backs of the legs, and point of the tail.

**Personality** Friendly with people; very energetic in the hunt.

**Uses** During the summer months it is used for hunting hares and foxes. It spends the winter months with the family. The Finnish hound is highly prized in Finland but little known elsewhere.

---

## 144 STEINBRACKE

**Origin** The Steinbracke was developed in Germany and is little known elsewhere.

**Description** It is a medium-sized dog, robust without being massive, with a light, elongated head. Height: 16 to 18 inches (40–45 cm.). Weight: 40 to 49 pounds (20–22 kg.). Eyes: dark chestnut, limpid, with a friendly expression. Ears: wide, close to the head. Teeth: strong, with a good bite. Tail: set high, ending in a brush. Limbs: thick-boned, with full thighs. Feet: oval, heavily covered with thick, hard hair. Its coat is black with areas of bright tan, or white with a dark back.

**Personality** Very combative and tireless in the hunt; affectionate and meek in the home.

**Uses** It is particularly adapted to hunting hares, but it will also pit itself against larger game.

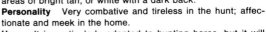

## 145  POLISH HOUND
### Ogar Polski

**Origin**   The Polish hound is indigenous to Poland.

**Description**   This is a well-constructed hound. Height for dogs: from 22 to 26 inches (56–65 cm.); weight: 55 to 71 pounds (25–32 kg.). Height for bitches: 22 to 24 inches (55–60 cm.); weight: 44 to 57 pounds (20–26 kg.). It has a noble, rectangular-shaped head; a large, dark nose; and a pendent lower lip. Jaws: powerful and meaty. Forehead: wrinkled. Eyes: large, oblique, brown, with a tranquil expression. Ears: pendent and close to the head. Tail: thick, covered with more hair than the rest of the body. Colors: black, dark gray, or dark brown in various shades. It has a beautiful, sonorous, clear voice.

**Personality**   Vigorous but not ferocious in the hunt, it is an obedient and affectionate dog.

**Uses**   Although its trot is a bit slow and its gallop a bit heavy, it is nonetheless highly prized for its perseverance, its "professional seriousness," and its great sense of smell. It is adapted to all types of hunting, even over difficult terrain and in bad weather.

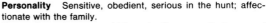

## 146  AUSTRIAN HOUND
### Österreichischer Bracke-Brandlbracke

**Origin**   The Austrian hound is indigenous to Austria.

**Description**   This is a medium-sized dog. Height: from 18 to 20 inches (46–52 cm.). Weight: 33 to 49 pounds (15–22 kg.). It has a very strong but, at the same time, loose-limbed body. It has a high forehead and a very straight muzzle. Eyes: chestnut, limpid, with an intelligent expression. Ears: pendent, rounded at the tips. Neck: very strong, leading to an ample chest. Tail: low, but carried high during the search for game. Perfect pincers bite. Its coat is flat and shiny like silk. Colors: black, with clearly defined shadings, or fawn. Small white spots on the chest are acceptable.

**Personality**   Sensitive, obedient, serious in the hunt; affectionate with the family.

**Uses**   A good runner and blessed with an excellent sense of smell, it is used for finding all types of game.

## 147 BAVARIAN MOUNTAIN HOUND
### Bayerischer Gebirgsschweisshund

**Origin**   The breed was developed by crossings between the old Bavarian hound and the Tyrolean hound.

**Description**   This is a dog with a light but muscular appearance. Height: not more than 20 inches (50 cm.). Weight: 55 to 77 pounds (25–35 kg.). It has a wide, slightly arched skull, a black or brown nose, and close-fitting lips. Eyes: chestnut, limpid. Ears: hanging close to the head. Neck and back: very robust. Abdomen: somewhat retracted. Its coat is thick, short, and rather hard to the touch, finer on the head and ears. Colors: deep red, yellow-ocher, light yellow to pale blond, or gray-red.

**Personality**   Lively, courageous, obedient during the hunt; very affectionate with its master.

**Uses**   Created specifically for the uneven Bavarian terrain, this is an agile, tough dog with fine instincts. It is largely used for tracking hares and game birds.

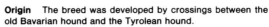

## 148 PETIT BLEU DE GASCOGNE

**Origin**   This is the smaller brother of the Grand Bleu de Gascogne. It has bloodhound blood in its veins.

**Description**   The Grand Bleu is 28 inches (70 cm.) high; the Petit Bleu measures around 20 inches (50 cm.) and weighs 44 pounds (20 kg.). Its reduced size makes it lighter in movement and gives it a more unified appearance. It has a long, noble head with a black open nose. Its skull is lean and narrow. Eyes: chestnut-colored with black-ringed lids. Ears: thin, slightly cone-shaped. Tail: long and thin. Hair: coarse and not too short. The blue of its coat comes from a thick speckling of color on a white background.

**Personality**   Proud, audacious, tenacious in its work; sweet and affectionate with its master.

**Uses**   Highly adept at finding and flushing wild rabbits. Going hunting with a Petit Bleu de Gascogne means never coming home with an empty game bag. Besides having an excellent sense of smell, this dog is prized by hunters for the ease with which it can be transported.

## 149   ARIÉGEOIS

**Origin**   This is a breed developed in the region of Ariège through crossing the Bleu de Gascogne, the Gascon Saintongeois, and the Briquet. Year of origin: 1912.

**Description**   It is a light and distinctive dog with a stature of 22 to 24 inches (55–60 cm.); weight: 66 pounds (30 kg.); bitches a little less. It has a lean, elongated head without wrinkles or dewlap; a black nose with open nostrils; dark, gentle eyes; and medium-length, soft, cone-shaped ears. Neck: slender and slightly arched. Tail: carried with a saber curve. Coat: fine and thick. Colors: white and black with slight shadings on the cheeks and under the eyes.

**Personality**   Passionate in the hunt; serene and affectionate in the family.

**Uses**   Outstanding for hunting hare whether on the plains, in the hills, or in rocky regions. It is fast and vigorous, with a very strong voice, a light step, and a good sense of smell. Nonetheless, it is a breed that is known and used only in the south of France.

## 150   BASSET ARTÉSIEN NORMAND

**Origin**   This breed was specifically developed with short legs to be able to go through bushes and brambles. There are two varieties: the Artésien, bred in Flanders, and the Normand, bred in Artois; however, the differences between them are negligible.

**Description**   It has a height of from 10 to 14 inches (26–36 cm.) and weighs 33 pounds (15 kg.). Its body is twice as long as it is high. Its head is dome-shaped and powerful with hairy cheeks and large dark eyes with an expression full of good will and melancholy. Its ears are very long, cone-shaped, soft, and pointed. Neck: with slight dewlap. Chest: round, with clearly visible sternum. Tail: long, thick at the root, but narrowing progressively, carried with a saber curve. Limbs: short, but not deformed. Coat: very short, bicolor (orange and white) or tricolor (orange, tan, and white).

**Personality**   Courageous and headstrong in the hunt. Because of its good nature it is also raised as a companion dog.

**Uses**   Used for hunting foxes and hares, sometimes in company with larger hounds. When the larger dogs are unable to penetrate the brambles, the Artésien Normand is ready to throw itself decisively into action. Like other bassets and terriers, it will go into the lair after its prey.

## 151 BASSET BLEU DE GASCOGNE

**Origin** The Basset Bleu de Gascogne was obtained through a breeding program involving the Grand Bleu de Gascogne.

**Description** It is the smallest of the Bleu de Gascogne family, only 12 to 15 inches (30–38 cm.) high. This low stature gives it a singular look. It weighs 35 to 40 pounds (16–18 kg.). Its head is long, with a somewhat ram-shaped muzzle and a black nose. Eyes: dark brown, with a sweet, sad expression. Ears: long, conical. Tail: carried gaily. Coat: blue or white with more or less extensive black markings and a trace of shading on the eyes and cheeks. The standard calls for crooked legs and black toenails clearly visible on particularly large and solidly soled feet.

**Personality** Audacious, curious, pleasant, affectionate.

**Uses** It is attentive, free-and-easy, fast, and has an outstanding sense of smell. It is adapted to hunting both furred and feathered game. Hunting with a Basset Bleu de Gascogne is a real pleasure. It is extremely lively, enthusiastic, joyous, and pleasant to look at; and it is ready to leap forth at any movement of a branch or the slightest smell of game.

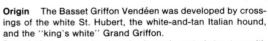

## 152 BASSET GRIFFON VENDÉEN

**Origin** The Basset Griffon Vendéen was developed by crossings of the white St. Hubert, the white-and-tan Italian hound, and the "king's white" Grand Griffon.

**Description** It was bred to give it an elongated structure with a height of between 15 and 17 inches (38–42 cm.). It weighs 40 to 44 pounds (18–20 kg.). It has an elongated muzzle with large mustaches on its lips. Eyes: large and dark, with an intelligent but meek expression. Ears: thin, long, oval. Tail: long, carried with a sickle curve. It has muscular thighs and well-boned front legs. Its coat is hard, not particularly long, never silky or woolly. Colors: tan, gray-white, white and orange, white and black, white and gray, white and fire red, white and hare color, or tricolor. There is also a smaller variety of Basset Griffon Vendéen that measures from 13 to 15 inches (34–38 cm.) high.

**Personality** Courageous, vigorous, tenacious. With the family, it is affectionate, docile, loyal, and lovable.

**Uses** Used individually or in packs, it is one of the best French hounds, especially for deer and wild-boar hunting. Because of its pleasing personality and its amusing expression, it has achieved a good deal of popularity as a companion dog.

## 153 BASSET FAUVE DE BRETAGNE

**Origin** The Basset Fauve de Bretagne is the result of numerous crossings between the Grand Griffon Fauve de Bretagne and the Basset Vendéen.

**Description** Height: from 13 to 14 inches (32–36 cm.). Weight: 36 to 40 pounds (16–18 kg.). It has a typical basset body with slightly crooked legs, an elongated head with a dark, open nose. Eyes: lively in expression. Ears: medium length, oval. Neck: short and muscular. Tail: sickle. Coat: hard, thick, short. Colors: various shades of fawn, and golden-wheat color. A white mark on the chest is admissible.

**Personality** Tranquil, affectionate, clean.

**Uses** It is a tenacious, vigorous, sturdy hound, adapted to hunting on plateaus, through heaths and brambles. It has also found a place as a companion dog. Outside France, however, it has not achieved the popularity it deserves.

## 154 GRIFFON NIVERNAIS

**Origin** The ancestor of the Griffon Nivernais is the Chien gris de Saint Louis, a great hound in the time of the Sun King, which has since disappeared.

**Description** The Griffon Nivernais is a sturdy-looking dog, similar to the Spinone, but smaller. It has a light but strong musculature, reaches a height of between 20 and 24 inches (50–60 cm.), and weighs 49 to 55 pounds (22–25 kg.). Head: light and elongated; chin, slightly bearded. Eyes: dark, with a penetrating gaze. Ears: soft, slightly conical. Tail: medium length, carried with a saber curve. Coat: long, strong, hard, bushy hair. Colors: gray-blue, wolf gray, boar gray, with shadings on the cheeks.

**Personality** Stubborn, tenacious, active.

**Uses** Because of its willingness to work and its adaptability to even the most difficult terrain, this breed is prized by Sunday hunters. It does not need any particular attention; it is resistant to the rain and does not suffer from heat or cold. It is a willing swimmer.

## 155    HARRIER

**Origin**   The harrier is similar to a foxhound. It was developed through crossings of the greyhound, the bulldog, and the fox terrier.

**Description**   About 21 inches (50 cm.) high, weighing 45 to 55 pounds (40–46 kg.), the harrier is a compact, perfectly perpendicular dog, speedy, hardy, and with the finest sense of smell. It has a broad head and a pointed muzzle with a well-developed nose. Eyes: small, oval. Ears: V-shaped, flat, pendent. Chest: well developed. Tail: medium length, carried rather high. Coat: flat, not overly short. Colors: white background with black spots; the back is sometimes entirely black.

**Personality**   Lively, distinguished, cheerful.

**Uses**   Its name, harrier, reveals the breed's specialty. Neither hare nor fox can escape its exceptional sense of smell, its cunning, and its unequaled hardiness. Prey chased by the indefatigable harrier has been known to collapse from sheer exhaustion.

## 156    BEAGLE

**Origin**   This breed was probably developed in Elizabethan times by crossings between the harrier and ancient English hounds.

**Description**   It is similar to the harrier, but with shorter legs. Hardy and extremely active, it is from 13 to 16 inches (33–40 cm.) high. Weight is 18 to 30 pounds (8.2–13.6 kg.). It has a powerful but not coarse head and a black nose with very developed nostrils. Its skull is dome-shaped; muzzle, pointed; stop, distinct. Eyes: chestnut or hazel, with a sweet expression. Ears: long and hanging against its cheeks. Neck: rather long, with slight dewlap. Thighs: very muscular. Feet: round and strong. There are two types of beagle distinguished only by their coats: one with smooth but not particularly fine hair and one with rough hair. Colors: blue with black tigering, white, black, orange, or typical hound tricolor.

**Personality**   Affectionate, cheerful, clean, tranquil, and pleasing, with a harmonious voice.

**Uses**   The breed is specialized for the hunting of hare, pheasant, and quail, but it has even been used for catching fish. It has also enjoyed periods of great popularity as a companion dog. There is a variety of miniature beagle, the Elisabeth beagle, which is not more than 12 inches (30 cm.) high and weighs just 22 pounds (10 kg.). In the past, mounted hunters carried this miniature beagle in their saddlebags.

## 157 BEAGLE HARRIER

**Origin** As its name indicates, this dog was obtained by crossing the beagle and the harrier. The instigator of this crossing of two English breeds was a Frenchman, Baron Gérard.

**Description** It is a distinguished, well-balanced dog. From the beagle it has inherited its passion for the hunt, its cheerfulness, and its harmonious voice. From the harrier it has taken its sense of smell, its pride, and its hardiness. It is from 17 to 19 inches (43–48 cm.) high and weighs 44 pounds (20 kg.). Skull: broad. Muzzle: narrowing in profile, but not pointed. Eyes: dark, with an intelligent expression. Ears: V-shaped, almost flat, not extremely long. Back: short and muscular. Front legs: perpendicular. Thighs: muscular. Coat: thick and flat, generally tricolor with bright or dark shadings.

**Personality** Courageous, lively, energetic, intelligent, elegant, sincere, affectionate. The appearance of fearfulness is a serious defect.

**Uses** Its best quality comes out in the hunting of hare and deer.

---

## 158 OTTERHOUND

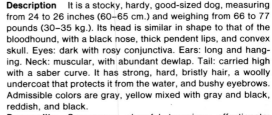

**Origin** This is a rather old breed obtained from crossings among the rough-haired terrier, the harrier, the Griffon Nivernais, and the bloodhound.

**Description** It is a stocky, hardy, good-sized dog, measuring from 24 to 26 inches (60–65 cm.) and weighing from 66 to 77 pounds (30–35 kg.). Its head is similar in shape to that of the bloodhound, with a black nose, thick pendent lips, and convex skull. Eyes: dark with rosy conjunctiva. Ears: long and hanging. Neck: muscular, with abundant dewlap. Tail: carried high with a saber curve. It has strong, hard, bristly hair, a woolly undercoat that protects it from the water, and bushy eyebrows. Admissible colors are gray, yellow mixed with gray and black, reddish, and black.

**Personality** Courageous, cheerful, tenacious, affectionate; esteemed as a companion dog.

**Uses** The otter, as the breed's name suggests, is this dog's preferred prey. The otterhound has a sense of smell so acute that it can smell in the morning an otter that passed through the water the night before. Defying the cold and wet, it will dive into the water seeking its prey and its prey's den.

## 159 BASSET HOUND

**Origin** This is a rather old breed, descended directly from the bloodhound. Shakespeare described the basset hound with the following poetic image: "Ears which sweep away the morning dew." However, the true fame of the basset hound began in 1863, when it was presented at the Paris Dog Show. Its popularity spread to England, and it was recognized by the Kennel Club in 1883. In England a lively dispute arose between two factions of breeders: those who wanted to keep the basset a hunting dog, and those who wished to transform it into a companion dog. Situated between these two factions were the American breeders who proceeded to develop an extremely pleasing companion dog without sacrificing any of the qualities of the hunter. The breed was recognized by the American Kennel Club in 1964.

**Description** The basset hound has short legs and a heavy bone structure but moves agilely and without clumsiness. Average height: 14 inches (35.5 cm.). Weight: between 40 and 51 pounds (18–23 kg.). It has a large well-proportioned head with a dome-shaped skull and accentuated occipital protuberances. The skin on its head is loose and falls in deep folds. Its nose is black; lips, pendent; teeth, well-developed, with a scissors bite. It has a powerful neck and pronounced dewlap. Eyes: dark, sweet, sad. Ears: long enough so that if pulled forward they would come well beyond the tip of the nose. The tail is slightly curved and carried gaily. The coat is short, hard, shiny. There are no rules concerning color, but it is usually white with chestnut or sand-colored markings.

**Personality** The basset is mild but not timid, very affectionate with its master and friendly with children. It is incapable of biting. It may be a bit stubborn. It has a pleasing voice. Housebreaking is difficult.

**Uses** Its natural bent is for hunting both in the den and in the open. It is, therefore, used for the hunting of fox, hare, opossum, and pheasant. It has an excellent sense of smell, but its reflexes are a bit slow. After a period of selective breeding in the United States, the basset hound gained international fame as a good-natured companion dog.

**Note** In order to keep its genetically somewhat unbalanced constitution within proper limits, overfeeding is to be avoided.

**ITALIAN HOUND**
**Segugio Italiano**

**Origin**  The first breeding of this hound took place in ancient Gaul with the crossing of the Egyptian racing hound (brought to Europe by the Phoenicians) and the Roman Molossus. However, its "golden age" came during the Renaissance when its looks and its hunting qualities were improved and its popularity spread through every class of society. After a period of neglect, accompanied by the breeding of dogs of questionable purity, the breed returned to vogue in the early twentieth century thanks to the efforts of various organizations of dog lovers that kept before the public the evidence of the dog's beauty and working qualities.

**Description**  This is a strong, muscular dog with no fat. Height: dogs, from 20 to 23 inches (52–58 cm.); bitches, from 19 to 22 inches (48–56 cm.). Its weight varies between 40 and 62 pounds (18–28 kg.). Its muzzle should be half the length of its head, which should be lean and thin-skinned. It has a black nose with open nostrils, a convex muzzle (ram-shaped), and thin, black-edged lips. Eyes: large and luminous, with dark-ocher irises. Ears: triangular, flat, wide, pendent. Neck: lean, without dewlap. Tail: carried sickle-shaped.

There are two varieties of Italian hound: short-haired and rough-haired. In the short-haired variety, the coat should be thick and gleaming. In the rough-haired variety, it should be coarse and not more than 6 inches (15 cm.) long on its body. All other characteristics, both physical and in personality, are the same. Admissible colors: all shades of solid tan and black with shadings. The shadings should be on the sides of the muzzle, eyebrows, chest, and limbs. The tan type may have white on its muzzle, skull, chest, feet, and the point of its tail.

**Personality**  Vivacious, ardent but not in any way vicious, this dog can adapt to frugal feeding and to a doghouse. While not demonstrative in its affection, it desires the presence and consideration of its master at all times.

**Uses**  The Italian hound only knows how to hunt. Robust, stubborn, untiring, it will deal with any type of terrain. It has a tendency toward independence and must begin training as a hunting dog during the first months of its life. It has a pleasing, harmonious bark.

## 161 CIRNECO DELL'ETNA

**Origin** This breed is descended from greyhounds brought to Sicily from Cyrenaica three thousand years ago. Due to the restricted space in which it developed, it became indigenous to the island. It was often used for hunting on the slopes of Mount Etna.

**Description** Height at the withers: dogs, 18 to 22 inches (46–56 cm.); bitches, 17 to 18 inches (42–46 cm.). Weight: dogs, 22 to 26 pounds (10–12 kg.); bitches, 18 to 22 pounds (8–10 kg.). It has the classic lines of the greyhound with pointed muzzle, flesh-colored nose, and straight nasal canal. It has an arched bite. Eyes: amber and gray, deep-set. Ears: triangular, stiff, upright. Tail: saber-shaped in repose. Coat: very short, all colors of solid tan with white lines on the chest.

**Personality** Dynamic, dignified, intelligent, loyal, tireless, obedient.

**Uses** It knows how to come up on a hare without the slightest noise. It is also used in hunting game birds and can easily be taught to retrieve. Although energetic and sportive, it is adaptable to the life of the city, where it has become an elegant and austere companion dog.

## 162 PODENGO PORTUGUÊS GRANDE

**Origin** This is a greyhoundlike dog that developed in the north of Portugal; however, the details of its origin are not known.

**Description** Height: from 22 to 28 inches (55–70 cm.). Weight: 66 pounds (30 kg.). It is a lanky dog with a pyramid-shaped head, honey or chestnut-colored eyes (depending on the color of its coat), and upright, extremely mobile ears. Its tail is carried horizontally when the dog is in motion and is slightly curved. Colors of coat: yellow, tan, dark gray, white with markings.

**Personality** Vivacious, tenacious, obedient.

**Uses** It is used in packs or alone in the hunting of rabbits. It has also been used with outstanding results as a guard dog.

**Note** This is a rare breed in danger of becoming extinct.

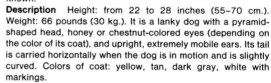

## 163 PODENGO PORTUGUÊS MEDIO

**Origin** Precise information regarding this dog's origin is not known; however, it is a greyhoundlike dog derived from the Podengo Grande.

**Description** Height: from 16 to 22 inches (40–55 cm.). Weight: from 35 to 44 pounds (16–20 kg.). It has good bone structure and strong musculature. Head: pyramid-shaped with tight-fitting lips; solid, white teeth; and clearly arched eyebrows. Eyes: honey or chestnut, with a lively expression. Ears: upright, inclined forward, extremely mobile. Neck: strong, muscular, without dewlap. Tail: hanging in repose, horizontal when the dog is in motion.

There are two varieties of the Podengo Medio: one with short, shiny hair and one with long, coarse hair. Colors: yellow, all shades of tan or faded black. All colors may be solid or marked with white.

**Personality** Lively, obedient, courageous, affectionate, intelligent.

**Uses** Used in hunting rabbits, it is also an attentive watchdog.

---

## 164 PODENGO PORTUGUÊS PEQUENO

**Origin** This is a small greyhoundlike dog derived from the Podengo Medio.

**Description** Height: from 8 to 12 inches (20–30 cm.). Weight: from 9 to 11 pounds (4–5 kg.). It has a convex skull; pointed muzzle; light-chestnut eyes with a lively expression; and upright, open, very mobile ears. Its neck is strong and without dewlap. Its body is longer than it is high. Tail: hanging in repose, horizontal when the dog is active, about 6 to 7 inches (16–18 cm.) long. Limbs: short; its forelegs may be straight or slightly curved. Coat: short, shiny, tight-fitting. Colors: yellow, tan (all shades), faded black. The colors may be solid or marked with white.

**Personality** Intelligent, lively, affectionate.

**Uses** It is normally used for hunting rabbits over rocky terrain. It will, however, gladly live indoors and is a good companion dog.

## 165 HAMILTON HOUND
### Hamiltonstövare

**Origin** This dog carries the name of its breeder, A. P. Hamilton, who created the breed by crossing the foxhound and the Hanover, Holstein, and Curlandia hounds.

**Description** This is a strong, sturdy, well-built dog. Height: not more than 24 inches (60 cm.) and not less than 20 inches (50 cm.). Weight: 55 pounds (25 kg.). It has a lean, elongated, rectangular head with a black nose and large nostrils, and a strong scissors bite. Skull: arched. Eyes: chestnut, with a tranquil expression. Ears: set high, hanging. Tail: almost in line with its back. It has long, muscular shoulders and straight perpendicular forelegs. Its feet have flexible toes and well-developed soles. Coat: especially thick in winter with a soft undercoat. Colors: black on the neck and back; chestnut on the head, the limbs, the underpart of the neck, and the chest; white under the muzzle down into the neck, on the point of the tail, and on the limbs.

**Personality** Courageous, aggressive, with a strong bite, but also obedient and intelligent.

**Uses** It is adapted to fairly large game such as deer and wild boar, especially over difficult, snowy terrain.

---

## 166 DREVER
### Swedish Dachsbracke

**Origin** The origin of the Drever is unknown. It is, however, an old breed that was officially recognized only in 1947.

**Description** Dogs are 14 to 15 inches (35–37 cm.) high; bitches are about 1 1/2 to 2 inches (4–5 cm.) shorter. Weight averages 33 pounds (15 kg.). It has an elongated head with a white muzzle ending in a pointed nose. Its bite is strong and scissors. Eyes: chestnut, limpid, expressive. Ears: wide, of medium length. Neck: long and strong. Tail: hanging, never carried on the dog's back. Its coat is thick, tight, and flat, a little long on the neck, back, and buttocks. All colors are admissible; however, there must be some white.

**Personality** Courageous, proud, obedient.

**Uses** It has mainly been used for hunting hares and foxes, but it is capable of risking its life against game more powerful than itself, such as the wild boar. In such cases, it will circle and dodge the prey and then attack, warning the hunter by barking furiously. It is one of the most common dogs in Sweden but is little known elsewhere.

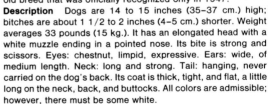

## 167 SWISS HOUND
### Schweizer Laufhund

**Origin**  This hound is descended from hunting dogs from the banks of the Nile. They were brought to Europe by the Phoenicians and to Switzerland by the Roman legionnaires. Its image (from a later date) appears in a painting done in 1100 and kept in the cathedral at Zurich. From the Swiss hound are descended the Jura, the Bernese, and the Lucernese hounds.

**Description**  It is a medium-sized, slightly elongated dog. Height: 18 to 22 inches (45–55 cm.). Weight: 40 to 44 pounds (18–20 kg.). It has a lean, well-proportioned head; extremely strong muzzle; black nose with wide nostrils; dark eyes, with a sweet expression; and very long, conical, pendent ears. Tail: carried horizontally or slightly curved. Limbs: strongly boned. Feet: hard, rugged soles. Its coat is thick and hard. Colors: white with orange or yellow markings; red-coated dogs are also acceptable.

**Personality**  Pugnacious, untiring, and intelligent in the hunt, it is at home one of the sweetest, most serene, and affectionate dogs imaginable.

**Uses**  It has an excellent sense of smell that makes it virtually infallible in the search for game. It will throw itself ferociously against such large adversaries as the wild boar. It will perform perfectly over the hardest terrain in any kind of weather.

---

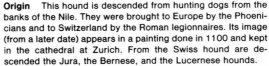

## 168 JURA HOUND
### Jura Laufhund

**Origin**  This breed is descended from Nile hunting dogs brought to Europe by the Phoenicians and introduced into Switzerland during the Roman domination.

**Description**  It is a medium-sized dog, about 16 inches (40 cm.) high, weighing 40 to 44 pounds (18–20 kg.). It has an elongated body, a lean head, and a strong muzzle. Its eyes are dark, with a sweet expression. Its ears are set low, very long, and conical. Tail: carried straight out or slightly curved. Coat: thick and abundant. Colors: solid brown, yellow, reddish, sometimes with a black saddle on its back; or black with lighter shadings. It sometimes has white markings on its chest.

**Personality**  Intelligent, a passionate hunter, tenacious. Serene and affectionate in the home.

**Uses**  Infallible in finding game, and tireless, even over difficult terrain, it is used for all kinds of hunting.

**Note**  There is also a variety of Jura hound known as the St. Hubert. It differs in having a stronger bone structure, dewlaps, and more massive head.

## 169 BERNESE HOUND
### Berner Laufhund

**Origin**   The Bernese hound is a variety of the Swiss hound.
**Description**   Minimum height: 16 inches (40 cm.). Average weight: 33 to 40 pounds (15–18 kg.). Body: elongated. Head: lean, with a strong muzzle. Eyes: dark, with a meek expression. Ears: very long, conical. Tail: carried horizontally or slightly curved. It has a thick, abundant coat. It is always tricolor: white, black, and more or less intense shadings. The white background has small black speckles.
**Personality**   Tenacious, proud, untiring in the hunt. Meek and serene when not at work.
**Uses**   Used for hunting all types of game.

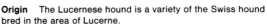

## 170 LUCERNESE HOUND
### Luzerner Laufhund

**Origin**   The Lucernese hound is a variety of the Swiss hound bred in the area of Lucerne.
**Description**   Minimum height: 16 inches (40 cm.). Average weight: 40 to 44 pounds (18–28 kg.). It has an elongated body with a lean head and a strong muzzle. Its eyes are dark, with a meek expression. Ears: very long, conical. Tail: carried horizontally or slightly curved. Its coat has a white background with gray or blue speckles and large dark or black markings. It also has reddish or dark-yellow markings on its head and body. When it is washed, the white seems to disappear, leaving only the darker markings.
**Personality**   Intelligent, tenacious in the hunt. Serene and affectionate at home.
**Uses**   It is gifted with a very fine sense of smell and is very secure in its work. It is used for hunting all types of game even over particularly impassable terrain.

## 171 SMALL SWISS HOUND
## Schweizer Niederlaufhund

**Origin** This is a smaller version of the true Swiss hound.

**Description** There are four varieties of these small hounds: the small Swiss hound, the small Bernese hound, the small Lucernese hound, and the small Jura hound, each bred in the region and descended from the larger dog of the same name. They all have the same standard, differing only in the color of the coat. These small Swiss hounds are from 12 to 15 inches (30–38 cm.) high with arched heads, large dark eyes, very long ears, elegant necks and slender chests, and hanging tails without any significant curvature. Average weight is 33 pounds (15 kg.).

**Personality** Active in the hunt, intelligent, mild when not at work.

**Uses** Like all Swiss hounds, these dogs are used for all types of game, even over very difficult terrain.

**Note** All the small Swiss hounds have full-bodied voices that resound pleasantly during the hunt.

## 172 SMOOTH-HAIRED ISTRIAN HOUND

**Origin** This is a rather old breed, known and used especially in Istria, but its exact origin is a mystery.

**Description** The smooth-haired Istrian hound is a distinguished-looking dog with a beautiful elongated head and muscular limbs. It is from 18 to 23 inches (46–58 cm.) high and weighs 40 to 44 pounds (18–20 kg.). It has oval eyes with a wide-awake expression; flat, pendent ears; and a medium-length tail with a slight upward curve (the thinner the tail, the more valued the dog). Its hair is fine in texture, thick, and brilliant. Color: snow white, generally with yellow-orange ears. There is also a variety of Istrian hound with rough hair (about 4 inches [10 cm.] long). This is a slightly larger dog, but it is otherwise just like the smooth-haired Istrian hound.

**Personality** A passionate hunter, it is tranquil and affectionate with the family.

**Uses** Gifted with a refined sense of smell, it is specialized in the hunting of hares and deer. It is often used in pairs or small packs, especially over rocky terrain or areas covered with thick brambles. Its bark during the hunt is continuous and of pleasing timbre.

### 173 POSAVAC HOUND
**Posavaski gonič**

**Origin** Born and bred in Yugoslavia, the Posavac hound is little known outside its native land.

**Description** Height: from 18 to 23 inches (46–58 cm.). Weight: around 40 pounds (18 kg.). It has an elongated head with a thick black or blackish nose, scissors bite, wide-awake eyes, pendent ears with rounded tips, muscular neck with nice lines, and a tail (sometimes slightly fringed) carried straight or curved. Its hair is about ¾ to 1½ inches (2–4 cm.) long, thick and hard. Colors: reddish, wheat yellow, fawn, with or without white markings on the chest, abdomen, and paws.

**Personality** Self-assured, obedient, lively, pleasing, affectionate with the family.

**Uses** The Posavac hound has a fine sense of smell, is resistant to fatigue even over rocky terrain, has an agile gait and a good bark, and is unremitting in its search for game. It is used especially in hunting for hare and deer.

---

### 174 RHODESIAN RIDGEBACK

**Origin** This breed was developed by the Boers at the end of the nineteenth century. Its standard, fixed in Rhodesia, dates from 1922.

**Description** Its name describes its most unique characteristic: a clearly defined symmetrical ridge running the length of its back, formed by hair that grows in the opposite direction from the rest of its coat. Height: dogs, 25 to 27 inches (63.5–68.5 cm.); bitches, 24 to 26 inches (61–66 cm.). Ideal weight: dogs, 75 pounds (33.9 kg.); bitches, 65 pounds (29.4 kg.). It has an elongated head with an extremely strong muzzle and jaws, a black or brown nose (depending on the color of its coat), very well-developed teeth, a flat skull, and a marked stop. Its eyes are round, shiny, intelligent. Its ears are wide, carried close to the head. Tail: slightly curved. Limbs: muscular. Its coat is short, thick, brilliant in colors that range from light wheaten to red wheaten. A little white on the chest and toes is admissible.

**Personality** It is ferocious in the hunt, but in the home it is a tranquil, obedient, good dog.

**Uses** It can be called a "safari dog" because in small groups it has been used for hunting lions and pumas. It withstands well the torrid heat of day and the damp cold of night, is insensitive to the bites of insects, and can go hungry and thirsty for many hours.

## 175　BASENJI

**Origin**　The first traces of a dog similar to the Basenji are found in Egyptian tombs and wall drawings of five thousand years ago. Also called the Congo dog, it was brought to Europe in 1934. English breeders refined it and exported it all over the world.

**Description**　It appears lively and intelligent, but wrinkles on its forehead also give it the look of a thoughtful old man. Its standard calls for a height of 16½ inches (42.5 cm.) for dogs and 16 inches (40 cm.) for bitches. Weight: from 22 to 24 pounds (9.9–10.8 kg.). It has a flat skull, pointed muzzle, and black or slightly rosy nose. Eyes: brown, almond-shaped. Ears: straight, opening toward the front. Tail: set high, forming two rings that rest on the side of its back. Thighs: muscular. Hair: short and silky, reddish with white markings. Skin: slack. Gait: light, like that of a horse.

**Personality**　Cheerful, affectionate, patient with children. It is an extremely clean dog without even a hint of bad odor. It also has a quality rare among dogs: it does not bark.

**Uses**　In Africa, it is used as a guide in the forests, to warn against the approach of dangerous animals, and as a hunter of small game. In Europe and America, it is considered an excellent companion dog.

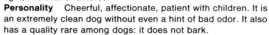

## 176　BLACK AND TAN COONHOUND

**Origin**　Descended from the bloodhound and the foxhound, the breed was developed in the United States on the basis of its colors (black and rich tan). Official recognition dates from 1945.

**Description**　This is a working dog, about 25 to 27 inches (63–68 cm.) high, weighing 50 to 75 pounds (45–64 kg.). It is very well-proportioned, with a finely modeled head. It has well-developed pendent lips; wide black nostrils; round chestnut eyes; long, pendent ears, falling in graceful folds; and a strong tail that is carried freely. Its coat is black with tan markings on the muzzle, limbs, and chest, and must be dense to protect it from bad weather.

**Personality**　A passionate worker, this dog is intelligent, vigilant, and aggressive, but obedient to its master.

**Uses**　As its name implies, the coonhound is a specialist in hunting raccoons. But it is also adapted to the hunting of stag, bear, and opossum, even over difficult terrain. It withstands well the rigors of winter as well as intense heat. Timid or nervous dogs may be disqualified from exhibitions.

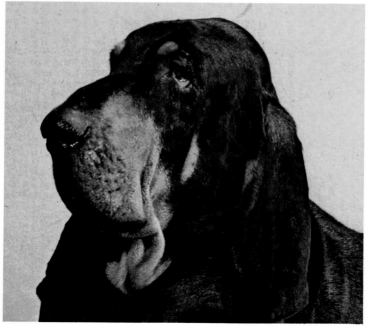

## 177 BLUETICK COONHOUND

**Origin** The bluetick coonhound was developed through crossings among various hounds especially for the hunting of raccoons.

**Description** Height: dogs, 22 to 27 inches (56–69 cm.); bitches, 20 to 25 inches (51–64 cm.). Weight: dogs, 55 to 80 pounds (25–36 kg.); bitches, 45 to 65 pounds (20–29 kg.). It has typical hound looks with an elongated head, pendent ears, and a tail carried horizontally. Coat: of medium length, soft, sleek, shiny. It has a light-colored base thickly speckled with blue with large markings over its body and head.

**Personality** A passionate hunter; kind with children.

**Uses** The bluetick is born with an obvious instinct for hunting. For this reason, its training is easily accomplished. It is extremely agile, attentive, able to work over difficult terrain in bad weather, and is specialized in the finding of raccoons, cougars, and foxes. It also thrives indoors, and if necessary can be an outstanding guard dog.

## 178 REDBONE COONHOUND

**Origin** This is a breed developed in Georgia, probably with the blood of the bloodhound and an ancient Irish hound.

**Description** The redbone has a more robust build than other coonhounds. Height: dogs, 22 to 26 inches (56–66 cm.); bitches, 21 to 25 inches (53–64 cm.). Weight: dogs, 50 to 70 pounds (23–32 kg.); bitches, 45 to 65 pounds (20–29 kg.). It has the hound's beautiful elongated muzzle, pendent ears, and long tail carried cheerfully. Its hair is dense, soft, and fine. Color: preferably solid red, though white traces on the chest and legs are permitted.

**Personality** Merry, mild, a passionate hunter.

**Uses** Gifted with an excellent sense of smell, a great hardiness, and a pleasing bark, it is specialized in the hunt for raccoons. However, it acquits itself equally well in the hunt for cougars and wildcats.

## 179 REDTICK COONHOUND

**Origin**   The result of crossings among a variety of hounds, the redtick is a close relative of the bluetick coonhound.

**Description**   Height: dogs, 22 to 27 inches (56–69 cm.); bitches, 20 to 25 inches (51–64 cm.). Weight: dogs, 55 to 80 pounds (25–36 kg.); bitches, 44 to 65 pounds (20–29 kg.). It has a massive head and elongated muzzle, pendent ears, and a tail carried horizontally. Hair: short, of medium coarseness, but soft and shiny. Color: reddish-chestnut, thickly speckled.

**Personality**   Mild, obedient, affectionate, good with children, an enthusiastic hunter.

**Uses**   Agile, hardy, and with an excellent sense of smell, the redtick gladly hunts raccoons, foxes, and cougars. It is easy to train and works excellently in variable weather and over the most difficult terrain. In the house, it can also fill the role of guard dog.

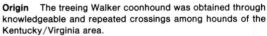

## 180 TREEING WALKER COONHOUND

**Origin**   The treeing Walker coonhound was obtained through knowledgeable and repeated crossings among hounds of the Kentucky/Virginia area.

**Description**   It has the noble aspect of some of the French hounds. It is energetic but of pleasing movement. Dogs are 22 to 27 inches (56–69 cm.) high; bitches, 20 to 25 inches (51–64 cm.) high. They weigh respectively 50 to 75 pounds (23–34 kg.) and 18 to 29 pounds (40–65 kg.). This dog has a robust head; a long, thin muzzle; and a very open nose. Its eyes have a dreamy expression. Ears: pendent. Tail: carried high. Its hair is soft, fine, dense, and shiny. Color: white with black and chestnut markings.

**Personality**   Courageous, untiring, ambitious, very attentive to orders.

**Uses** As its name suggests, this is a raccoon hunter that "climbs trees to follow its prey." It has an excellent sense of smell and good speed. It is an enthusiastic hunter and knows neither fear nor fatigue.

## 181 TENNESSEE TREEING BRINDLE

**Origin** This is a very recently developed breed, but it is descended from very old mountain dogs used for hunting by the Indians.

**Description** It has a robust build like that of the pointer. Height: dogs, 18 to 24 inches (46–61 cm.); bitches, 16 to 22 inches (46–56 cm.). Weight: dogs, 35 to 50 pounds (16–23 kg.); bitches, 30 to 40 pounds (14–18 kg.). It has a robust head and a prominent muzzle with slightly hanging lips. Its front legs are very straight; the back legs, very muscular. Hair: soft, short, slightly crinkly. Colors: brindle or black with streaks.

**Personality** A most enthusiastic hunter, the Tennessee treeing brindle nonetheless has need of a loving master. It thrives in any environment but likes best the warmth of the house.

**Uses** Like its ancestors, the modern Tennessee has an outstanding sense of smell, and is extremely fast. It prefers treeing its prey to trailing and often will almost grab it directly, climbing the tree. Its favorite prey is the raccoon.

**Note** Although of recent creation the breed is already very popular in the U.S.

---

## 182 WESTPHALIAN BASSET
### Westfalischer Dachsbracke

**Origin** This breed is the product of crossing German hounds and bassets.

**Description** Height: from 12 to 14 inches (30–35 cm.). Weight: 33 to 40 pounds (15–18 kg.). It is a robust, moderately long dog with a noble, pointed head; a ram-shaped muzzle; and pendent lips. It has light-brown eyes with a lively cheerful look and hanging ears that are rounded at the tips. Its bite is strong, either scissors or pincers. Tail: carried with a saber curve. Front legs, perpendicular; hind legs, strongly muscular. Its hair is thick and heavy. All colors common to the German hound are admissible with white areas on the neck, chest, muzzle, feet, and point of the tail.

**Personality** Combative, intelligent, friendly.

**Uses** The Westphalian basset combines the hunting qualities of the hound and the basset. It is capable of following the trail of game, alerting the hunter, and penetrating even into the lair. Because of its pleasing looks, its melancholy but at the same time spirited expression, it has also gained popularity as a companion dog. This is a little-known breed, rarely presented at dog shows.

## 183    BOSNIAN HOUND

**Origin**    Developed during the last century, this breed is not known outside its native land of Yugoslavia.

**Description**    Height: 18 to 22 inches (46–56 cm.). Weight: 35 to 53 pounds (16–24 kg.). Its standard demands that the length of its trunk be 10% greater than its height. It has a strong rectangular muzzle with beard and mustaches, and an evident stop. Nose: black, with well-developed nostrils. Teeth: strong, scissors bite. Eyes: oval, chestnut, with a lively expression. Ears: meaty, pendent. Tail: folded slightly upward. Hair: long, hard, bristly, with a thick undercoat. Colors: grain yellow, reddish-yellow, earth gray, blackish. Dogs with white markings, bicolor dogs, and tricolors are also admissible.

**Personality**    Courageous and fervent on the hunt field, the Bosnian hound is tranquil in the home.

**Uses**    This is an untiring dog adapted to hunting all kinds of game even over impassable terrain. It has a pleasing, well-modulated voice.

## 184    YUGOSLAVIAN MOUNTAIN HOUND

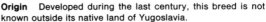

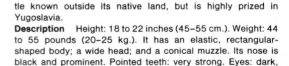

**Origin**    This is a relatively old breed of local formation. It is little known outside its native land, but is highly prized in Yugoslavia.

**Description**    Height: 18 to 22 inches (45–55 cm.). Weight: 44 to 55 pounds (20–25 kg.). It has an elastic, rectangular-shaped body; a wide head; and a conical muzzle. Its nose is black and prominent. Pointed teeth: very strong. Eyes: dark, with an intelligent expression. Ears: hanging, without folds, rounded tips. Tail: saber, reaching the hocks. Coat: thick, coarse, flat, with an abundant undercoat. Its base color is black with red or rust markings over the eyes. Grayish-white markings on the chest are also admissible. This dog has a sure and elastic gait.

**Personality**    Audacious, intelligent, resistant, calm in the most dramatic hunting situations, good-natured, affectionate.

**Uses**    As its name suggests, it is a dog specifically created for hunting in the mountains, in the bush, and over difficult terrain. It has an outstanding sense of smell and a good voice.

## 185 YUGOSLAVIAN TRICOLOR HOUND

**Origin** This is a breed of local formation.

**Description** It is a medium-sized dog 18 to 22 inches (45–55 cm.) high, weighing 44 to 55 pounds (20–25 kg.), well-constructed, with a strong, elegant body. It has a rather long head, a well-developed black nose, and a prominent nasal canal. Eyes: brown or black, with a mild expression. Ears: lying flat against the cheeks. Tail: straight or slightly curved. Thighs: muscular. The soles of its feet are hard. Coat: short, dense, brilliant. As its name indicates, its coat should be tri-color: black (dominant), bright red, and yellow or white.

**Personality** Audacious, steady, good-natured, affectionate.

**Uses** Its wonderful sense of smell and its well-known resistance to wear and weather make it adaptable for any type of hunting, even over difficult terrain and in terrible storms.

## 186 BLACK FOREST HOUND
### Slovensky Kobov

**Origin** This is the Czechoslovakian national hound. It is of ancient origins but was recognized only after World War II.

**Description** It has an elongated body and a rather light bone structure. Height: 18 to 20 inches (45–50 cm.). Weight: 44 to 49 pounds (20–22 kg.). Skull: rounded. Nose: black, pointed. Muzzle: strong, with well-developed teeth. The frontal stop forms a 45-degree angle. Its eyes are always dark, deep-set, with a look of liveliness and courage. Ears: rounded at the tips, hanging close to the cheeks. Tail: sickle-shaped, reaching the hocks. It has a thick, rough coat from 3/4 to 2 inches (2–5 cm.) long. It is always black with red or mahogany shadings on the lips, cheeks, throat, chest, eyes, and limbs.

**Personality** Independent, intelligent, trainable, blessed with a great sense of direction.

**Uses** It is specialized in the hunting of wild boar and is widespread in the mountainous areas of Czechoslovakia. Because of its tough temperament, it can also be used as a watchdog.

## 187 GRAND ANGLO-FRANÇAIS

**Origin**   The breed was established by crossing French hounds with the English foxhound.

**Description**   The Grand Anglo-Français is an elegant dog. Height: from 24 to 27 inches (60–68 cm.). Weight: 66 to 71 pounds (30–32 kg.). Head: long and noble. Eyes: dark, with a meek expression. Ears: pendent, but not long. Tail: carried low with a slight curve. There are three varieties: tricolor, black and white, and black and orange. In turn these three varieties are divided into three sizes: small, medium, and large. The hair is very short, strong, and close to the skin.

**Personality**   Courageous, energetic, tenacious; an enthusiastic hunter, but mild in repose.

**Uses**   The Grand Anglo-Français is used in all sorts of hunting. It is one of the most highly thought of French hunting dogs because of its excellent sense of smell and its knowledge of game. It is probable that the breed will become more widespread and more specialized in the future.

## 188 PORCELAINE

**Origin**   The Porcelaine is the oldest of the French hounds. The breed disappeared during the French Revolution but was "reconstructed" in 1845 with the help of Swiss breeders.

**Description**   Its name, Porcelaine, or porcelain dog, refers to its shining coat, which makes it look like a porcelain statuette. Dogs are between 22 and 23 inches (55–58 cm.) high; bitches, from 21 to 22 inches (53–56 cm.). Weight averages 55 to 62 pounds (25–28 kg.). It is a very distinguished-looking dog with a finely chiseled head, a black nose with wide-open nostrils, and a flat forehead. Eyes: dark, with a sweet expression. Ears: thin, conical, pointed. Neck: long and slender. Tail: hefty at the base, narrowing to a point at the end. Hair: very short, fine, shiny, very white with roundish orange markings.

**Personality**   Energetic, impetuous, and fierce in the hunt, but serene when not hunting.

**Uses**   Vigorous and tireless, with a wonderful sense of smell and a sonorous, modulated bark, it is a hound used for hunting all types of wild game. It is one of the few French hunting dogs that has overcome the confines of its native land and aroused interest abroad.

## 189 ANGLO-FRANÇAIS TRICOLOR

**Origin** This dog was bred by crossing French hounds (Poitevin, Porcelaine) with the English harrier.

**Description** Height: around 20 inches (50 cm.). Weight: 49 to 55 pounds (22–25 kg.). Eyes: small, round, dark. Ears: V-shaped, pendent. Tail: sickle-shaped. Coat: sleek, not too short, tricolor (white, black, orange). There is no official standard for this breed, but in 1957 three varieties were established: tricolor, black and white, orange and white.

**Personality** Clever, untiring, obedient.

**Uses** It is a very fast hound with an excellent sense of smell and a sonorous voice. It is used for hunting small game over any type of terrain.

---

## 190 PETIT ANGLO-FRANÇAIS

**Origin** This breed is the result of crossings of medium-sized French hounds and the beagle.

**Description** The Petit Anglo-Français has not been recognized officially and therefore does not have a standard. However, in general, its height is between 16 and 18 inches (40–45 cm.) and it weighs 35 to 44 pounds (16–20 kg.). Eyes: dark hazel. Ears: hanging, not too long. Tail: carried cheerfully. Coat: shiny; normally in three colors: white, black, and orange. However, there are black-and-white and orange-and-white dogs.

**Personality** Reserved but pleasant.

**Uses** This is a good tracking hound used in the hunt for rabbit, pheasant, and quail. It gladly adapts to indoor life, where it has proved to be tranquil and clean.

## 191 TRANSYLVANIAN HOUND
### Erdelyi Kopo

**Origin**   The breed was developed by crossing dogs brought to Hungary by the Magyars in the ninth century with local dogs and Polish hounds.

**Description**   This is a hound of medium size weighing 66 to 77 pounds (30–35 kg.). There are two varieties: a long-legged variety that is 22 to 26 inches (55–65 cm.) high, and a short-legged variety that is 18 to 20 inches (45–50 cm.) high. It has a short but not pointed head; unwrinkled skin; a straight nose; and strong, well-developed teeth. Eyes: oblique, dark brown. Ears: hanging, without folds. Limbs: well-constructed, ready to spring. Tail: hanging when the dog is at rest; twisted on its back during the hunt. Its coat is short, strong, close to its body. The long-legged variety is black with white markings on its forehead, chest, feet, and the point of its tail. For the short-legged variety, the base color is red-brown with white markings.

**Personality**   Courageous, tenacious, obedient, trainable, good-natured, with an excellent sense of direction.

**Uses**   The Transylvanian hound developed in the Carpathian Mountains, an area rich in forests, meadows, and rivers. Thus it is used to hunting over all types of terrain during frozen winters and sultry summers. The long-legged variety is used for hunting boar, stag, and lynx. The short-legged dogs are used for hunting fox and hare.

---

## 192 SMALL GRAY ELK DOG
### Grähund

**Origin**   This is a very ancient elk dog. Archeological findings show that six thousand years ago the dog was the same as it is today.

**Description**   It is a square, compact, foxlike dog about 19 to 20 inches (49–52 cm.) high. Weight: not over 66 pounds (30 kg.). It has an elegant wedge-shaped head, tight lips, pointed muzzle, and scissors bite. Eyes: dark brown. Ears: stiff and pointed. Tail: short and rolled on the dog's back. Hair: strong and shiny, with a soft undercoat. Colors: various shades of gray, lighter on the abdomen, chest, and limbs. The ears and muzzle, on the other hand, are dark.

**Personality**   Balanced, obedient, good.

**Uses**   As in centuries past, it is still used for hunting elk, bear, and lynx over difficult terrain and vast expanses. Because of its good nature and cordial temperament it has also won esteem as a companion dog. If brought to live in warm countries it needs frequent brushing and bathing.

## 193 BALKAN HOUND
### Balkanski Gonič

**Origin** The Balkan hound belongs to the great dynasty of hounds brought to Europe by the Phoenicians. This particular breed became acclimatized to Yugoslavia and was perfected through selective breeding.

**Description** Height: dogs, from 18 to 21 inches (46–54 cm.); bitches, from 17 to 20 inches (44–52 cm.). Average weight: 44 pounds (20 kg.). It is a strong dog of medium build with a long head and a wide forehead. The stop is only slightly marked. Premolars: strong. Eyes: brown, limpid, intelligent. Ears: hanging, flat, rounded. Tail: not longer than the hocks. Shoulders and limbs: muscular. Feet: round, with strong nails. Hair: thick, fox red or rust-brown with a broad black saddle.

**Personality** Tenacious, energetic, intelligent.

**Uses** Adapted to hunting all types of game over all sorts of terrain in any weather. This is an untiring dog with an outstanding voice. It is used particularly for hunting hare, deer, and boar.

## 194 LUNDEHUND

**Origin** This breed is indigenous to the islands to the north of Norway.

**Description** Height: dogs, 13 to 14 inches (32–36 cm.); bitches, 12 to 13 inches (30–34 cm.). Weight: about 13 pounds (6 kg.). Eyes: brown, not prominent. Ears: upright, opening forward. Tail: short, carried on its back. Coat: long and stiff in black, gray, or brown combined with white.

**Personality** Vivacious, tenacious, attentive, intelligent.

**Uses** This hound has been specially trained for "hunting" black-and-white birds known as puffins (*Fratercula arctica*), whose nests are edible. The Lundehund climbs up on the cliffs or trees where the bird nests, avoiding the bird's strong beak. It puts the bird to flight and grabs the nest and takes it to its master. Aiding it in performing this singular task, the Lundehund has five toes and eight plantar cushions. When working in caves, it is able to close its ears to protect its ear passages from dripping water.

## 195 NORWEGIAN ELKHOUND
## Norsk Elghund

**Origin** This breed is thousands of years old. It has been by man's side since the time he hunted with slingshots.

**Description** There are two varieties of Norwegian elkhound: gray and black. For the gray type the standard requires a height of 20 inches (52 cm.) for dogs, 19 inches (49 cm.) for bitches; a short, compact body; a muzzle of moderate length; strong jaws; dark-brown eyes with a friendly expression; pointed, mobile ears; a tail rolled on its back; and thick, coarse hair. It may be any shade of gray. For the black type, the standard requires a height of between 18 and 20 inches (45–50 cm.); a short, compact body; a light, conical head; dark eyes with an energetic expression; pointed, very mobile ears; a tail rolled on its back; and dense, coarse hair. Its color should be brilliant black. Weight, which is not specified in the standard, is about 44 pounds (20 kg.).

**Personality** Loyal, affectionate, trainable, clean, docile, intelligent.

**Uses** It is specialized in hunting elk, which it can scent from a distance of several kilometers. It is also highly prized as a sled dog; in case of war the Norwegian Defense Minister has the power to mobilize all privately owned elkhounds. It loves the hunt and vast unconfined areas, but due to its outstanding character and its adaptability, it can be a perfect companion dog, especially with children.

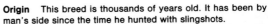

## 196 SCHILLERSTÖVARE

**Origin** The Schillerstövare is a hound that has been known since the Middle Ages. The breed was perfected by the breeder Per Schiller, who gave it his name. It was officially recognized in 1952.

**Description** It is a robust-looking dog, but at the same time noble, light, and dynamic. Optimum height: dogs, 22 inches (57 cm.); bitches, 21 inches (53 cm.). Weight: 40 to 53 pounds (18–24 kg.). It has an elongated head that, seen from above, looks conical. Its nose is black and well-developed; its lips are tight to the jaw. It has a clearly visible stop and a scissors bite. Eyes: chestnut, full of vitality. Ears: soft to the touch, hanging. Tail: carried straight or slightly saber. Shoulders: muscular. Toes: elastic. Soles of feet: tough. Its coat is composed of a strong, shiny outer coat and a thick undercoat. Colors: black and tan. The neck, shoulders, sides of the chest, and top side of the tail are black.

**Personality** Vivacious, active, intelligent, good-natured.

**Uses** It is a hound that specializes in hunting over the snow.

## 197 GREEK HOUND
### Ellinikós ichnilátis

**Origin** This is a native breed known only in Greece.

**Description** Height: from 19 to 22 inches (47–55 cm.) for dogs; from 18 to 21 inches (45–53 cm.) for bitches. Weight: 38 to 44 pounds (17–20 kg.). It has an elongated head with a somewhat ram-shaped nasal canal, a black nose, strong white teeth, and a stop that is only slightly pronounced. Eyes: brown, with an intelligent expression. Ears: flat, hanging. Tail: not long, carried saber. Hair: very short, thick, a little coarse. Colors: black and fire red with small white markings on the chest.

**Personality** Lively, very attentive, good-natured.

**Uses** Gifted with an extremely fine sense of smell and able to endure running over rocky terrain, this hound is used either alone, in pairs, or in packs for all kinds of hunting. It has a resonant, harmonious voice.

## 198 SMÅLANDSSTÖVARE

**Origin** This breed is native to central Sweden. Its standard was established in 1921 and updated in 1952.

**Description** The Smålandsstövare is a compact, robust, but noble-looking dog about 20 inches (50 cm.) high. Weight: 33 to 40 pounds (15–18 kg.). It has a narrow head, a black nose with very open nostrils, strong teeth, and a blunt muzzle. Eyes: dark, with a tranquil expression. Ears: flat, pendent. Back: slightly hollowed. Abdomen: muscular, retracted. The tail may be hock length or docked at birth. The hair of its coat is thick and heavy but at the same time sleek and shiny; it is black with lighter shadings over the eyes, at the bottoms of the front legs, and in the anal area.

**Personality** Steady, intelligent, affectionate.

**Uses** This dog is used above all for hunting fox and hare because of its wonderful sense of smell and the lightness with which it runs over any kind of terrain in any season.

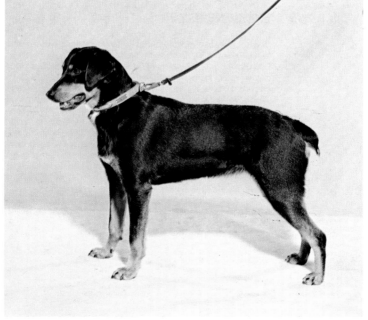

## 199 HYGENHUND

**Origin** This is an indigenous breed, widespread through Norway but little known elsewhere.

**Description** Its height varies from 19 to 22 inches (47–55 cm.); however, very sturdy males may reach 24 inches (60 cm.). Weight: 44 to 53 pounds (20–24 kg.). Bitches are somewhat smaller. It has a regular conical-shaped head, a black nose, tight lips, scissors bite, and a well-defined stop. Eyes: dark, adapted in color to the hue of its coat. Ears: soft and wide, reaching the middle of its muzzle. Tail: carried gaily, but not rolled on the back. Limbs: solid, nervous. Thighs: wide and muscular. Hair: straight, dense, shiny, not too short. Colors: chestnut, yellow-red (with or without black shadings), black with areas of bright chestnut. These colors may be combined with white.

**Personality** Lively but steady, active, good-natured.

**Uses** This dog has an outstanding sense of smell and is a great and untiring runner. It is used for all types of hunting, even in weather and over terrain that seem prohibitive.

## 200 HALDENSTOVER

**Origin** This is a very old breed that took shape in Norway and has not spread to other countries.

**Description** It is a compact, solid, hardy dog with an elongated body. Height: dogs, 19 to 22 inches (47–55 cm.); bitches, 10% less. Weight: 44 to 55 pounds (20–25 kg.). It has a well-proportioned head, a straight muzzle, and a black nose. Its skull is dome-shaped, and its lips should not be too pendent. Eyes: dark brown, with a serene expression. Ears: reaching to the middle of its muzzle. Neck: long and curved, without dewlap. Tail: thick, carried low. Limbs: well-boned, with muscular thighs. Feet: oval, with strong soles. Its hair is shiny and dense. Colors: white with black and brown markings, but the black must not predominate.

**Personality** Steady, active, intelligent, good-natured.

**Uses** Built for fast chases over wide-open spaces, it is used for all types of hunting over difficult terrain and over snow.

## 201 DUNKER

**Origin** This is a native breed that has not spread beyond the confines of Norway.

**Description** The Dunker is strong but not heavy. It has a rectangular body from 19 to 22 inches (47–55 cm.) high. Weight: 35 to 49 pounds (16–22 kg.). It has a beautiful elongated head with slender cheeks, a black nose and wide nostrils, and a scissors bite. Eyes: dark, with a tranquil expression. Ears: soft, of medium length, carried close to its head. Neck: long, without folds of skin. Tail: strong, never rolled. The bone structure of its legs is robust, and its feet are compact with thick soles. Hair: thick and straight. Colors: black or marbled blue.

**Personality** Steady, serene, good.

**Uses** Esteemed more for its hardiness in working situations than for its speed, it is adapted to any kind of terrain. It withstands cold well.

---

## 202 SOMERSET HARRIER

**Origin** Obtained in 1800 after repeated crossings among various hounds and the harrier.

**Description** This is a strong, well-constructed dog about 22 inches (55 cm.) high. Weight: 33 to 40 pounds (15–18 kg.). It has a rather long head with a wide skull, only a slight stop, and a well-developed black nose. Eyes: chestnut or dark hazel, with a lively, intelligent expression. Ears: flat, not too long, thin and soft. Neck: with slight dewlap. Well-boned sides and legs. Hair: thick and flat. Colors: solid white, white and light red, white and orange, white and gray, white and tan.

**Personality** Lively, distinguished, cheerful, intelligent.

**Uses** Gifted with a fine sense of smell, great speed, sturdiness, and cunning, the Somerset harrier is especially adapted to the hunting of rabbits and foxes.

## 203    SABUESO ESPAÑOL

**Origin**    Originally brought in by the Phoenicians, this breed developed and changed slowly in the confines of the Iberian peninsula.

**Description**    This is a strong, slender dog. Height: dogs, 20 to 22 inches (51–56 cm.); bitches, 19 to 20 inches (49–52 cm.). Weight: about 55 pounds (25 kg.). It has a long head; a large pigmented nose with open nostrils; a large convex skull; and slightly pendent lips, sometimes with pouches. Eyes: chestnut. Ears: very long and flexible. Tail: extending beyond the hocks. Hair: fine, not fringed. Color: usually white with round orange or black markings. There is also a variety of Sabueso Español that is lighter in weight than the above. It has thin, elastic skin and short shiny, glossy hair. It is white with red or black markings that are sometimes so extensive they cover its entire body except for the neck, muzzle, and chest.

**Personality**    Steady but lively, loyal, affectionate.

**Uses**    This is an outstanding hound, adapted to all types of hunting. It is capable of working long hours even in very hot weather.

---

## 204    RASTREADOR BRASILEIRO

**Origin**    This dog was bred in large part from the American foxhound.

**Description**    This is a strong, lively dog about 26 inches (65 cm.) high. Weight: about 55 pounds (25 kg.). It has a triangular head, dark nose, straight muzzle, and only a slight stop. Eyes: almond-shaped; dark, with metallic reflections. Ears: pendent, rounded at the tips. Neck: strong, with slight dewlaps. Chest: wide and deep. Back: long and straight. Saber tail, always carried flaglike. Feet: wide with strong, elastic soles. Its coat is composed of very short, dense hair, coarse to the touch. Colors: white background with small blue markings and small chestnut markings on the legs; white background with large black or chestnut markings; brown with black head, back, and tail.

**Personality**    Ardent, intelligent, obedient, not aggressive.

**Uses**    The Rastreador Brasileiro was bred and trained to hunt jaguar, which it will follow tenaciously through the bush, over marshes, and across the most difficult terrain.

## 205 LEVESQUE

**Origin** This breed was created in 1873 by a French breeder named Rogatien Levesque, who obtained it by crossings among the foxhound, the Bleu de Gascogne, the Virelade, the Saintongeois, and the Vendéen. Today, it is extremely rare.

**Description** This is a thin, bony, lively dog 26 to 28 inches (65–72 cm.) high. Weight: 55 to 66 pounds (25–30 kg.). It has a strong elongated head with a rounded skull and thick pendent lips. Eyes: brown, deep-set, with a serene and intelligent expression. Ears: slightly curled. Neck: short and strong, with slight dewlaps. Tail: long and curved. Shoulders and thighs: muscular. Hair: very short and thick. Colors: always black and white; the black sometimes has violet reflections.

**Personality** Exuberant, affectionate, an enthusiastic hunter.

**Uses** Originally bred to hunt in packs, the Levesque has a fine sense of smell and is fast and sturdy. The few remaining examples of this breed are used for searching out all kinds of game.

## 206 BRIQUET GRIFFON VENDÉEN

**Origin** Bred in the department of Vendée in France.

**Description** A short but well-proportioned dog, the Briquet male is 20 to 22 inches (50–55 cm.) high; bitches, 19 to 21 inches (48–53 cm.). Weight: 35 to 53 pounds (16–24 kg.). It has a short, rather light head; a black, open nose; and mustaches on its lips. Eyes: dark, large, with a lively expression. Ears: soft, pointed, not too long. Chest: deep. Tail: carried with a sickle curve. It has good bone structure and hard-soled feet. Hair: long, thick, and bushy with a thick undercoat. Colors: fawn, light brown, white and orange, white and gray, or tricolored in the above-mentioned hues.

**Personality** Decisive, active, intelligent.

**Uses** Capable of rousing all kinds of game over varied terrain—sandy, hilly, or even flooded. It is used in small groups, but also as the personal hunting dog of individual hunters.

## 207  PETIT GRIFFON BLEU DE GASCOGNE

**Origin**  Developed by crossing the wirehaired griffon with the Bleu de Gascogne.

**Description**  Height: 17 to 20 inches (43–52 cm.). Weight: around 33 pounds (15 kg.). It has a straight or slightly ram-shaped nasal canal and a black nose. Eyes: golden chestnut, expressive. Ears: not very long, slightly curled. Neck: thin but with a slight dewlap. Back: short. Tail: long, very thin toward the end. Its hair is coarse and flat to its body, wavy on its thighs and chest. Color: speckled white with black markings and shaded areas on its cheeks, chest, and paws. Over all, this is a rustic-looking dog.

**Personality**  Audacious but wise.

**Uses**  The breed is adapted to all kinds of hunting, furred or feathered game, over a wide variety of terrain, wet, dry, or wooded. It is methodical and untiring, blessed with an excellent sense of smell and a light, nervous gait.

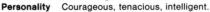

## 208  GRIFFON FAUVE DE BRETAGNE

**Origin**  Well known during the Middle Ages, this dog had its moment of splendor in the second half of the nineteenth century. It is still known in France but little known elsewhere.

**Description**  Height: 20 to 22 inches (50–55 cm.) for dogs; 19 to 20 inches (47–52 cm.) for bitches. Weight: around 44 pounds (20 kg.). It is a muscular dog with a strong bone structure. It has an elongated muzzle; a black or brown nose; dark eyes; and long, pointed ears. Its tail is of medium length, often with twill-like hair patterns. It has rather long hair that is very stiff, not curled: Colors: golden wheat, brown-red, tan.

**Personality**  Courageous, tenacious, intelligent.

**Uses**  At one time, the breed specialized in hunting the wolves that menaced the flocks in Bretagne. Ten of these dogs can wipe out the most ferocious predators. Later, it became a fine hound for hunting rabbits and foxes.

**Note**  Because the breed was becoming bastardized, a very strict standard has been applied. Dogs with short muzzles, wide skulls, hanging lips, ears that are too short or too long, excessively round thighs, soft wide feet, or weak-looking dogs are not allowed in shows.

**GERMAN SHORT-HAIRED POINTER**
**Kurzhaar**

**Origin**  This German pointing dog is descended from the Spanish pointer, which was introduced into Germany in 1600 by Flemish hunters. Crossings with the Italian pointer and the English pointer made it faster and more energetic. The modern short-hair quickly became very popular throughout Europe.

**Description**  The German short-haired pointer is a distinguished, elegant-looking dog 24 to 25 inches (62–64 cm.) high, weighing 55 to 70 pounds (25–32 kg.). According to its standard, it should have a lean, well-delineated head with a broad skull with a flat arch; a very prominent brown nose (a flesh-colored nose is not desirable); slightly pendent lips; and a strong, tight-fitting bite. Eyes: brown (yellow eyes are a defect). Ears: moderately long, flat, tight to the cheeks, with rounded points. Chest: higher than it is broad, with well-arched ribs, but not barrel-shaped. The tail is docked to avoid injuries during the hunt. The hair is short, thick, coarse to the touch. Admissible colors: solid chestnut; chestnut with small white markings on the chest and limbs; dark-chestnut roan with a chestnut head and markings; white with a chestnut mask, markings, and speckles; or black with any of the above variations. Yellow is not considered a defect.

**Personality**  Exuberant, trainable, forthright, decisive, intelligent, cheerful, obedient, friendly with children.

**Uses**  The German short-haired pointer is used by every type of hunter for pointing, for following game, and for guarding. It is all together a dog of extraordinary hunting capability in the mountains, in the woods, in marshes, and in all climates. It is a somewhat rustic-looking dog, and although it has an outstanding temperament, it should not be considered an apartment dog. Nonetheless, it can adapt itself to any situation so long as it has adequate space for outdoor exercise when hunting season is over.

## 210 GERMAN WIREHAIRED POINTER
### Drahthaar

**Origin** The German wirehaired pointer was bred in the first years of the twentieth century with careful crossings of the German pointer, the wirehaired griffon, the pointer, the bloodhound, and the Airedale. The German Drahthaar Club will register only the six best puppies from every litter in order to maintain the high quality of the breed.

**Description** Height: dogs, 24 to 26 inches (60–67 cm.); bitches, 22 to 24 inches (56–62 cm.). Weight: 60 to 70 pounds (27–32 kg.). Muzzle: wide, long, robust. Dentition: strong, scissors bite. Lips: not pendent. Eyes: dark and limpid. Ears: of medium length, pendent. Neck: slender and robust. Chest: wide and deep. Back: short. Tail: moderately docked. Hair: hard and bristly, like steel wool; bushy eyebrows and beard. Colors: from dark to medium chestnut.

**Personality** Steady, lively, vigorous. Very affectionate with its master and jealous of other dogs.

**Uses** The German wirehaired pointer inherited the best qualities of each of its ancestors: a fine sense of smell, a secure point, a ready intelligence, and elegant lines. This is a dog that can fully respond to the needs of the hunter.

---

## 211 GROSSER MÜNSTERLÄNDER

**Origin** Breeding of the Münsterländer began in the early 1900's in the German city of Münster. It is the result of crossings between the spaniel and the German long-haired pointer.

**Description** Height: from 23 to 24 inches (58–62 cm.). Weight: about 44 pounds (20 kg.). It has an elongated head and a lean muzzle. Eyes: dark, heavily lidded. Ears: light, very hairy. Tail: carried horizontally, docked by several centimeters. Hair: sleek, in white with black markings, or with markings and speckling. An all-black coat is not desirable.

**Personality** Courageous, cheerful, intelligent, obedient.

**Uses** This is a dog adapted to any terrain (valleys, prairies, forests, water) and to every type of hunting. It is resistant to fatigue and to bad weather. Particularly appreciated for the sureness of its point and the precision with which it retrieves, the breed has also shown itself to be a dedicated enemy of birds of prey that try to attack farm animals. It is also an excellent guard dog.

## 212 KLEINER MÜNSTERLÄNDER

**Origin** The Kleiner Münsterländer was developed in the early 1900's in the town of Münster in Westphalia through crossings of the spaniel and the German long-haired pointer.

**Description** Height: dogs, from 19 to 22 inches (48–56 cm.); bitches, 17 to 20 inches (44–52 cm.). Weight: around 33 pounds (15 kg.). Head: distinguished-looking, lean. Nose: brown with no flesh-colored markings. Muzzle: elongated, with tight lips. Eyes: dark, with an expression of good will. Ears: pointed and hairy. Neck: arched and muscular. Chest: large, with well-rounded ribs. Tail: slightly curved, with feathering. Front legs: solid and straight; muscular thighs. Its hair is sleek and tight to its body. Colors: white and chestnut.

**Personality** Courageous, gay, obedient.

**Uses** Resistant to fatigue and to the worst weather, the Kleiner Münsterländer is adapted to all types of hunting in open spaces or in woods. It is sure in the point and precise in its retrieval. It is also an amiable companion dog. Its most pleasing and attractive characteristics are its beautiful ears, which are held pricked, as if in continual alarm; its distinctive carriage; its cleanliness; and its happy, always-wagging tail.

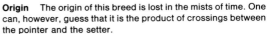

## 213 GERMAN LONG-HAIRED POINTER

**Origin** The origin of this breed is lost in the mists of time. One can, however, guess that it is the product of crossings between the pointer and the setter.

**Description** Height: from 25 to 28 inches (63–70 cm.). Weight: 55 to 65 pounds (25–30 kg.). Skull: convex. Muzzle: elongated. Nose: brown and flat. Dentition: sturdy. Eyes: dark. Ears: flat to the head, rounded at the tips. Back: short and solid. Body: robust and muscular but noble-looking. Tail: slightly docked, feathered. Its hair is about 2 inches (5 cm.) long, short on the head and feathered on the legs. Color: chestnut.

**Personality** Steady, trainable, docile, very obedient. It always seeks a close affectionate bond with its master.

**Uses** Known only in Germany, it is esteemed for its indomitable interest in every kind of game, for its excellent sense of smell, for its tirelessness in the search for game, and for its calmness even at the most dramatic moments of the hunt.

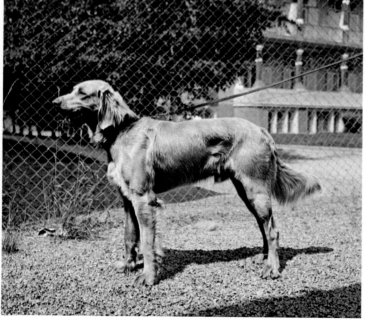

## 214 WEIMARANER

**Origin** The breed is several centuries old. A Weimaraner appears in a Van Dyck painting of the early 1600's. There are various theories as to its origin: Some feel it is the result of albinism that overtook some ancient German pointing dogs. Others feel it is descended from the German hound, the Braken. And still others feel it is the fruit of crossings overseen by Grand Duke Karl August of Weimar between a regular pointer and a certain yellow pointer.

**Description** The Weimaraner is a beautifully formed, medium-weight dog. Height: dogs, 23 to 28 inches (59–70 cm.); bitches, 22 to 26 inches (57–65 cm.). Weight: 70 to 85 pounds (32–38 kg.) for males. It has a broad, lean head; a long, strong muzzle; a minimal stop; and a dark-flesh-colored nose. Eyes: amber, with an intelligent expression. Ears: broad and long, with rounded points. Tail: docked to 1½ inches (4 cm.) when the dog is two days old. Limbs: long and muscular. Hair: short and fine. Colors: all shades of gray. The head and ears are slightly lighter in color.

**Personality** Lively, cheerful, affectionate, tends to be stubborn.

**Uses** Very hardy, with a good sense of smell, and a passionate worker, the Weimaraner can be used for all kinds of hunting.

## 215 PERDIGUERO DE BURGOS

**Origin** This is an ancient hunting dog indigenous to the province of Burgos in northern Spain.

**Description** It is a bony, muscular, tough dog with a massive head; noticeable dewlap; and thick, pendent lips. Its height is from 26 to 30 inches (65–75 cm.) and it weighs from 55 to 66 pounds (25–30 kg.). It has an almost square muzzle; a dark, but not black, nose; dark eyes with a melancholy expression; and wide, long, pendent ears. Its neck is round and strong; its chest, deep; its back, rounded. Tail: docked to a third its original length, carried high and cheerfully. Legs: long, with muscular thighs. Hair: short and fine. Colors: white with liver markings or speckles, or liver with white speckling.

**Personality** Docile, affectionate, likable.

**Uses** The Perdiguero de Burgos loves all types of hunting and is used for hunting pheasant, hare, and deer. It is easy to train and is undeterred by bad weather and difficult terrain. It has a most sensitive sense of smell and is a perfect pointer and retriever. It does not seem to suffer from even the hot Spanish summers.

## 216 PODENCO IBICENCO

**Origin**   This is a greyhoundlike dog native to the Balearic island of Ibiza.

**Description**   Height: dogs, 24 to 26 inches (60–66 cm.); bitches, 22 to 25 inches (57–63 cm.). Weight: dogs, about 50 pounds (22.5 kg.); bitches, about 42 pounds (19 kg.). It has a long, narrow head with a flesh-colored nose; a convex muzzle; thin lips; and exceptionally healthy teeth. Eyes: oblique, light amber. Ears: erect, rigid. Neck: long and slightly arched. Tail: down when the dog is in repose, raised to a sickle curve in action. There are three varieties of the Podenco Ibicenco: sleek-coated, wirehaired, and long-haired. Colors: white and red, white and tan, or solid white or red.

**Personality**   Very lively, active, intelligent; males can be quarrelsome with other male dogs.

**Uses**   This is a very fast dog with an innate pride. It is used especially for hunting wild rabbits. It is also used in nocturnal hunting.

## 217 BRAQUE ARIÉGEOIS

**Origin**   The Braque Ariégeois is an ancient breed that originated in the department of Ariège, near the Pyrenees, and was modified by breeding with the Braque Saint-Germain.

**Description**   This is a solid, powerful, but elegant dog from 24 to 26 inches (60–67 cm.) high. Weight: 55 to 66 pounds (25–30 kg.). It has a convex skull, square muzzle, and red or light-chestnut nose. Eyes: a frank and intelligent expression. Ears: long and scrolled. Neck: with slight dewlap. Tail: docked. Hocks: nervous. Its coat, which is made up of fine opaque hair, is white with orange or chestnut markings and light speckling.

**Personality**   Lively and independent. It needs thorough training and a master who knows how to dominate it.

**Uses**   This is the most powerful of the French pointing breeds. It is a tenacious walker and is resistant to illness. It has a fine sense of smell and is an outstanding retriever. It is adapted to hunting all kinds of game in the mountains or over very difficult terrain. It is mainly popular in France.

## 218    BRAQUE D'AUVERGNE

**Origin**    There are different opinions about the origin of this breed: indigenous to the region of Auvergne, descended from an ancient French pointer; or imported at the end of the eighteenth century by the cavalry driven out of Malta by Napoleon.

**Description**    This is a powerful, elegant dog with robust limbs. Height: 22 to 25 inches (57–63 cm.) for dogs; 22 to 23 inches (55–60 cm.) for bitches. Weight: 49 to 62 pounds (22–28 kg.). It has an elongated head; a shiny black nose with open nostrils; a square muzzle; strong white teeth; an oval skull; and arched, raised eyebrows. Eyes: large, dark hazel, with a loyal expression. Ears: light, fine in texture, long, slightly scrolled. Neck: strong and slightly arched. Back: short and straight. Tail: docked by two-thirds (ideal length: 6 to 8 inches [15–20 cm.]). Hair: shiny, short, not hard. Colors: a white background with or without black markings and speckling, or charcoal (a mixture of black and white). The head should always have ample black markings.

**Personality**    Lively, sensitive, obedient, affectionate.

**Uses**    Light and elegant in the chase, where it displays its solid and effective musculature, this "provincial" French dog is adapted to any kind of hunting over any terrain, be it volcanic or woodsy.

---

## 219    FRENCH POINTER
### Braque Français

**Origin**    Against the view that all pointers come from Italy, the result of crossings between the Molossus and the hound, some authors maintain that the French pointer is a native breed.

**Description**    Powerful but not heavy, this is a noble-looking animal with an imposing head. It has a slightly convex skull, a rectangular muzzle, and a thick chestnut-colored nose. Eyes: chestnut or dark yellow, with a serious and friendly expression. Ears: pendent, slightly pleated. Tail: docked. Chest: broad and deep. Shoulders and limbs: very muscular. Height: from 22 to 26 inches (56–65 cm.). Weight: from 55 to 71 pounds (25–32 kg.). Hair: thick and dense, finer on the head and ears. Color: white with chestnut markings, with or without trout markings.

**Personality**    Obedient, loyal, tranquil in the family.

**Uses**    It has an excellent sense of smell, is adapted to difficult terrain, and has a beautiful statuelike point. It is thus fitted for use in any kind of hunting. However, it bites the game too hard.

## 220 BARBET

**Origin** The barbet is descended from the ancient *canis aquaticus* and is extremely rare. Its name comes from the French *barbe* (beard).

**Description** The barbet is a pointing breed. Height: 22 to 24 inches (55–60 cm.). Weight: about 33 pounds (15 kg.). It has a thick, shiny, tasseled coat. Colors: black, gray, or chestnut with white markings.

**Personality** Gay, obedient, intelligent.

**Uses** This is an excellent water dog, reflecting its famous origins. It is, however, used only by a very few admirers in France.

**Note** The barbet is the progenitor of many pointing breeds and is often mentioned as the father of the poodle.

## 221 VIZSLA

**Origin** The Vizsla is probably descended from two ancient breeds: the Transylvanian hound and the Turkish yellow dog. In more recent times the blood of the German short-haired pointer and the pointer has been added to the Vizsla.

**Description** The Vizsla is a medium-sized dog, distinguished, robust, with an elastic gait. Height: dogs, 22 to 24 inches (57–62 cm.); bitches, 21 to 23 inches (53–58 cm.). Weight: from 49 to 62 pounds (22–28 kg.). It has a squared-off muzzle with a dark-brown nose, developed jaws, and porcelain-white teeth. The color of its eyes blends with the color of its coat. Ears: long, pendent, with rounded tips. Neck: muscular, without dewlap. Tail: docked by a third. Its musculature is well developed over its entire body. Its hair is short, abundant, and tight to the body. All shades of dark sandy yellow are admissible (brown is a defect). Besides this short-haired Hungarian pointer there is a variety with hard hair. It developed by spontaneous mutation and has been encouraged by crossings with the wirehaired German pointer.

**Personality** Intelligent, trainable, steady, obedient, affectionate.

**Uses** Adapted to all types of hunting, it has an exceptional sense of smell and a masterful retrieval over any terrain, even marshes. It is known and esteemed beyond the confines of its native Hungary.

## 222 BRITTANY SPANIEL
### Épagneul Breton

**Origin** The origin of the Brittany spaniel is controversial. According to some experts, it formed autochthonously in France and is called "spaniel" not because it came from Spain but from the verb *espanir*, which means to crouch or to flatten out oneself, both typical actions of this dog in the presence of game. According to another hypothesis, the Brittany spaniel may be the fruit of a crossing between the orange-and-white setter and some not clearly identified French dog. In either case, the Brittany spaniel was first shown at a French dog show in 1896. Its official recognition dates from 1938, so before receiving a standard, the Brittany spaniel underwent several changes of fortune.

**Description** Height: dogs, 19 to 20 inches (48–50 cm.); bitches, 18½ to 19 inches (47–49 cm.). Weight: 35 to 40 pounds (15–18 kg.) for males. This is an elegant, sturdy, vigorous dog with an intelligent-looking face. It has a rounded skull of medium length with a straight or slightly ram-shaped muzzle, a pronounced stop, and a nose that is more or less dark depending on the color of its coat. Eyes: amber, expressive. Ears: rather short, slightly rounded, with a little feathering. Back: short, with high withers. Tail: not more than 4 inches (10 cm.) long. Shoulders and thighs: muscular. Its hair is always thick and fine, flat and a little wavy. Colors: white and orange, white and chestnut, white and black, or tricolor.

**Personality** Intelligent, trainable, naturally well mannered, very sweet, playful. It can become timid if treated roughly.

**Uses** The Brittany is adapted to all types of terrain: woods, plains, hills. It is resistant to cold and damp. It is used especially for hunting woodcock, partridge, and hare, and is always active, enthusiastic, and untiring. It also has an outstanding instinct for retrieving from water. The Brittany spaniel has earned great popularity among millions of hunters because of its moderate size, which allows them to transport it easily. Because of its jovial character, it is also popular as a companion dog. While always remaining a sporting dog, it adapts easily to apartment life.

## 223 FRENCH SPANIEL
### Épagneul Français

**Origin** There are varying opinions regarding the origin of this breed. It may come from Spain, as its name "spaniel" suggests, or it may be of native formation with help from a so-called quail pointer, which is now extinct.

**Description** This is a powerful, elegant dog with harmonious lines and a passion for its work. Height: dogs, 22 to 24 inches (55–60 cm.); bitches, from 21 to 23 inches (54–58 cm.). Weight: 44 to 55 pounds (20–25 kg.). It has a slightly convex skull; a strong head with an elongated, slightly ram-shaped muzzle; and a brown nose with open nostrils. Eyes: large, dark amber, with a very sweet expression. Ears: long, with a silky fringe, rounded at the tips. Tail: with an S curve, feathered. Shoulders and thighs: muscular. Hair: long, soft, flat or wavy. Curls are only allowed on the ears, neck, limbs, and tail. Color: always white with chestnut markings.

**Personality** Docile, expansive, intelligent, trainable.

**Uses** Outstanding for finding and standing both furred and feathered game. Appreciated also for the ease with which it can be transported. It is not widespread outside France.

## 224 PICARDY SPANIEL

**Origin** The breed is a native of the ancient French province of Picardy. At the end of the nineteenth century, the breed suffered a sudden decline; however, new breeders have brought it justifiably back into vogue in recent years.

**Description** Height: 22 to 24 inches (55–60 cm.). Weight: around 44 pounds (20 kg.). Skull: round and broad. Muzzle: slightly ram-shaped. Nose: brown. Eyes: dark amber, very expressive. Ears: with wavy fringes, pendent. Neck, shoulders, and thighs: muscular. Tail: well feathered. Hair: heavy, slightly wavy. Color: speckled gray with chestnut markings spread over its body.

**Personality** Very good, cheerful, intelligent, sensitive.

**Uses** With its excellent sense of smell and great hardiness, it is used in hunting hare and wild duck in prairies, woods, and marshes.

## 225    PONT-AUDEMÈRE SPANIEL
### Épagneul de Pont-Audemère

**Origin**   The breed was created at Pont-Audemère, on the river Aude, by crossings between the ancient French spaniel and the Irish water spaniel.

**Description**   The Pont-Audemère is a vigorous dog about 20 to 23 inches (52–58 cm.) high. Weight: 40 to 53 pounds (18–24 kg.). It has a rounded skull, a brown pointed nose, and a somewhat ram-shaped muzzle. Eyes: small, dark amber, with a meek expression. Ears: pendent, richly feathered. Long fringes gather into a saucy little toupet, which gives it the look of an old woman. Tail: docked to a third its length; always in motion. Hair: rich, slightly ruffled, shiny. Color: chestnut with gray reflections.

**Personality**   Vigorous in the field; mild at home.

**Uses**   Its close relationship to the Irish water spaniel ("the dog that loves the water like a fish") and its origins near the river Aude have contributed to make it an outstanding retriever in marshy areas. It is, however, also used a great deal over difficult terrain in all types of hunting. Its pleasing looks and the sweetness of its expression have also opened to it the role of companion dog. Nonetheless, it is little known outside southern France.

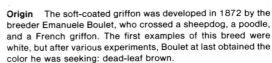

## 226    SOFT-COATED GRIFFON
### Boulet

**Origin**   The soft-coated griffon was developed in 1872 by the breeder Emanuele Boulet, who crossed a sheepdog, a poodle, and a French griffon. The first examples of this breed were white, but after various experiments, Boulet at last obtained the color he was seeking: dead-leaf brown.

**Description**   Height: from 22 to 24 inches (55–60 cm.) for dogs; from 20 to 22 inches (50–55 cm.) for bitches. Weight: 44 to 55 pounds (20–25 kg.). It has a long, broad muzzle with big mustaches; a blond or brown nose with open nostrils; yellow eyes with thick eyebrows; and pendent hairy ears. Chest: broad. Tail: straight, carried low. Hair: sleek or wavy but never curly. Color: dead-leaf brown with or without white markings (large white markings are a defect).

**Personality**   Active, intelligent, cheerful, mild.

**Uses**   The soft-coated griffon is an excellent hunter whether in the woods or in the marshes. It is robust and has a fine sense of smell. It has also earned esteem as a companion dog.

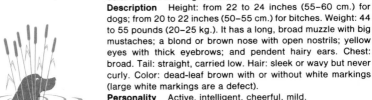

## 227 WIREHAIRED POINTING GRIFFON
## Korthals

**Origin** The wirehaired pointing griffon was developed in the period between 1870 and 1873 by the Dutch breeder E. K. Korthals with the blood of the otterhound, setter, pointer, and spaniel.

**Description** Height: dogs, 22 to 24 inches (55–60 cm.); bitches, 20 to 22 inches (50–55 cm.). Weight for males: 50 to 60 pounds (23–27 kg.). It has a large, long head with mustaches and thick eyebrows. Eyes: large, with blue or yellow irises, and a lively but mild expression. Ears: pendent. Neck: rather long, without dewlap. Tail: docked, carried horizontally. Limbs: vigorous and muscular. Hair: hard and coarse, like that of a wild boar, with a thick undercoat. Colors: steel gray with chestnut markings, or white and chestnut, or chestnut.

**Personality** Lively, intelligent, active, affectionate.

**Uses** Gifted with an exceptionally fine sense of smell and a great passion for the hunt, especially for quail and hare.

---

## 228 GRAND GRIFFON VENDÉEN

**Origin** The ancestors of this breed are the St. Hubert hound, the Italian pointer, and the Griffon Nivernais. Its native land is the region of Vendée. Used for centuries by French kings, it was known as the *chien blanc du roi*.

**Description** The Grand Griffon Vendéen is a well-proportioned animal with a distinguished gait. It is 24 to 26 inches (60–65 cm.) high and weighs 44 to 55 pounds (20–25 kg.). It has an elongated head, a thick black nose, and lips with mustaches. Eyes: dark, large, and lively. Ears: thin, in the form of an elongated oval. Back: solid and short. Flanks: retracted. Tail: carried with a saber curve. Limbs: well boned. Its coat is composed of long, bushy hair. Colors: tan, gray brown, white and orange, white and gray, white and gray brown, or tricolor. Woolly hair is a disqualification at dog shows.

**Personality** Active, passionate and courageous.

**Uses** This is a truly professional hunter: with a great sense of smell, good over all terrain. However, it becomes too excited at the beginning of the hunt. Thus, after a few hours, it tires and the hare gets away. The hunter can only let his dog rest. For this reason, the breed is especially good for hunters who plan to hunt for only half a day.

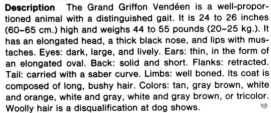

## 229 BRIQUET
### Chien d'Artois

**Origin** Derived from crossings between the hound and an ancient pointing breed, the Briquet also carries the name of Artois, the province in northern France in which it was developed.

**Description** This is a dog of medium size with good conformation and musculature. Height: 20 to 23 inches (52–58 cm.). Weight: 40 to 53 pounds (18–24 kg.). Head: broad, with a square muzzle and a black nose. Eyes: dark, with a melancholy expression. Ears: broad and flat. Neck: long and powerful. Tail: long, carried with a sickle curve. Back, shoulders, and thighs: very muscular. Hair: thick and strong. Color: tricolor (white, dark tan, and charcoal).

**Personality** Active, intelligent, gay.

**Uses** It has inherited the personalities of the pointer and the hound, from which it is descended. Thus it demonstrates in the hunt a strong sense of orientation, an excellent ability to scent, and a perfect point. Once used for hunting deer, it is today a fine hunter of hare, hardy over even impenetrable terrain.

## 230 GAMMEL DANSK HONSEHUND

**Origin** The breed is of indigenous formation.

**Description** Height: 20 to 23 inches (52–58 cm.) for dogs; 19 to 21 inches (48–54 cm.) for bitches. Weight: 40 to 53 pounds (18–24 kg.). The Gammel Dansk Honsehund has a strong constitution; broad, muscular thighs; and an elastic gait. Its head is rather short, with a liver-colored nose and well-developed nostrils; slightly pendent lips; and a scissors bite. Eyes: light or dark hazel. Ears: very long, rounded at the tips. Neck: strong and muscular, with dewlap. Tail: thick at the base, narrowing toward the tip. Hair: dense, short, tight. Color: white with light or dark liver markings.

**Personality** Thanks to excellent Danish breeders it is a tenacious, tranquil, affectionate dog.

**Uses** Used in all kinds of hunting, always with excellent results. It is, however, a dog that has not become popular outside Denmark.

## 231 WETTERHOUN

**Origin** This is an ancient breed of indigenous formation.
**Description** Height: about 22 inches (55 cm.). Weight: 33 to 44 pounds (15–20 kg.). It has a lean, strong head; a muzzle that narrows toward the nose without being pointed; tight lips; and strong dentition with a scissors bite. Eyes: medium size, oblique, chestnut. Ears: spatulate, with wavy hair. Tail: rolled in a spiral. Its whole body, except for its head, is covered with thick curls. The hair may seem oily to the touch. Colors: black, brownish-white, or bluish-white.
**Personality** Active, courageous, aggressive.
**Uses** At one time it was used for hunting otter. Today, it is adapted to any type of hunting. Because of its strong temperament, it is also used with excellent results for guarding property.

## 232 STABY-HOUN

**Origin** The origin of the Staby-Houn is not clearly identifiable. The breed is probably of native formation that was then continuously improved.
**Description** Body: elongated. Maximum height: 20 inches (50 cm.). Weight: 33 to 44 pounds (15–20 kg.). It has a lean head that narrows to a black nose; a broad, straight nasal canal; and strong dentition. Eyes: brown (yellow is a serious defect). Ears: folded in the shape of a trowel; the upper halves are covered with hair. Tail: long, hanging straight, lifted when the dog is active. Its hair is short on its head and long and sleek over the rest of its body. Colors: dappled black, dappled blue, dappled brown, dappled orange.
**Personality** Docile, tranquil, loyal, obedient, intelligent, not a biter.
**Uses** This is a simple pointer, attentive, enthusiastic, useful for the Sunday hunter. Because of its excellent temperament, it is also much esteemed as a companion dog and can adapt to living with children.

## 233 SPINONE ITALIANO

**Origin** The official theory is that this breed is a direct descendant of a wirehaired hound bred in Piedmont in 1600 and later exported to France where it became the progenitor of the French griffon. A dog similar to the spinone, however, was painted by Mantegna in the fifteenth century.

**Description** This is a solid, sturdy dog with strong bones and well-developed muscles. The height prescribed by its standard is 23 to 26 inches (58–65 cm.) for dogs and 24 to 28 inches (60–70 cm.) for bitches. Weight: dogs, 71 to 82 pounds (32–37 kg.); bitches, 62 to 71 pounds (28–32 kg.). The total length of the head should be two-fifths the height at the withers. Its large nose is meat red or brown, depending on the color of its coat. Its jaws are strong, with an arched dentition that meets perfectly. Eyes: yellow or orange. Ears: triangular, not to hang more than 2 inches (5 cm.) below the throat. Its name, spinone, comes from the word *spino* (thorn or bramble). It refers to the dog's coat, which is hard, like thorns, thick, and tight to its body. Longer hair covers the arched eyebrows, cheeks and lips, giving the dog a characteristic beard. Colors: white, white with orange markings, white uniformly speckled with orange, white with chestnut markings, or white uniformly speckled with chestnut (chestnut roan).

**Personality** Sociable, patient, affectionate, courageous, equally adaptable to stable life or apartment life.

**Uses** Popular with both commoners and nobility in the 1700's, it was used for all types of hunting until the French Revolution. After a long decline, it returned to vogue at the end of the nineteenth century, and its popularity is still high. Extremely robust and untiring, with an immediate and statuesque point, an excellent sense of smell, and oily, leathery skin that allows it to hunt in water without ever becoming ill, it is the ideal dog for modern hunting. At the end of the hunting season, the spinone is an excellent house dog, since it is tranquil, clean, polite, and good-natured. No one has ever been bitten by a spinone.

### 234 ITALIAN POINTER
### Bracco Italiano

**Origin**  This is the oldest pointing breed in Europe. It was known by Pliny, Xenophon, Dante, and Cellini. However, its popularity increased greatly in the sixteenth century when hunting with firearms began.

**Description**  The Italian pointer is an elegant, vigorous dog with a serious-looking face and a long, fast trot. According to its standard, it should be 22 to 26 inches (55–67 cm.) high and weigh 55 to 88 pounds (25–40 kg.). It has a long, angular head with pronounced arched eyebrows; a thick nose, meat red or brown; and pendent lips. Eyes: yellow or ocher, depending on the color of its coat. Ears: well developed, pendent, scrolled. Tail: docked to 6 to 10 inches (15–25 cm.) in length. Hair: short and fine. Colors: solid white; white with orange, amber, or chestnut markings; or white speckled with orange or chestnut. An exaggerated dewlap is a fault.

**Personality**  Thoughtful, docile, obedient, trainable, loyal, not excessively cheerful.

**Uses**  It is an excellent finder of game and has a secure point and an impeccable retrieval. It is adapted to all types of game and knows how to cooperate fully with the hunter. Tranquil and clean, the Italian pointer also fits in well with the family.

---

### 235 PERDIGUERO PORTUGUÊS

**Origin**  This dog was derived from the Italian pointer.

**Description**  This is a dog with elegant lines, solid and slender. Dogs are 22 inches (56 cm.) high; bitches are 20 inches (52 cm.) high. It weighs 44 to 60 pounds (20–27 kg.). It has a broad but not bony head; a long, straight muzzle; pendent lips; and a very visible stop. Eyes: chestnut, expressive. Ears: about 6 inches (15 cm.) long and 4½ inches (11 cm.) wide, soft and thin. Tail; normally docked to a third its length. Hair; short, strong, uniform, velvety on its head and ears. Colors: yellow or chestnut, either solid or with markings.

**Personality**  A passionate hunter, lively, astute, intelligent, not very tolerant of other dogs.

**Uses**  It has a model, even theatrical, point. It is adapted to hunting for all types of game. It makes up for a lack of burning speed with silence in the search for game, perseverance, a perfect accord with the hunter, tirelessness, and an excellent sense of smell.

## 236 ROUGH-COATED BOHEMIAN POINTER
### Český Fousek

**Origin** The breed is native to Bohemia and was very popular between the mid-nineteenth century and World War I. It then disappeared from shows but was redeveloped during the 1930's with the addition of German short-haired pointer blood.
**Description** This is a noble-looking dog. Height: dogs, 24 to 26 inches (60–66 cm.); bitches, 23 to 24 inches (58–62 cm.). Weight: dogs, 62 to 75 pounds (28–34 kg.); bitches, 49 to 62 pounds (22–28 kg.). It has a thin, long head; a slightly ram-shaped muzzle; a dark-brown nose; powerful jaws; and a strong scissors bite. Eyes: dark amber or chestnut, with a meek expression. Ears: pendent, broad at the base, narrowing to a point. Tail: docked by three-fifths its length. It has a dense undercoat about ½ inch (1.5 cm.) long. The outer coat is made up of coarse hair an inch or two (3–4 cm.) long and hard, straight bristles 2 to 3 inches (5–7 cm.) long, especially on its chest, back, and groin. Admissible colors are dirty white with or without brown markings or brown without markings.
**Personality** Aristocratic, impetuous, affectionate.
**Uses** This dog is appreciated for all types of hunting. It is quick in the search for game, adapted to every kind of terrain (even marshes), a tireless worker in any climate, and scrupulous in its messages to its master.

## 237 DRENTSE PATRIJSHOND

**Origin** Probably descended from crossings between the pointer and the setter.
**Description** Average height: 26 inches (65 cm.). Weight: about 44 pounds (20 kg.). It has a well-developed nose; a wedge-shaped muzzle; strong teeth; and a wide, flat head. Eyes: amber-colored, intelligent. Ears: not heavy; they are fringed and fall along the cheeks without folds. Neck: short and powerful, without any hint of dewlap. Chest: deep, with long ribs. Tail: turned upward only when the animal is in action. Its hair, while not long, seems to be because of the fringe on its chest and neck. Color: white with brown or orange markings.
**Personality** Obedient, docile, wise, extremely loyal, can be trained successfully, naturally well mannered.
**Uses** It is adapted to all kinds of hunting whether in the country or in wetlands. It is greatly appreciated for its indomitable temperament, its excellent sense of smell, and the silence with which it points. Despite its outstanding qualities, this breed has not spread beyond the confines of its native Holland.

**Origin**   According to the most credible hypothesis, the pointer was developed two centuries ago by crossings among the Italian pointer, the foxhound, the bloodhound, the greyhound, the Newfoundland, the setter, and the bulldog. This is an almost unbelievable mix, but it certainly has produced an outstanding result. The modern pointer has existed for about eighty years.

**Description**   The pointer has an athletic body with long muscles. It is powerful and agile. Height: dogs, 22 to 24 inches (55–62 cm.); bitches, 21 to 24 inches (54–60 cm.). Weight: 44 to 66 pounds (20–30 kg.). Its very beautiful head shows mettle and intelligence. Seen from the side, its nose is markedly raised above the horizontal line of its muzzle. Its upper lip is full but not slack. Its dental arch fits together perfectly. Further characteristics prescribed by its standard are the following: eyes: hazel or chestnut, depending on the color of its coat; ears: medium length, lying flat to the head; tail: thick at the root, narrowing toward the tip; front legs: straight; back legs: with muscular thighs; strong oval feet. Its coat is made up of a fine, short, stiff, shiny hair, well distributed and with no hint of feathering. Admissible colors: white and lemon, white and orange, white and liver, white and black; unicolor or tricolor dogs are also acceptable. The nose should be the same color as the dark markings of the coat.

**Personality**   Aristocratic, patient with children, affectionate, intelligent, clean; an ardent, passionate hunter. In the home it is reserved, wise, and adaptable to every situation. It will bark at suspicious noises, but it is not a watchdog.

**Uses**   Its name, pointer, describes its stance when in the presence of game. Its point is always spectacular as it assumes a statuesque, motionless pose. Untiring, obedient, and with an exceptional sense of smell, it is best adapted to hunting such feathered game as woodcock, quail, or pheasant; but it is adaptable to all kinds of hunting.

## 239 ENGLISH SETTER
### Lawerack

**Origin** The first rudimentary setter was developed in France in 1500, obtained from the Spanish pointer and the French pointer. Three centuries later it was brought to Great Britain, where its true developer was an extremely intelligent breeder, Edward Lawerack. Lawerack molded the setter into the beautiful shape and splendid character of the dog we know today.

**Description** The setter is a slender, powerful-looking dog. Height: dogs, from 22 to 26 inches (56–62 cm.); bitches, 21 to 23 inches (53–58 cm.). Weight: 60 to 70 pounds (27–32 kg.). It has an elongated head with a pronounced frontal stop. Its muzzle is half the length of the head and has well-developed but not pendent lips; tight-fitting jaws; and a large, wide black or near-black nose. Eyes: large and brilliant, with a sweet expression; hazel in color. Ears: hanging in fine folds. Tail: slightly curved, fringed. Its hair should be flat and silky, never curled or rippled. It forms long fringes on the back of the neck, legs, and buttocks. Preferred colors for the English setter are black and white, white and lemon, white and orange, white and chestnut, or tricolor (black, white, and red). Speckling may be more or less heavy and the markings may be of any size.

**Personality** Mild, sensitive, lively, friendly, and affectionate, with good reflexes. Disciplined but exuberant. It is very receptive to patient, persuasive training.

**Uses** The setter, as its name indicates, takes a half-sitting stance to indicate the presence of game to the hunter. Among its most valuable gifts is its exceptional sense of smell, which allows it to scent game even hours after it has gone by. Besides this, the English setter is fast, tireless, active, vigorous, and adapted to any terrain, even wetlands. It is resistant to bad weather and to the heat of summer. It can be used for all kinds of hunting but it works best for its own master.

**Note** The setter has a good appetite and has therefore a tendency to become heavy. It will behave itself well in the house and garden, but it has been known to jump over hedges or to dig tunnels to gain a few hours of freedom.

## 240  IRISH SETTER

**Origin**   The Irish setter is probably older than the English setter. Their common ancestor, however, is the Spanish pointer.

**Description**   Height of males should vary from a minimum of 21 inches (54 cm.) to a maximum of 24 inches (62 cm.); that of females, from 20 to 23½ inches (52–60 cm.). Weight: dogs, 40 to 55 pounds (18–22.5 kg.); bitches, 33 to 49 pounds (15–22 kg.). The length of the muzzle should be equal to half the length of the entire head. The nasal canal is straight; the nose, black or nearly black. The jaws have a close-fitting dental arch. The stop is not greatly accentuated. Eyes: chestnut or dark hazel. Ears: triangular, thin, soft to the touch. The chest is rather narrow; the thorax, deep and streamlined. The tail, carried horizontally, is fringed. Its coat is long and silky except on the head, where it is short and fine. Even the feet should be well covered with hair. Color: mahogany red, gilded and shiny without the slightest trace of black.

**Personality**   Energetic and full of feeling, expansive, independent. Not always tolerant with strangers.

**Uses**   Extremely swift, with an excellent sense of smell and hardy over any terrain and in any climate, the Irish setter is used for all types of hunting. It even works well in wetlands. It is a long-lived dog.

## 241  GORDON SETTER

**Origin**   The breed was developed at the end of the 17th century by the Scottish Duke Alexander IV of Gordon.

**Description**   It differs from the English and Irish setters in that it has a more robust structure, a more massive head, and more fully developed lips, as well as by the color of its silky, wavy coat. Height: dogs, 23 to 25 inches (59–64 cm.); bitches, 22 to 24 inches (56–61 cm.). Weight: 55 to 75 pounds (24–33 kg.). It has a slightly rounded head and a pronounced nasal stop. Nose: black, with very open nostrils. Jaws: strong, with a black palate. Eyes: brown, lively, intelligent. Ears: somewhat pointed, hanging flat. Tail: straight or carried with a saber curve. Color: deep black with mahogany markings. A small white mark on the chest is admissible.

**Personality**   Intelligent, diligent, helpful, polite, a pleasant companion.

**Uses**   Less agile and fast than its English and Irish cousins, it is nonetheless one of the most conscientious and intelligent of the standing breeds. It has an outstanding sense of smell and is a perfect retriever, working as well in marshes as it does over plains and in woods. It is a general hunting dog that excels in hunting woodcock. Among the Gordon's good qualities are excellent health and its adaptability to guarding and to family life.

## 242 BRAQUE DU BOURBONNAIS

**Origin** This is a provincial French breed, developed principally by crossings between an ancient French pointing breed and the pointer.

**Description** Characteristically, the Braque du Bourbonnais is born without a tail or with only a rudimentary tail about 2 inches (5 cm.) long. Its average height is 22 inches (55 cm.). Weight: 40 to 57 pounds (18–26 kg.). It has an elongated skull and muzzle, a brown nose, and slightly pendent lips. Eyes: dark amber, with a good-natured expression. Ears: pendent, slightly curled. Neck: short and muscular, with a slight dewlap. Chest: deep. Back: convex. Front legs: very straight. Back legs: very muscular in the thighs. Hair: strong and short. The background color is white or light chestnut with numerous dark speckles.

**Personality** Serene, sweet, affectionate.

**Uses** It is adapted to all kinds of hunting. It is most especially esteemed for its good sense of smell, its spectacular point, and the ease with which it adapts to the difficulty of the terrain. It is, however, not often found outside France.

## 243 BRAQUE DUPUY

**Origin** This breed, known since 1700, was saved from extinction during the French Revolution by a gamekeeper named Dupuy. It is probably the result of crossings between the Braque Poitou and the greyhound.

**Description** This is an elegant, noble dog. It is thin and light, with a maximum height of 27 inches (68 cm.) for dogs; 26 inches (65–66 cm.) for bitches. Weight: 49 to 62 pounds (22–28 kg.). Its head is long and narrow with a ram-shaped nasal canal and a thick, dark nose. Lips: tight and thin. Teeth: powerful. Eyes: golden or brown, dreamy. Ears: long and curled. Neck: light, with no trace of dewlap. Tail: of medium thickness, carried low, reaching the hocks. The Braque Dupuy has short, shiny hair. Color: a white background with dark chestnut markings or a chestnut saddle.

**Personality** Lively, intelligent, dignified.

**Uses** It is very fast and has an excellent sense of smell. It can be used for all kinds of hunting, especially over wide-open plains.

## 244  BRAQUE SAINT-GERMAIN

**Origin**  The Braque Saint-Germain was bred in the mid-1800's from a French pointer sire and a pointer dam with yellow markings.

**Description**  This is an elegant well-proportioned dog of moderate musculature. Height: dogs, from 20 to 24 inches (50–62 cm.); bitches, from 21 to 23 inches (54–59 cm.). Weight: 40 to 57 pounds (18–26 kg.). It has a long muzzle, pink nose with open nostrils, slightly pendent lips as red as its palate, and strong white teeth. Eyes: golden yellow, with a sweet expression. Ears: folded at an angle, pendent, thin and soft. Neck: long and muscular (a slight dewlap is allowed). Tail: carried horizontally; it must not be longer than the hocks. Its hair is short, neither fine nor hard. Color: opaque white with some orange hairs mixed in and bright-orange markings.

**Personality**  Mild, intelligent, affectionate, stubborn.

**Uses**  Used for hunting pheasant and rabbit. It is especially at home in the woods, where it exhibits a good gallop and a very attentive search for game. The breed is not very popular and has a limited circle of admirers.

## 245  STICHELHAAR

**Origin**  This breed was developed during the early 1900's at Frankfort on Main. It is the result of crossings among rough-haired "standing" dogs and German sheepdogs, but more detailed information regarding its progenitors is not known.

**Description**  The Stichelhaar is a robust but not heavy dog. Height: from 24 to 26 inches (60–66 cm.). Weight: around 44 pounds (20 kg.). It has a slightly arched skull; a long, wide, straight nasal canal with a wide-open nose; a rather square muzzle; and a stop that should not be too pronounced. Eyes: oval and chestnut (never yellow), with thick eyebrows. Ears: flat to the head, not scrolled. Tail: of medium length, sometimes docked. Its hair is about 1½ inches (4 cm.), long and bristly. Colors: brown and white mixed or with larger chestnut markings.

**Personality**  Tough and indomitable. It is aggressive with strangers and ferocious with game. It will accept only one master.

**Uses**  Adapted to any kind of hunting over varied terrain. It is a breed that has not become overly popular.

## 246 PUDELPOINTER

**Origin** The Pudelpointer was developed at the end of the nineteenth century through crossings of the French poodle and the English pointer. It inherited the best qualities of character and hunting from its parents.

**Description** Resembling a heavy pointer, the Pudelpointer is from 24 to 26 inches (60–65 cm.) high. Weight: 55 pounds (25 kg.). It has a head of medium length with thick eyebrows and beard. Eyes: round, lively, yellow or yellow-chestnut. Ears: flat, tight to the sides of the head, well covered with hair. Neck: thin and muscular, arched at the nape. Tail: carried horizontally, covered with hair. The dog's entire body is covered with hard, coarse, thick, tousled hair. Colors: chestnut or the color of dead leaves.

**Personality** Lively, full of enthusiasm, energetic, affectionate, intelligent, obedient, loyal.

**Uses** It is a dog of all work: hound and retriever in any place and any temperature. It specializes in the hunting of partridge, rabbits, foxes, and marsh birds. Its love of the water is inherited from its ancestor the poodle.

## 247 CURLY-COATED RETRIEVER

**Origin** Developed in 1800, this breed carries the blood of the Irish water spaniel, the Labrador, and the Poodle.

**Description** It is an agile, elegant, hardy dog. Height: around 26 inches (66 cm.). Weight: from 65 to 70 pounds (29 – 32 kg.). It has a well-proportioned skull, a black nose with wide nostrils, a pointed muzzle, and strong teeth. Eyes: large, black or chestnut. Ears: small, tight to the head, covered with little curls. Limbs: muscular. It is covered from head to foot with a mass of little curls. Colors: black or liver.

**Personality** Affectionate, loyal, easy to train.

**Uses** As its name indicates, it is adapted to retrieving game that has been shot and returning it to the hunter. In particular, the curly-coated retriever knows how to carry dead or wounded animals gently in its mouth. It is an excellent worker over difficult terrain and in water. Its thick coat protects it from the damp and from thorny bushes.

## 248 FLAT-COATED RETRIEVER

**Origin** The breed was developed in 1800 by crossings among the Labrador, the Irish setter, the curly-coated retriever, and probably the Newfoundland.

**Description** Height: from 22 to 23 inches (56–58 cm.). Weight: 60 to 70 pounds (27–32 kg.). Head: long and molded. Muzzle: wide and powerful. It has chestnut or dark-brown eyes with an intelligent expression, and small ears that lie flat to the head. Its chest is deep and wide; its back, short and square. It carries its plumy tail gaily. Front legs: perfectly straight; back legs, muscular. Feet: round and strong. Coat: thick, fine, and flat, in colors of black or liver.

**Personality** Obedient, trainable, intelligent, affectionate, patient with children.

**Uses** Gifted with fine intuition and an excellent sense of smell, this is a dog for connoisseurs. It is used above all for retrieving on plains and in areas thick with trees and bushes. It is a good swimmer and also works well in marshy areas.

## 249 GOLDEN RETRIEVER

**Origin** This breed was probably developed through crossings of the bloodhound with unspecified golden-coated dogs belonging to a Russian circus that visited England in the mid-nineteenth century.

**Description** Height: dogs, from 23 to 24 inches (58–61 cm.); bitches, 21½ to 22½ inches (55–57 cm.). Average weight: dogs, 65 to 75 pounds (29–34 kg.); bitches, 60 to 70 pounds (27–32 kg.). It has a large, powerful muzzle; a scissors bite; and a clear frontal stop. Eyes: dark, with a meek expression. Ears: medium-sized, falling. Neck: muscular. Chest: ample. Its tail is long but never curled. Its legs are well boned and have muscular thighs. Its hair must be shiny and wavy with feathering and a water-resistant undercoat. Colors: all shades of gold and cream. Reddish shades are a defect.

**Personality** Active, sweet, well mannered, affectionate, lovable.

**Uses** Solid and vigorous, with a fine sense of smell, the dog works well on land or in water. Beautiful and with a good temperament, the golden retriever is also highly prized as a companion and family friend. Wonderfully patient and gentle with children and even infants.

## 250 LABRADOR RETRIEVER

**Origin**   Native to Newfoundland, this breed was first brought to Great Britain in 1800 by English ships coming from Labrador.

**Description**   It is a short, solid dog, from 22 to 22½ inches (55–57 cm.) high and weighing 55 to 75 pounds (24–36 kg.). Bitches are from 21 to 22 inches (54–56 cm.) high. It has a robust, pointed head with a thick nose, scissors bite, and pronounced stop. Eyes: chestnut or hazel, with an intelligent expression. Ears: hanging against the head. Neck: powerful. Its tail is of medium length and is completely covered with special short, thick hair (otter tail). Its limbs have a good bone structure. Hair: dense and hard without waves; water-resistant undercoat. Colors: black, yellow, liver—always solid colors. There will sometimes be one yellow pup in an otherwise black litter.

**Personality**   Lively, affectionate, lovable.

**Uses**   The Labrador has an excellent sense of smell and knows how to work in perfect synchronization with its master. It is an outstanding retriever in marshes and in water. Accustomed for centuries to plunging into the water, often to help fishermen draw in their nets, it is a healthy, hardy dog of excellent bloodlines.

---

## 251 CHESAPEAKE BAY RETRIEVER

**Origin**   In the winter of 1807, an English ship with two Newfoundlands on board was wrecked off the coast of Maryland. Everyone was saved, and the two dogs were given to a family of dog lovers and were subsequently mated with local retrievers. The new breed, which was first used for hunting in the Chesapeake Bay, proved to be excellent.

**Description**   Height: dogs, from 23 to 26 inches (58–66 cm.); bitches, from 21 to 24 inches (53–61 cm.). Weight: dogs, 64 to 75 pounds (29–34 kg.); bitches, 55 to 64 pounds (25–29 kg.). It has a wide, round head with a short, pointed muzzle and thin lips. Eyes: yellowish. Ears: pendent. Neck: very muscular. Chest: strong and wide. Tail: 12 to 15 inches (30–37.5 cm.) long. It has short, thick hair with a woolly undercoat. All colors from dark chestnut to light red to hay color are admissible.

**Personality**   Lively, cheerful, an enthusiastic hunter, trainable, affectionate, courageous.

**Uses**   This is a dog that loves the water and can be used for hunting in any weather. It specializes in retrieving from water. It will come out of a river or marsh with only a few drops of water remaining on its coat, and these are quickly eliminated with a shake.

**Origin**   The first information we have of the existence of the spaniel comes from a description by Gaston Phebus in 1300. However, it was five hundred years later that the various English spaniels were divided into seven breeds: the Clumber, the Sussex, the Welsh springer, the English springer, the field, the Irish water spaniel, and the cocker. All these spaniels derive from a spaniel-type dog imported into England centuries ago.

**Description**   The English cocker spaniel is a cheerful, hardy, sporty dog with an elegant appearance. Height: dogs, 15½ to 16 inches (39.5–41 cm.); bitches, 15 to 15½ inches (38–39.5 cm.). Weight: from 28 to 32 pounds (12.7–14.5 kg.). It has a square muzzle with a pronounced stop, a generous nose, sturdy jaws, and a scissors bite. Eyes: brown, cheerful, brilliant. Ears: set at eye level, covered with silky hair. Neck: muscular between sloping shoulders. Tail: set low, carried gaily (may be moderately docked). Legs: well boned, feathered. Feet: solid and round. Its hair is silky but not wavy and is feathered. Many colors are admissible, but on solid-colored dogs white is acceptable only on the chest.

**Personality**   This is a good-natured, sweet, affectionate dog—a great friend of children. It is sociable with strangers, is a moderate barker, and obeys respectfully the orders it is given.

**Uses**   In the past, it was a marvelous finder of game. Its name comes from that of the woodcock. It was also prized for its tenacity and tirelessness, the skill with which it maneuvered over difficult terrain, and its perfect retrieval with a delicate grip. Potentially, the cocker is still a hunting dog today, but in reality, it has passed, bag, baggage, and wagging tail, into the ranks of the companion dog.

This is an emotional and sensitive dog and must be trained gently without recourse to humiliation or blows.

**Note**   Because it has a tendency to gain weight, the cocker should be fed judiciously. Its silky coat needs frequent brushing. During the summer, the ears should be checked often. Hanging close to the ground as they do, they can become host to ticks or burrs, often the cause of deafness.

## 253  COCKER SPANIEL

**Origin**  The cocker spaniel is descended through careful breeding from the English cocker spaniel.

**Description**  It is aesthetically very pleasing, especially because of the beautiful coat that covers it completely. Maximum height: dogs, 15 inches (38 cm.); bitches, 14 inches (36.8 cm.). Weight: 24 to 28 pounds (10.9–12.7 kg.). Dogs larger than these limits are disqualified from shows. The cocker has a rounded head; a wide, deep muzzle; an upper lip that covers the lower jaw; strong teeth with a scissors bite; and well-developed nostrils. Eyes: intelligent and mild, in various colors depending on the color of its coat. Ears: very long, wavy, pendent. Neck: muscular, without dewlap. Tail: carried on a line with its back, constantly in motion. It has medium-length hair with a silky texture. Colors: solid black, black with lighter shadings, chamois, cream, roan, brindle.

**Personality**  Cheerful, sweet, an inseparable friend of children, and respectful of its master's authority.

**Uses**  Although it still possesses the gifts of a hunting dog, the cocker's daily role is that of companion dog. It is very popular, especially in America.

## 254  CLUMBER SPANIEL

**Origin**  The Clumber was developed in France by one of the dukes of Noailles. Threatened by the Revolution, he transferred his dogs to England, close to his friend the Duke of Newcastle. Here the Clumber was perfected and was successfully presented at its first shows in the nineteenth century.

**Description**  The Clumber is a massive dog, from 16 to 18 inches (41–46 cm.) high, weighing 55 to 70 pounds (25–31.5 kg.). It has a large, square head, wide across the top, with a generous flesh-colored nose; a deep stop; and well-developed lips. Eyes: dark amber, slightly deep-set. Ears: large, in the shape of vine leaves, hanging forward, well covered with hair. Neck: thick and heavy, feathered at the throat. Tail: short, fringed, carried level with the back. Shoulders: robust and muscular. Limbs: short, straight, strong boned. Its hair is thick, straight, and silky in pure white with lemon markings.

**Personality**  Playful, silent, intelligent, pleasant.

**Uses**  In the past, Clumbers were used in small packs, but today they gladly hunt alone, preferring to hunt for pheasant and partridge. They are also well adapted to family life, where they behave themselves in a well-mannered fashion. They are not very widespread, but they do enjoy great esteem within the limited circle of their admirers.

## 255  ENGLISH SPRINGER SPANIEL

**Origin**  This is the founder of all the English hunting spaniels. During the Renaissance, it was considered the ideal companion for the European hunter. Its popularity in America began in 1700.

**Description**  The English springer is a symmetrical, strong, compact dog with an average height of 20 inches (50 cm.) and a weight of between 49 and 53 pounds (22–24 kg.). It has a wide, somewhat rounded head; full lips; well-developed nostrils; and strong jaws. Eyes: dark hazel or brown, depending on the color of its coat. Ears: tight to the head. Neck: strong and muscular. Its coat is of medium length and is fringed at the throat, chest, and thorax. Preferred colors are white and liver or white and black, with or without shadings.

**Personality**  Cheerful, courageous, meticulous. In the family it is affectionate, good-natured, and sincere.

**Uses**  The springer is attentive and precise in the search for game and in retrieving it. It is used over all types of terrain, especially that which is thick with brambles. A hardy, relatively long-legged dog, it is more powerful and faster than the other spaniels. Its behavior as a companion dog is much like that of the cocker spaniel.

**Note**  It has a tendency toward overweight.

## 256 WELSH SPRINGER SPANIEL

**Origin** The Welsh springer spaniel was bred from spaniel stock, exclusively for hunting.

**Description** It is a hardy, compact dog weighing from 35 to 45 pounds (15.75–20.25 kg.). Height: 15 to 17 inches (38–43 cm.). It has a rather square muzzle of medium length with powerful jaws and a conspicuous stop. Eyes: dark hazel. Ears: pendent, covered with fringe, like those of a setter. Neck: long and muscular, without dewlap. Tail: low and slightly feathered. Hair: straight, thick, silky. Color: white and bright red.

**Personality** Cheerful, sensitive, independent.

**Uses** Highly adapted to hunting and retrieving over the most difficult terrain and resistant to any kind of bad weather. It is said that for the Welsh springer "it is always sunny." It is not afraid of icy-cold water and can work for many hours without signs of tiring.

**Note** It has a tendency to wander too far from the hunt field, and it is therefore necessary to give it constant training beginning at about six months of age.

## 257 IRISH WATER SPANIEL

**Origin** This breed was developed in the early 1800's, probably through crossings between the poodle and the Irish setter.

**Description** It is a compact, well-built, tireless dog. Height: from 21 to 23 inches (53–58 cm.) for dogs; 20 to 22 inches (51–56 cm.) for bitches. Weight: 55 to 60 pounds (25–27.22 kg.) for the male. It has a rather large head with an arched skull; a long, square muzzle; and a large, well-developed nose. Eyes: small, brown, brilliant. Ears: hanging along its cheeks, covered with ringlets. Neck: powerful. Tail: thick at the base, narrowing toward the point. Front legs: straight and well boned. Back legs: long and nervous. Its coat is thick, with little curls and crinkles, but the muzzle is smooth. Its hair is oily and thus waterproof. Color: deep liver with a tendency toward violet.

**Personality** Cheerful, obedient, intelligent.

**Uses** It loves the water and is therefore used for hunting wild ducks in marshes and lakes.

**Note** Although descended from two breeds with outstanding characters (the poodle and the Irish setter), it has nonetheless had little success as a companion dog, mainly due to the difficulty of keeping its curly coat neat.

## 258 SUSSEX SPANIEL

**Origin**   The breed was developed in the 1800's in Sussex, England. Official recognition came in 1885.

**Description**   The Sussex is a strong, massive dog measuring from 15 to 16 inches (38–40 cm.) high and weighing 40 to 44 pounds (18–20 kg.). Its standard demands a well-balanced head, a liver-colored nose, scissors bite, and a well-marked frontal stop. Eyes: hazel, with a sweet expression. Ears: rather large, tight to the head, covered with soft, wavy hair. Neck: slightly arched. Chest: deep and well developed. Tail: docked to 5 to 7 inches (12.5–17.5 cm.). Coat: thick and flat without curling. Color: golden liver.

**Personality**   Tranquil and intelligent when at rest, it reaches the enthusiasm of a warrior in its work.

**Uses**   On the hunt field it barks continuously, moving with a characteristic swinging gait. It is adapted to hunting and retrieving small game, especially in wooded areas. It is also a good companion dog.

**Note**   The golden-red color of its coat, especially at sunset, blends with the color of the trees and the game. Thus it can inadvertently be shot by the hunter. This may be why the breed is not widespread.

---

## 259 FIELD SPANIEL

**Origin**   The same as those of the cocker.

**Description**   The field spaniel looks much like the cocker, but it has a longer body and shorter legs. Average height: 18 inches (46 cm.). Weight: from 35 to 50 pounds (16–22.5 kg.). Its muzzle is regular, neither too wide nor too pointed. Its nose has very open nostrils. Below the eyes, it is lean and thin (this is an important characteristic). Eyes: dark hazel or chestnut, with a thoughtful expression. Ears: rather long and wide, covered with fringe, like those of a setter. Neck: strong and muscular. Tail: fringed, carried low. Hair: flat or slightly wavy, but never curly, thick and silky in texture, abundantly fringed at the chest, abdomen, and limbs. Colors: it is always one-colored in black, liver, golden liver, or mahogany red, possibly with shaded areas in a lighter hue.

**Personality**   This is the spaniel with the best personality. It is sweet, affectionate, tranquil, and intelligent.

**Uses**   Hardy, fast, agile, active, and especially well adapted to hunting over open country, as its name indicates. Because of its exceptionally mild temperament, the field spaniel enjoys great esteem as a companion dog, especially in Great Britain and the United States.

## 260 AMERICAN WATER SPANIEL

**Origin**  Precise information regarding the origin of this breed does not exist. The Irish water spaniel and the curly-coated retriever probably contributed to its development. It was recognized by the American Kennel Club in 1940.

**Description**  The American water spaniel is an active, muscular, hardy dog about 15 to 18 inches (38–45 cm.) high, weighing 29 to 44 pounds (13–20 kg.). It has a wide, full head with a pronounced stop and a square medium-length muzzle. Its teeth are straight and well shaped; its nostrils, very well developed. Eyes: hazel or chestnut, with an intelligent expression (yellow eyes are a serious defect). Ears: wide and long. Body: well developed, with solid limbs. Tail: of medium length, slightly curved. Its coat is formed of thick, tight curls, but the hair is not coarse; it provides a good defense against water and brambles. Colors: liver or dark chocolate (a little white on the chest and toes is permitted).

**Personality**  Enthusiastic about its work, tenacious, obedient, affectionate, extremely responsive to training.

**Uses**  It is a wonderful hunter in difficult waters, in the woods, and over uneven terrain. It is used above all for hunting duck, quail, pheasant, grouse, and rabbit. It is also greatly appreciated as a guard dog and companion.

## 261 BOYKIN SPANIEL

**Origin**  Probably obtained by crossing the cocker spaniel and the American water spaniel.

**Description**  Very similar to the American water spaniel, it is 15 to 17 inches (38–43 cm.) high and weighs 30 to 38 pounds (14–17 kg.). Bitches are slightly smaller. It has an elongated muzzle, a chestnut nose, yellow eyes, and long ears covered with little curls. Its tail is curved and feathered. Its coat, wavy or curly and waterproof, is dark mahogany or liver.

**Personality**  Cheerful, docile, sensitive.

**Uses**  It usually works in the water, retrieving pigeons and ducks, but due to its infallible sense of smell it is also highly thought of for hunting game in the woods. It is a good companion dog, and should the need arise, it becomes a watchdog.

# COMPANION DOGS

**POODLE**
**Barbone**

**Origin** Its origin is controversial: was it developed in France, Germany, Denmark, or the ancient Piedmont? In any event, it is certain that the poodle is descended from a now nearly extinct French water dog, the barbet.

**Description** There are three types of poodle: the standard, the miniature, and the toy. The standard must measure 15 inches (38 cm.) or more at the highest point of the shoulder; the miniature must measure at least 10 inches (25.4 cm.) but less than 15 inches (38 cm.); and the toy must be under 10 inches (25.4) high. Average weight for the three types is 49 pounds (22 kg.), 26 pounds (12 kg.), and 15 pounds (7 kg.) respectively.

The poodle has a distinguished rectilinear head proportionate to its body. The nose of black, white, blue, gray, silver, and cream-colored dogs must be black, while that of brown and café-au-lait dogs is liver-colored. The poodle has a well-modeled skull, flat cheeks, and a scissors bite. Eyes: black or brown, with a lively expression. Ears: falling along its cheeks, covered with wavy hair. Neck: solid, slightly arched. Head: carried proudly. Tail: set high, docked to a half or a third its length. Hair: curly or corded. It is always unicolored in the hues mentioned above. As a rule, poodles are clipped periodically in either puppy clip, English saddle clip, or continental clip. Other clips are not admissible in shows.

**Personality** Fundamentally good-natured, most intelligent, bold, cheerful, sensitive, trainable.

**Uses** In France, this breed is known as *caniche,* a name derived from *canard* (duck), because in the past the poodle was an outstanding retriever of game from marshes, an ability it inherited from its ancestor the barbet.

Due to its attractive personality, its beauty, and its intelligence, however, the poodle quickly passed into the ranks of the companion dog. It has excellent hearing and a noteworthy sense of orientation. More than most other dogs, it can understand the meaning of the spoken word. It is patient during bathing and clipping and loves to play with children. It will not accept, however, heavy-handed training.

## 263  GREAT SPITZ

**Origin**  Descended from *Canis familiaris palustris*, the great spitz can be considered the ancestor of all breeds of dogs. Fossil remains of the spitz dating from tens of thousands of years ago have been found in Asia, Africa, and northern Europe.

**Description**  Its height is never less than 16 inches (40 cm.); weight about 40 pounds (18 kg.). It has a medium-sized head with a wedge-shaped skull and a round, slightly flattened black or brown nose, depending on the color of its coat. Eyes: dark, oblique. Ears: small, pointed, triangular, erect. Its tail folds forward over its back. Its hair is abundant over its body and short on the muzzle, ears, and paws. The color of its coat determines to which of the following four varieties it belongs: wolf spitz (silver-gray with black shadings), black spitz (skin, undercoat, and outer coat all black), white spitz (true white with no yellowish nuances), brown spitz (deep brown, unicolor). The wolf spitz may be somewhat larger than the other varieties.

**Personality**  Lively, loyal, intelligent, a barker, suspicious of strangers.

**Uses**  This is a companion dog that becomes so attached to its home that it will defend it like a true guard dog. It reaches physical and psychological maturity at the age of three years.

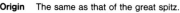

## 264   SMALL SPITZ

**Origin**   The same as that of the great spitz.

**Description**   The small spitz is a small-sized copy of the great spitz. It must not be more than 11 inches (28 cm.) high or weigh more than 8¼ pounds (3.75 kg.). It has a wedge-shaped head; dark, slightly almond-shaped eyes; pointed, upright ears; and carries its tail folded over its back. It is wrapped in a thick coat, which makes it look like a toy. Its standard divides the breed into five varieties depending on the color of the coat: small black spitz, white, brown, wolf gray, or orange.

**Personality**   Extremely affectionate with its family, suspicious of strangers, intelligent, proud.

**Uses**   It has all the qualities of beauty and temperament to be an outstanding companion dog. It loves its home and will defend it against intruders.

**Note**   It is extremely resistant to illness, but great care must be taken with its feeding to prevent intestinal disturbances.

## 265   VOLPINO ITALIANO

**Origin**   It has the same origin as all the spitzes. In the eighteenth century it was known as the Volpino di Firenze (Florentine spitz) and in the nineteenth century as the Cane del Quirinale.

**Description**   There are only slight differences between the Volpino Italiano and the Pomeranian. The Italiano has a slightly more robust head with larger eyes, and its coat is either white or red, while the Pomeranian may also be gray, black, or orange. According to its standard, the Volpino Italiano dog should be 11 to 12 inches (27–30 cm.) high, while the bitch should be from 10 to 11 inches (25–28 cm.) high. Its weight should not exceed 9 pounds (4 kg.). It has a pyramid-shaped head, a damp black nose, regular white teeth, and an accentuated stop. Eyes: ocher, with a lively, intelligent expression. Ears: triangular, carried erect. Tail: about 5½ inches (14 cm.) long, covered with long hair and carried rolled up on its back.

**Personality**   Lively, exuberant, noisy, affectionate with its family, suspicious of strangers.

**Uses**   It is a sympathetic companion dog, resistant to illness and long-lived.

**Note**   Its thick, long, straight coat needs very frequent brushing. When white dogs have a tendency to become yellowish, it is advisable to treat the hair with a cake of talcum followed by a light brushing.

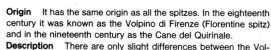

## 266  JAPANESE SPITZ

**Origin**  The Japanese spitz is a direct descendant of the Nordic spitz, which was imported into Japan centuries ago. There it found outstanding breeders and popularity.

**Description**  Height: dogs, 12 to 16 inches (30–40 cm.); bitches, 10 to 14 inches (25–35 cm.). Weight: around 22 pounds (10 kg.). It has a rather large head, a slight stop, a pointed muzzle, and a small black nose. Its teeth are solid and without prognathism. Eyes: oblique and dark. Ears: small, pointed, upright. Tail: covered with long hair, carried rolled on the dog's back. It has a thick pure-white coat.

**Personality**  Cheerful, bold, proud, most intelligent, affectionate toward its master, but like all spitzes, suspicious of strangers.

**Uses**  It is a well-loved companion dog that, should the need arise, will protect its house, barking and growling at intruders. Its coat needs a good deal of care—frequent brushing and occasional baths.

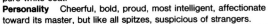

## 267  HARLEKINPINSCHER

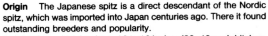

**Origin**  This is an ancient breed derived from the German smooth-haired pinscher.

**Description**  The Harlekinpinscher is a sturdy-looking, lean, muscular dog around 12 to 14 inches (30–35 cm.) high, and weighing 22 to 26 pounds (10–12 kg.). It has a moderately elongated head, a well-fused skull and muzzle, and a black nose. Prognathism and enognathism are defects. Eyes: dark, in harmony with the color of the coat. Ears: small, carried upright with the points sometimes folded down. Tail: docked, carried slightly upright. Hair: short, flat, tight to the skin. The background color is white or gray with black or dark markings that justify the appellation "harlequin."

**Personality**  Lively, affectionate, amusing.

**Uses**  Because of its unusual coat, the dignity of its carriage, and its outstanding temperament, it is an ideal companion dog. It thrives on indoor life.

**Origin** There is total disagreement concerning the origin of this breed. It is certainly very ancient, since traces of it are found on Egyptian bas-reliefs and Hellenic friezes. In 1700, a dog known as the Bengal pointer, similar to the Dalmatian, existed in England, calling into question the Dalmatian's Yugoslavian origins.

**Description** The Dalmatian is a muscular, symmetrical dog, 22 to 24 inches (55–60 cm.) high. Bitches measure from 20 to 22 inches (50–55 cm.) Weight: about 55 pounds (25 kg.). Its head is rather long, with a vigorous muzzle and a moderate stop. Its nose is black or brown depending on the color of its coat. Eyes: black or brown, round and brilliant, with an intelligent expression. Ears: soft to the touch, carried against the head. Tail: strong at the base, narrowing toward the point, carried with a slight upward curve. The Dalmatian's hair should be short, hard, dense, and shiny. The base color is always pure white with black or liver spots. The more defined and well distributed the markings, the more valuable the dog. Puppies are born completely white.

**Personality** Serene, loyal, independent but domesticated, extremely sensitive. It needs human company without which it is likely to become melancholy. It is fond of playing with children. It has an excellent memory and can remember for years any bad treatment it has received.

**Uses** In the Middle Ages, it was used as a hound. In the nineteenth century, it became a "carriage dog" and its popularity shot up. It followed its master with exceptional reliability and hardiness whether its master was on foot, on horseback, or in a carriage. Later, it found wide acceptance as a companion dog that could also act as a guard dog. It is clean and neat, avoids puddles, and loves soap and water.

## 269  KROMFOHRLÄNDER

**Origin**  The Kromfohrländer was developed in the nineteenth century, but the breeds that contributed to its formation are not recorded.

**Description**  Height: from 15 to 18 inches (39–46 cm.). Weight: 26 pounds (12 kg.). Head: elongated and wedge-shaped. It has a black open nose, either a scissors or a pincers bite, dark oval eyes, and triangular ears that lie flat to its head. Neck: slightly arched. Front legs: straight. Tail: carried with a slight curve. There are three varieties of Kromfohrländer: a coarse-haired variety; one with short coarse hair; and one with long coarse hair. All are white with light-chestnut markings. Black is not admissible.

**Personality**  Lively, loyal, obedient.

**Uses**  Being purely a companion dog, it is well adapted to apartment life. Its abilities as a watchdog and bodyguard are also much appreciated. It has an excellent sense of hearing and will react to the smallest noise.

---

## 270  PINSCHER

**Origin**  Dating from ancient times, the breed was recognized officially at the end of the nineteenth century.

**Description**  The pinscher is a medium-sized elegant-looking dog. Height: from 18 to 19 inches (45–48 cm.). Weight: 13 to 18 pounds (6–8 kg.). It has a long, narrow head with a straight muzzle, a vigorous bite, dark oval eyes, and upright ears (docked). Its neck is long, thin, and arched. Its body is square. Its tail is docked to the first three vertebrae and carried vertically. Hair: short, hard, shiny, tight to the body. Colors: black with dark shadings, pure black, chestnut, stag red, blue-gray with shadings, or pepper-and-salt.

**Personality**  Although the word ''pinscher'' in German means biter, this is a docile, devoted, affectionate dog, which is also clean and intelligent. It is, however, a menacing barker; and it knows how to use its sharp teeth against enemies.

**Uses**  It is a companion dog that is used as a guard for houses, gardens, and automobiles.

## 271 MINIATURE SCHNAUZER
### Zwergschnauzer

**Origin** Like its larger brothers the giant and standard schnauzers, the miniature schnauzer is descended from ancient terriers, but it also carries in its veins the blood of the affenpinscher.

**Description** Both males and females are from 12 to 14 inches (30–35 cm.) high and weigh 13 to 15 pounds (6–7.3 kg.). Dwarfism is considered a defect. It has a long head, a strong muzzle, a well-developed nose, and a scissors bite. Eyes: dark and oval. Ears: docked to a point. Neck: long, arched, and elegant. Tail: docked to the third vertebra. Its hair is hard and coarse and sticks out in spiny eyebrows and a bristly beard. It is black or pepper-and-salt.

**Personality** Most affectionate, energetic, obedient, trainable, pleasant, a barker.

**Uses** Besides looking like a miniature version of the other two schnauzers, it possesses the same temperament. It is a vigilant guard and a mouser. It is, however, considered exclusively an apartment dog.

---

## 272 SCHIPPERKEE

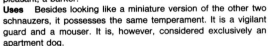

**Origin** The schipperkee was bred in Flanders by a canal boat captain named Renssens. It first appeared at a dog show in 1880. From that point on it was exported throughout the world.

**Description** There are three varieties of schipperkee: large, weighing from 11 to 20 pounds (5–9 kg.); medium, weighing from 7 to 11 pounds (3–5 kg.); and miniature, weighing less than 7 pounds (3 kg.). The heights are 13 inches (33 cm.), 11 inches (28 cm.), and 10 inches (25 cm.) respectively. It has a foxlike head with a pointed muzzle; a small nose; and a wide, slightly rounded forehead. Eyes: oval, dark brown. Ears: triangular, erect, very mobile. Body: short and compact. It has no tail. Its hair is abundant, hard, short on its head and the fronts of its legs, but forming an ample mane. The only acceptable color according to the Belgian standard is totally black.

**Personality** Exuberant, trainable, intelligent, curious, suspicious with strangers.

**Uses** At one time it was a boatsman's and shoemaker's dog and was trained to swim, to guard, and to hunt. Today it is a companion dog, apparently indifferent but really bound to its master. Among its best qualities are the ability to defend its home against intruders with tenacity and of being an excellent friend to children.

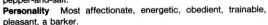

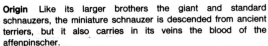

## 273 BELGIAN GRIFFON
### Griffon Belge

**Origin**   The Belgian griffon was developed in the 1800's through crossings of the Yorkshire, the affenpinscher, the miniature schnauzer, and the pug.

**Description**   According to the standard, the small variety must not weigh more than 6½ pounds (3 kg.); height 7 to 8 inches (25.5–40.6 cm.); the large variety, not more than 11 pounds (11 kg.). Thus the Brussels griffon is a tiny dog with a round convex forehead, a thick black nose, and a short muzzle with bushy beard and mustache. Its bite is undershot; its eyes are large, round, and black; and its ears are upright, docked to a point. It has a strong neck and a deep chest. Its tail, docked to two-thirds its length, is carried high. Hair: hard, abundant, disordered. Color: black, black with lighter areas, or red and black mixed. It needs stripping twice a year.

**Personality**   Despite its sullen expression, it is a rather sweet, affectionate, obedient, trainable, lively dog.

**Uses**   Originally a farm and stable dog and a great mouser, it still loves the freedom of the woods and fields; but it is considered a pleasant companion dog. It is not very fond of children.

**Note**   Due to the round skull of the puppies, the dam may have difficulty delivering; Cesarean section is often necessary.

---

## 274 GRIFFON BRABANÇON
### Piccolo Brabantino

**Origin**   The same as that of the Belgian griffon.

**Description**   The Griffon Brabançon is similar to the Belgian griffon. It differs only in its hair, which is short, and the color of its coat, which is red (sometimes with a dark mask) or black with areas of lighter shading.

**Personality**   Affectionate, lively, curious, intelligent, moody.

**Uses**   It is a rather rare but pleasant companion dog.

## 275  ENGLISH BULLDOG

**Origin**  The breed is descended from the ancient Asiatic mastiff, but its development took place completely in Great Britain. The name bulldog, which is medieval in origin, refers not only to the robust look of a little bull, which this aggressive dog has, but also to the power with which this dog attacked bulls in arena combat before the practice was prohibited by law in the nineteenth century.

**Description**  The bulldog is small in stature, but wide and compact, with a thick, massive head. Optimum weight: dogs, 53 to 55 pounds (24–25 kg.); bitches, 49 to 51 pounds (22–23 kg.). Its height is not indicated in the standard, but ranges from 12 to 14 inches (30–35 cm.). Its head should be broad (the broader the better) with cheeks that extend to the sides of the eyes. The skin on its skull and forehead should fall in dense folds. Its muzzle is short and pug; its nose, broad and black, with large nostrils. Its upper lip is pendent and its lower jaw should be very undershot. Eyes: round, far apart, very dark. Ears: small and thin, folded back, in the form of a rose. Neck: arched, with dewlap. Tail: short, carried low. Hair: short and soft, either tan and white or variegated white. Black is not acceptable.

**Personality**  Until the nineteenth century, when the bulldog was still used in combats, it was aggressive, ferocious, and bloodthirsty, so much so in fact that the Romans promulgated a decree that forbade taking a bulldog through the streets, even if held on a chain. Breeding over the last hundred years, while maintaining the bulldog's menacing look, has made of it a good-natured, reserved, dignified, loyal, domesticated dog, clean and aristocratic, "beautiful in its ugliness."

**Uses**  At the end of its career as a gladiator, it was used as a guard dog, a police dog, and an auxiliary in the army. In the United States, one bulldog was decorated with five ribbons and a Bronze Star for its war work and another was promoted to corporal. Today, the bulldog is esteemed as a companion dog.

**Note**  Because of their big heads, the puppies are difficult to deliver. It is often necessary to have recourse to Cesarean section. Furthermore, many bitches are infertile. These factors tend to keep the price of bulldogs high.

## 276 FRENCH BULLDOG

**Origin**   This is a native French breed, possibly with some English bulldog blood. It reached its greatest popularity in the second half of the nineteenth century.

**Description**   The French bulldog is a small dog, 12 inches (30 cm.) high and weighing 13 to 26 pounds (6–12 kg.). It has a strong, square head with a short pug nose and loose black lips that cover its teeth; a broad, powerful muzzle; and a very pronounced stop. Eyes: dark, round, slightly protruding. Ears: broad at the base and rounded at the tips, carried erect. Neck: without dewlap. Barrel chest, with rounded ribs. Tail: docked, carried low. Hair: smooth, shiny, soft. Colors: tiger (a mixture of black and reddish hairs) or quail (a white background with tiger markings).

**Personality**   Courageous, active, steady, affectionate, sensitive, intelligent.

**Uses**   The French bulldog is a companion dog that also makes itself useful as a guardian of the apartment. It is also a ruthless hunter of mice.

**Note**   It should not be allowed to get fat, because a swollen abdomen can impair its breathing.

---

## 277 BOLOGNESE

**Origin**   This breed was developed centuries ago in Bologna. Known since the thirteenth century, it became famous during the Renaissance at the courts of the Medici, the Gonzaga, and Este.

**Description**   Height: dogs, 11 to 12 inches (27–30 cm.); bitches, 10 to 11 inches (25–28 cm.). Weight: from 5½ to 9 pounds (2.5–4 kg.). It has a squarish trunk and a medium-length head with a straight muzzle and a cold, damp black nose. It has a close-fitting dental arch. Eyes: large, with an intelligent expression. Ears: long and pendent, but held slightly away from the head. Tail: curved over the back. Its hair is gathered in tufts that cover it from head to toe. Color: pure white.

**Personality**   Very serious, but most affectionate and intelligent, attached to the family.

**Uses**   Although it occasionally likes to wander beyond the confines of its garden, the Bolognese, since its creation, has always been a delightful companion dog. Today, however, it is rather rare.

## 278 BICHON AVANESE

**Origin** There are two versions concerning the origin of this breed: (1) crosses between Bolognese and toy poodles effected in Argentina; (2) crosses between the Maltese and small dogs from the Antilles.

**Description** According to its standard, it should never weigh more than 13 pounds (6 kg.). Height approximately 10 inches (25 cm.). It has a flat, broad skull; very flat cheeks; a pointed muzzle; and a black nose. Eyes: large, preferably black. Ears: pointed and hanging. Body: longer than it is high. Tail: carried up. Limbs: straight and lean. Hair: long and flat; white, beige, gray, or speckled white.

**Personality** Lively, affectionate, dignified, clean.

**Uses** This is a pleasant but rare companion dog.

## 279 HAIRLESS DOG
### Cane Nudo

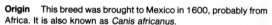

**Origin** This breed was brought to Mexico in 1600, probably from Africa. It is also known as *Canis africanus*.

**Description** The hairless dog is an elegant animal with a fine but sturdy bone structure and overall lines similar to those of the small Italian greyhound. It is from 10 to 16 inches (25–40 cm.) high and weighs 9 to 18 pounds (4–8 kg.). It has a sculpted head; regular dentition; small, bright eyes; and upright rose-shaped ears. Its skin is shiny and smooth. Its only hair is on the top of its head. The color of its skin is elephant gray, gray with reddish markings, or flesh-colored with gray or black markings. The body of the hairless dog is very warm to the touch—average temperature 102° F.

**Personality** Lively, sensitive, affectionate, devoted.

**Uses** This is solely a companion dog whose popularity is limited to Mexico.

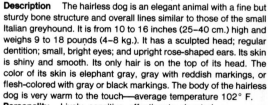

**Origin** The first images of a chow chow appear in a two-thousand-year-old Chinese bas-relief. Its popularity in Europe, however, dates back only to the second half of the nineteenth century when it was brought to England by English merchant ships along with various other goods from the East, and one was given to the Prince of Wales, the future Edward VII.

**Description** It has a leonine appearance and a proud bearing. Its head is broad and its skull flat. The muzzle is broad near the eyes and narrows toward a black nose without becoming pointed. Eyes: small, oblique, dark. Ears: triangular, erect, turned forward. The tongue, palate, gums, and lips must be purple. It has an abundance of long, thick hair and a woolly undercoat. Its ample collar is what gives it its lionlike looks. Colors: tan, red, cream, blue, black, silver-gray, or, rarely, white. It is always unicolored. Markings are not admissible. The height of the chow chow should be between 19 and 20 inches (48.4–50.8 cm.) and must not be under 18 inches (45.7 cm.). Average weight is 55 to 60 pounds (24–27 kg.). Its chest is broad and deep; its kidney area, short and strong. Tail: thickly covered with hair, carried over its back.

**Personality** In China the chow chow was used for guarding junks and for pulling carts. Its flesh was eaten and there was a market for its fur. This sad history plus the lack of a single master has dampened the personality of this extremely beautiful dog. It thus appears introverted, detached, and indifferent. It is, however, a loyal, sincere dog that is very affectionate toward its master. It does not accept muzzles and leashes gladly, but is otherwise polite, clean, and patient.

**Uses** The chow chow is a companion dog adapted to tranquil people. It needs frequent brushing, especially in summer. In the past it was used as a guard dog, a wolf hunter, and a sled dog.

## 281    PUG

**Origin**    Brought from China to Holland four hundred years ago, the pug was later perfected in England.

**Description**    It has a compact body and well-developed musculature. Height: 10 to 11 inches (25.4–28 cm.). Weight: 14 to 18 pounds (6.3–8 kg.). It has a round, massive head; a short, square muzzle; and deep wrinkles on its forehead. Eyes: prominent, with a sweet expression. Ears: pendent, soft as velvet. Tail: twisted over its haunches. Limbs: straight and strong. Hair: soft and shiny. Colors: apricot-yellow, silver, black, with as dark a mask as possible.

**Personality**    The pug is an affectionate, loving dog, especially with its master. It is miserable in hot weather and should not be left in closed cars or stuffy apartments when the weather is hot.

**Uses**    It has always been a companion dog, especially popular with women.

## 282    SHAR-PEI
## Chinese Fighting Dog

**Origin**    The ancestry of the Shar-Pei is uncertain. It may be a descendant of the chow chow; however, the only clear link between these two breeds is their purple tongue.

**Description**    It is a compact, agile, strong dog covered with a soft skin that falls in large folds. Height: dogs, 18 to 20 inches (46–51 cm.); bitches, 16 to 18 inches (41–46 cm.). Weight: dogs, 45 to 55 pounds (20–25 kg.); bitches, 35 to 45 pounds (16–20 kg.). It has small ears that lie flat to the head, a ringed tail carried high, and moderately soft hair. Colors: fawn, cream, red, or black.

**Personality**    It gives the impression of being slightly sad, but it is happy to live in the home. It is tranquil, good, loyal, and particularly friendly to children.

**Uses**    In the past, it was a ferocious combat dog. Dog fighting was very popular in China and for years the Shar-Pei was an applauded protagonist in these battles. Later, after careful and loving breeding, it was brought to the United States where it has become almost exclusively a companion dog.

## 283    TIBETAN SPANIEL

**Origin**    The breed originated in Tibet. It is supposed that in its veins runs the blood of the Pekingese, the pug, and the Japanese spaniel (Chin).

**Description**    It is a medium-sized dog, weighing 9 to 15 pounds (4.1–6.8 kg.) and 10 inches high (51 cm.). It has a strong muzzle, a dome-shaped skull, and chestnut eyes. Its ears are pendent and feathered at the lower edge. Its tail has a plumed pennant and curves over its back. Hair: abundant and flat, in the following colors: fawn, golden, black, black with areas of bright tan, cream, white, or chestnut.

**Personality**    Lively, merry, kind, alert to any noise, lovable and affectionate in the family, cool to strangers.

**Uses**    A fine family companion, very independent, good watchdog.

## 284    CAVALIER KING CHARLES SPANIEL

**Origin**    Same rootstock as the English toy spaniel, greater resemblance to spaniels in paintings of the fifteenth and sixteenth centuries than to spaniels of the present day.

**Description**    Height: from 12 to 13 inches (30.5–34 cm.). Weight: from 13 to 19 pounds (4.45–8.81 kg.). It has a conical muzzle and a flat skull. Its nostrils are quite open; its stop, shallow. Eyes: dark, large, not prominent. Ears: long, with abundant feathering. Tail: medium length (sometimes docked). Hair: long, silky, not tufted. Like the English toy spaniels, this breed has four varieties: black with areas of bright tan, solid red, white with chestnut markings, or tricolor (black, white, chestnut).

**Personality**    Lively, sportive, outgoing.

**Uses**    The Cavalier King Charles spaniel is a pleasant companion dog. It has noteworthy senses of smell and vision and can be used in short hunts in open country.

**Note**    Not all breeders dock the tail, and this factor is not taken into account in shows.

## 285 TELOMIAN

**Origin** This is a very ancient breed raised by Malaysian aborigines. It was brought to the United States in 1963, where, aided by a better diet and a new environment, it developed and improved both in size and in temperament.

**Description** This is a vigorous, rustic-looking dog, somewhat similar to the Basenji, with whom it probably shares a distant relationship. Dogs are 16 to 19 inches (41–48 cm.) high; bitches, from 15 to 18 inches (38–46 cm.) high. They weigh respectively 25 to 30 pounds (11–14 kg.) and 22 to 27 pounds (10–12 kg.). The Telomian has a wedge-shaped head, a compact body, a sickle tail, sturdy limbs, retracted abdomen, and broad chest. Its hair is short and soft. Colors: all shades of brown with white markings on its chest and feet.

**Personality** Lively, intelligent, cheerful, a great friend of children, but difficult to train.

**Uses** In its country of origin it is a dog of all work: hunter, watchdog, shepherd, companion. In America, however, it is exclusively a companion dog, appreciated for its cleanliness; dignity; its subdued, polite bark; and its happy yodeling, similar to that of the Basenji.

**Note** This breed is studied and raised by members of the Telomian Club of America through which the puppies are sold.

## 286 SHIBA INU

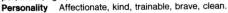

**Origin** This is a very ancient breed, probably with chow chow and Kyūshū blood. It was brought to Japan from China two thousand years ago.

**Description** Height: dogs, 15 to 16 inches (37.9–40.9 cm.); bitches, 13¾ to 14½ inches (34.9–37 cm.). Approximate weight 44 pounds (20 kg.). It has a pointed muzzle, a broad forehead, and a dark nose. Eyes: small, dark brown. Ears: triangular, upright. Neck: sturdy. Tail: thick and strong, carried either in a ring or with a sickle curve. Its coat is made up of hard, thick hair with a fine undercoat. Colors: red, pepper-and-salt, red pepper, black pepper, black, tiger, or white.

**Personality** Affectionate, kind, trainable, brave, clean.

**Uses** This is an amiable, much appreciated companion dog used also for hunting small game and for guarding property.

## 287 POMERANIAN

**Origin** The Pomeranian has the same prehistoric origins as all the spitz-type dogs, but the breed was developed in the Prussian region of Pomerania.

**Description** Maximum height: 12 inches (30 cm.). Average weight: 11 pounds (5 kg.). It has a wedge-shaped head, small dark eyes with an intelligent expression, and pointed upright ears. Its tail is folded over its back. Its hair is thick and long. Colors: unicolor white, red, orange, black, or gray. Its coat is at its most perfect when the dog is three years old. When the dog is old, it may become mottled with bald spots.

**Personality** Lively, cheerful, proud, obedient, with a tendency to bark at strangers.

**Uses** After being a watchdog and a shepherd, it became a luxury companion dog during the Renaissance. It loves its home, and when necessary, it will improvise as a guard.

**Note** Pomeranian puppies are born very small and delicate. Three newborns can be held in the palm of one's hand.

---

## 288 AFFENPINSCHER

**Origin** No precise data about the affenpinscher's origin exist. It is certainly related to the Brussels griffon and probably to the terrier.

**Description** It measures from 10 to 15 inches (25–38 cm.) high and weighs 7 to 8 pounds (3–3.6 kg.). It has a wide, round head; a strong muzzle; a short nose; an accentuated stop; and a convex skull covered with ruffled hair—all giving it the look of a little monkey. Eyes: dark, round, prominent, intelligent. Ears: upright and pointed. Neck: short and arched. Body: compact, with a wide chest. Tail: carried high, docked to two-thirds its length. Limbs: straight, well boned. Its coat is composed of long hair that is coarse to the touch and dry. The undercoat is slightly curly. Colors: grayish-black, bluish-gray, or reddish-yellow. It does not need grooming.

**Personality** Authoritarian, aggressive, exuberant, a barker, most affectionate in the family, curious.

**Uses** This is an apartment dog that also loves open spaces. It is a ruthless hunter of mice and an outstanding watchdog.

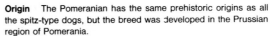

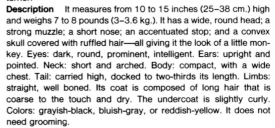

**289**　**ENGLISH TOY SPANIEL**
**King Charles Spaniel**

**Origin**　It is presumed that among the ancestors of this breed are
the Japanese spaniel (Korean), the pug (English), and the Maltese
(Italian). Its name comes from Charles II, the king who promoted
the popularity of the breed.

**Description**　Height: 10 inches (25 cm.). Weight: from 9 to 12
pounds (4.1–5.4 kg.). Muzzle: square, deep, pug. Nose: black,
with very open nostrils. Skull: dome-shaped. Eyes: large and dark,
with a sweet expression. Ears: long and feathered, hanging along
its cheeks. Hair: long, straight, silky, with feathering on the limbs
and tail. There are four varieties of King Charles spaniel: the true
King Charles, which is black with areas of bright fawn; the ruby,
which is chestnut red; the Prince Charles, which is white, tan and
black, and the Blenheim, which is red and white.

**Personality**　Timid, but sociable with those who approach it af-
fectionately. Needs little exercise.

**Uses**　It is exclusively a companion dog.

## 290 TOY TERRIER

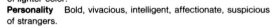

**Origin**   The toy terrier was obtained by repeated crossings among the smallest of the Manchester terriers.

**Description**   Maximum height: 10 inches (25 cm.). Weight: never less than 5½ pounds (2.5 kg.). It has a wedge-shaped head with a flat, narrow skull; scissors bite; dark, protruding eyes; and erect, pointed ears. It has a sturdy tail that is slightly docked. It has a thick, smooth, shiny coat that is either all black or black with areas of lighter color.

**Personality**   Bold, vivacious, intelligent, affectionate, suspicious of strangers.

**Uses**   It has always been a companion dog, loved by women, who carried it in their muffs or in the pockets of their fur coats. Despite its Lilliputian appearance (it is one of the smallest breeds known), it has not forgotten its terrier blood and is in fact a bitter enemy of mice.

## 291 TOY FOX TERRIER

**Origin**   The toy fox terrier is directly descended from the English fox terrier, whose standard dates from 1876. It was miniaturized in the United States through careful breeding.

**Description**   Height for both dogs and bitches: 10 inches (25 cm.). Weight: 3½ to 7 pounds (1.5–3 kg.). It has an elongated muzzle, erect ears, and a short tail carried high. Eyes: dark and round. Hair: short and thick, white with black or chestnut markings.

**Personality**   Curious, intelligent, pleasant, sensitive.

**Uses**   It is a companion dog that has not forgotten its ancient terrier instincts, and will therefore fight mice and small animals.

## 292 BRUSSELS GRIFFON
### Griffon Bruxellois

**Origin** The same as that of the Belgian griffon.

**Description** It differs from the Belgian griffon in its hair, which is long, hard, disheveled, and a uniform lively red in color. Its coat requires daily brushing and stripping twice a year. Baths should be limited to those necessary for hygiene in order that its coat not lose its characteristic coarseness.

**Personality** Affectionate, lively, curious, intelligent, moody.

**Uses** This is a companion dog that expresses its terrier temperament by hunting mice and defending the house with irrepressible barking.

## 293 MALTESE

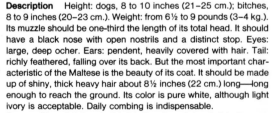

**Origin** This ancient dog was described by the Greek philosopher Theophrastus as belonging to the "Melita" breed, an archaic name for Malta. It was developed in Italy with the addition of miniature spaniel and poodle blood.

**Description** Height: dogs, 8 to 10 inches (21–25 cm.); bitches, 8 to 9 inches (20–23 cm.). Weight: from 6½ to 9 pounds (3–4 kg.). Its muzzle should be one-third the length of its total head. It should have a black nose with open nostrils and a distinct stop. Eyes: large, deep ocher. Ears: pendent, heavily covered with hair. Tail: richly feathered, falling over its back. But the most important characteristic of the Maltese is the beauty of its coat. It should be made up of shiny, thick heavy hair about 8½ inches (22 cm.) long—long enough to reach the ground. Its color is pure white, although light ivory is acceptable. Daily combing is indispensable.

**Personality** Astute, playful, intelligent, and devoted to its master. It is easily alarmed by suspicious noises.

**Uses** It is a classical companion dog, graceful and lovable. It may live to be as old as eighteen, but it is important to keep it out of the damp.

**Note** It does not shed in spring and fall. Its coat, therefore, always looks luxurious.

## 294 LITTLE LION DOG

**Origin** This breed originated in southern Europe several hundred years ago and is said to be the rarest purebred dog in the world. It has appeared in tapestries and appears with the Duchess of Alba in Goya's portrait.

**Description** Height: from 8 to 14 inches (20–35 cm.). Weight: from 4½ to 9 pounds (2–4 kg.). It has a short head with a broad skull; a black nose; round, dark, intelligent eyes; and pendent, feathered ears. Its body is short and well proportioned, with a medium-length tail. Hair: long and wavy. The most sought-after colors are white, black, and lemon, but speckled dogs are also acceptable. The body of the little lion dog should be clipped like the toy poodle: from the middle of the body to the rear, including the tail. A pennant should be left on the tail to give the dog the look of a little lion, as its name demands.

**Personality** Kind, cheerful, affectionate, intelligent.

**Uses** This is purely a companion dog, but, if necessary, it will defend its house with intense barking. It has been known almost exclusively in France, but recently it has been introduced into the United States.

---

## 295 BICHON FRISÉ

**Origin** The Bichon Frisé was derived from the Maltese in the fifteenth century.

**Description** Maximum height: 12 inches (30 cm.). Average weight: 7 to 12 pounds (3–5 kg.). The Bichon Frisé has a moderate muzzle that is not pointed. Its stop is only slightly accentuated. It has a scissors bite; round, dark, intelligent eyes; and hanging ears, well covered with hair. Neck: long. Chest: developed. Tail: curved over its back. Hair: fine and silky, 2¾ to 4 inches (7–10 cm.) long, all white, sometimes with brown or gray markings. It can be shown clipped like a poodle or long-haired, with clipping only at the feet and muzzle.

**Personality** Bold, lively, dignified, intelligent, affectionate, with a strong temperament.

**Uses** Its great period of splendor was the Renaissance. It was immortalized in several of Goya's paintings. Even today, however, it is well known and has fans in Europe and America.

## 296 SMALL CONTINENTAL SPANIEL
### Phalène

**Origin** Widespread in Italy during the Renaissance, the breed was later perfected by French breeders.

**Description** Of elegant structure and lively looks, the small continental spaniel should not be more than 11 inches (28 cm.) high and should weigh from 5½ to 10 pounds (2.5–4.5 kg.). However, bitches weighing as little as 3 pounds (1.5 kg.) are admissible. It has a light head; a skull with an accentuated stop; a little, black, slightly flat nose; and rather strong dentition. Eyes: wide, almond-shaped, dark, expressive. Ears: fine, pendent, mobile, covered with long, wavy hair. Tail: well plumed, carried curved over the dog's back. Its hair is abundant and wavy, but short on its muzzle and the fronts of its legs. All colors are admissible (red, yellow, tricolor, bicolor).

**Personality** Lively, steady, obedient, a quiet traveler.

**Uses** This is an ideal companion dog. Its coat reaches full splendor at eighteen months. It is hardy and resistant to all climates, but it likes the comfort of home.

---

## 297 PAPILLON

**Origin** The same as that of the small continental spaniel.

**Description** Unlike the small continental spaniel, which has pendent ears, the papillon, or butterfly dog, carries its ears erect, wide open, and turned to the sides, in such a way as to suggest the spread wings of a butterfly. The insides of the ears are covered with fine, wavy hair, while the outer surfaces are covered with a falling fringe. Avoid crossing the papillon with the small continental spaniel in order to keep from having puppies with mixed ear formation (semierect). This formation is considered a serious defect. The papillon is an elegant, sporting small dog. Height: 11 inches (28 cm.). Weight: 9 to 10 pounds (4.1–4.5 kg.). Its profuse coat is either black and white, brown and white, or white and black with tan patches. It needs careful grooming.

**Personality** Steady, obedient, silent.

**Uses** The papillon is a most gracious companion, robust despite its small size, and very adaptable.

## 298 COTON DE TULÉAR

**Origin** This breed has been known for centuries in Tuléar, in southern Madagascar. It was brought to the United States in 1971.
**Description** This is a delightful small dog similar to the Maltese. Height: dogs, 12¼ inches (31 cm.); bitches, 11 inches (28 cm.). Weight: dogs, 8¾ pounds (4 kg.); bitches, 7¾ pounds (3.5 kg.). The most outstanding characteristic of the Coton de Tuléar is its coat, composed, as its name suggests, of long, heavy cottonlike hair. It is white with slight yellowish markings on its ears.
**Personality** Devoted, affectionate, very attached to its home and its master.
**Uses** It is a companion dog that loves wide-open spaces, enjoys swimming, and can follow its master on horseback for many miles.

## 299 MEXICAN HAIRLESS DOG
### Xoloitzcuintle

**Origin** This breed is native to Mexico and is widespread throughout South America. It is named after the ancient god Xoloti.
**Description** The Mexican hairless is about 20 inches (50 cm.) high, although there exists a variety only 12 inches (30 cm.) high. It weighs 20 to 30 pounds (9.1–13.6 kg.). It resembles a robust Manchester terrier. It has a broad skull and a long muzzle with a black or flesh-colored nose. Eyes: of medium size, slightly almond-shaped, with a color that may vary from black to yellow and with a lively, intelligent expression. Ears: batlike but elegant, about 4 inches (10 cm.) long. Neck: graceful, like that of an antelope. Back: straight and flexible. Tail: long and sleek, with short hair at the end. It does not have a coat, only one lone tuft of hair on its head. Its skin, which falls in heavy folds over its body and neck, is reddish-gray. The puppies are born pink, like baby pigs, and only reach the lines demanded by the standard when they are a year old.
**Personality** Cheerful in the family, reserved with strangers, very intelligent.
**Uses** Natives used to eat the flesh of this dog. At the end of the nineteenth century, it became completely a companion dog. Due to its abilities as a barker, it is also esteemed as a watchdog.

## 300 CHIHUAHUA

**Origin** This is the oldest breed on the American continent and the smallest breed in the world. Native to Mexico (its name is that of a Mexican state), nonetheless it seems to have been introduced by the Chinese. It was only brought to Europe at the end of the nineteenth century.

**Description** It is from 6 to 9 inches (16–22 cm.) high and weighs proportionally little: from 2 to 5¾ pounds (.9–2.6 kg.). Little dogs are the most highly prized. It has an apple-shaped head with a short, pointed muzzle. Eyes: round and very black. Ears: large, held erect when the dog is alert. Body: compact, longer than it is high. Tail: carried curved over the back or to the side. There are two varieties of Chihuahua: a short-haired variety and a wavy-haired variety (rare). The most frequent colors are light fawn, sand, chestnut, silver, or steel blue. The coat may be unicolored or dappled.

**Personality** Courageous, extremely lively, proud, affectionate, loyal, intelligent, enterprising.

**Uses** The Chihuahua is a companion dog and knows how to defend itself even against somewhat bigger dogs. It needs exercise, and it is a mistake to keep it cooped up in an apartment because of concern for its health.

## 301 CHINESE CRESTED DOG

**Origin** No exact information exists about the origin of this breed. Some scholars, however, doubt that it is of Chinese nationality, naming Ethiopia or Turkey as its country of origin.

**Description** This is a little-known hairless dog. It is about 12 inches (30 cm.) high. Weight: not over 10 pounds (4.5 kg.). It has a broad skull and a long muzzle. Eyes: dark. Ears: erect. Tail: with hair at the end. There is also a tuft of hair at the top of its skull. Otherwise it is hairless and its skin is any color, plain or spotted.

**Personality** Lively, cheerful, intelligent, never noisy or aggressive.

**Uses** This is a companion dog that needs a warm atmosphere.

## 302  CHINESE IMPERIAL CH'IN

**Origin**  Related to the Chinese temple dog, the Pekingese, and the Japanese spaniel, this is a very ancient breed. Until the early 1900's, it was exclusively the property of the Chinese imperial family.

**Description**  There are four sizes of Ch'in: the giant, 9 to 10 inches (23–25 cm.) high, weighing 15 pounds (7 kg.); the classic, 4 to 6 inches (10–15 cm.) high, weighing 4 to 5 pounds (1.8–2.5 kg.); the miniature, 4 inches (10 cm.) high, weighing 3 to 4 pounds (1.4–1.8 kg.); and the sleeve dog, 3 inches (8 cm.) high, weighing 1.5 to 2 pounds (.7–.9 kg.). It has a large head that appears flat in profile; a short, wide nose; fringed ears that are long and pendent; a tail that is rolled on its back; and an abundant cottony coat. Colors: black and white, solid black, or, rarely, red.

**Personality**  It has been described as the most sensitive, the most regal, the most intelligent, and the most demanding of dogs, which spends its days "meditating."

**Uses**  It has always been a companion dog. The last empress of China kept fifty Ch'ins in the throne room. When the empress entered the room, the Ch'ins lined up, upright on their hind legs, and remained that way until she was seated.

**Note**  This is a dog that withstands the cold well.

---

## 303  CHINESE TEMPLE DOG

**Origin**  Belonging to the same family as the Ch'in, the breed was used for centuries as guardians in the temples.

**Description**  It has a large head, a short muzzle, a pug nose, extremely hardy teeth, and a ferocious look. There are four sizes of Chinese temple dog: giant, 12 to 14 inches (30–36 cm.) high, weighing 20 pounds (9 kg.); classic, 10 to 12 inches (25–30 cm.) high, weighing 10 to 15 pounds (4.5–6.8 kg.); miniature, 4 to 5 inches (10–13 cm.) high, weighing 4 pounds (1.8 kg.); and sleeve, 3 inches (7.6 cm.) high, weighing 1.5 to 2 pounds (.7–.9 kg.). Its hair is extremely long and silky and is normally black and white. It can withstand low temperatures and loses its undercoat when it is warm.

**Personality**  Despite its ferocious looks, this is a quiet, loyal dog that even has a sense of humor.

**Uses**  It has been bred to be a gentle companion dog. However, it becomes a barking watchdog when strangers approach the door.

## 304　PEKINGESE

**Origin**　The Pekingese probably has spitz blood, but its origin is lost in the shadows of a four-thousand-year history. For many centuries the Pekingese was the favorite of the imperial family in Peking. It was brought to Europe in 1860 by British and French soldiers who found the dogs in the ruins of the Summer Palace.

**Description**　Height: 6 to 9 inches (30.4–45 cm.). Weight: from 8 to 10 pounds (3.6–4.5 kg.). It has a broad head that is wide between the eyes, a short but very visible nose, a wrinkled muzzle, and a deep stop. When its mouth is closed, neither teeth nor tongue should show. Eyes: large, dark, and lucid, slightly prominent. Ears: heart-shaped, with long feathering. Neck: short and thick. Hair: long and straight, with a heavy mane and abundant feathering. All colors are permissible except liver and albino.

**Personality**　Sensitive, extremely affectionate with its master, suspicious of strangers, dignified, loyal, obedient, courageous to the point of foolhardiness.

**Uses**　This is a classic apartment and lap dog. When necessary, however, it can change into a barking watchdog.

**Note**　It should be combed very often. Its teeth need cleaning to avoid their premature loss.

---

## 305　SHIH-TZÛ

**Origin**　Documents and paintings dating from the sixth century show a dog resembling a small lion. In the seventeenth century, dogs were brought from Tibet and bred in the Forbidden City of Peking. From these dogs the Shih-Tzû was developed. They were brought to England in 1930.

**Description**　Maximum height: 10½ inches (27 cm.). Maximum weight: 14 pounds (6.4 kg.). It has a round head that is wide between the eyes; a thick beard and mustaches; a short, square muzzle; and a black nose. It is often called the "chrysanthemum-faced dog" because its face hair grows in all directions. Eyes: dark, large, and round. Ears: long and pendent, with so much hair that they blend into the dog's neck. The thick tail is rolled over the dog's back. The coat is composed of abundant, long hair (not curly) with a good undercoat. All colors are admissible, but a white marking on the forehead and the point of the tail is highly appreciated by dog-show judges.

**Personality**　Royally arrogant, plucky and alert. Trustworthy with polite, careful children.

**Uses**　The Shih-Tzû is a typical drawing-room dog, but it has the hardiness of a working dog. It is also long-lived, easily reaching fifteen years. Its coat needs daily care.

## 306 LHASA APSO

**Origin** The land of Tibet was the home of the Lhasa Apso, the breed taking its name from the sacred city of Lhasa.

**Description** Ideal height: dogs, 10 to 11 inches (25–28 cm.); a little less for bitches. Weight: 13 to 15 pounds (5.9–6.8 kg.). According to its standard, its hair should cascade from its head over its eyes; it should have a dark beard and mustaches; a muzzle that is of medium length but not square; small, dark, deep-set eyes; and heavily feathered ears. Its neck has an abundant scarf of hair, and its feathered tail is carried over its back. Coat: straight, hard, heavy, but not silky. Colors: honey, sand, slate, or black brindle.

**Personality** Stubborn, self-confident, affectionate with its master, but will not tolerate rough, badly behaved children.

**Uses** The Lhasa Apso is a hardy dog with an excellent sense of hearing. It will give good early warning at the approach of strangers.

## 307 JAPANESE SPANIEL
### Chin

**Origin** The Japanese spaniel is probably native to Korea, the breed being developed in Japan at a later date and spread to Europe in 1700. Its greatest moment of popularity came in 1853 when one was given as a gift to Queen Victoria.

**Description** The Japanese spaniel should not be more than 9 inches (30 cm.) high and its weight should not be less than 7 pounds (3.2 kg.). The smaller the dog, the more it is appreciated. It has a rather large head, open nostrils, an extremely short nasal canal, a small undershot muzzle, and a distinct stop. Its skull is rounded forward. Eyes: almond-shaped, dark, expressive. Ears: shaped like an upside-down V, well covered with hair. Tail: falling on its back. Its coat is white with black or red markings; it is soft and long over its entire body, except for its head.

**Personality** Extremely devoted to its master, docile, affectionate, intelligent, but peevish with strangers.

**Uses** It is exclusively a companion dog. It is very susceptible to distemper.

**YORKSHIRE TERRIER**

**Origin**  The breed was developed during the last century by miners in the English county of Yorkshire who hoped to obtain a dog adapted to catching the terrible rats that infested the mine shafts. Crossings among the Skye terrier, the black-and-tan toy terrier, the Dandie Dinmont, and the Maltese all contributed to the makeup of this dog. The first Yorkshire with the characteristics demanded by its standard today appeared in a dog show in 1870.

**Description**  The Yorkshire is a well-proportioned, even vigorous dog about 9 inches (23 cm.) high, weighing at most 7¾ pounds (3.5 kg.). It has a small flat head, a medium-length muzzle, a black nose, and regular teeth. Eyes: dark, extremely vivacious. Ears: V-shaped, small, erect or semierect. Tail: docked to a medium length and carried level with the back. Limbs: straight, with round feet and black nails. Its coat is composed of straight, long, shiny, silky hair that is steel blue with golden areas on the head, chest, and limbs. The hair on its head is so abundant that it is almost always necessary to gather it in a band to keep it from dragging in the dog's food and to give the animal maximum visibility.

**Personality**  Like all terriers, the Yorkshire is lively, courageous, stubborn, affectionate with its master, suspicious of strangers, and not very sociable with other animals.

**Uses**  The Yorkie, as it is known, has found great popularity as a companion dog all over the world. This is due to its exceptional good looks and general lovableness. It has, however, not forgotten its terrier blood and can localize even the smallest noise, which makes it useful as a watchdog. It loves the outdoors but behaves well in an apartment.

**Note**  Bitches often have difficulty delivering their pups, so veterinary supervision is advisable. The puppies are born almost black, and it is only after a year that they develop the coat demanded by their standard. In winter, they have a tendency to suffer from the cold and should wear woolen jackets when taken out.

## 309 BLACK-AND-TAN TOY TERRIER
## Small English Terrier

**Origin** This breed was obtained in the 1800's through breeding of the Manchester terrier.

**Description** Height: from 10 to 12 inches (25–30 cm.). Weight: from 6 to 8 pounds (2.7–3.6 kg.). It has a long, narrow, conical head with a flat skull, just the slightest stop, a black nose, and tight lips. Eyes: almond-shaped, black. Ears: erect and pointed, turned to the front. Neck: long and slightly arched. Tail: not to reach below the hocks. Hair: thick, sleek, and shiny. Colors: black and mahogany in mutually distinct areas.

**Personality** Most affectionate, lively, very intelligent.

**Uses** This tiny companion dog can be a ferocious mouser.

## 310 AUSTRALIAN TERRIER

**Origin** This breed was developed in Australia in the early years of this century by crossings among the Yorkshire, Skye, Norwich, and cairn terriers. It was officially recognized in 1933.

**Description** Average height: 10 inches (25 cm.). Weight: 10 to 11 pounds (4.5–5 kg.). The Australian terrier is a short-legged, active, vivacious dog. It has a long head, black nose, powerful jaws, and a scissors bite. Eyes: small and dark. Ears: erect or folded forward. Tail: docked. Its hair is straight and hard and about 2 to 3 inches (5–6.5 cm.) long. Colors: blue-black or silver-gray with shadings on the paws and muzzle; light sand; or reddish-sand. Pups are born black and change color after two to three months.

**Personality** Lively, impetuous, spirited, dignified.

**Uses** Once used as a hunter of small game and even as a shepherd, this dog has retained all the characteristics of a terrier. Today, however, it is esteemed solely as an affectionate companion.

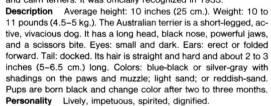

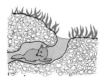

## 311 SILKY TERRIER

**Origin** Developed by crossings among the Skye, cairn, and Yorkshire terriers, the silky is cousin to the Australian terrier. Its standard was first established in 1962 and was updated in 1967. It is also known as the Sidney terrier.

**Description** This is a compact but lightly built dog. Average height: 9 inches (22.5 cm.). Weight: from 9 to 11 pounds (4–5 kg.). Its head is of medium length, wide between the ears, strong, and typically terrier. It has sturdy jaws, a black nose, round dark eyes, and erect V-shaped ears. Its body is moderately elongated, and its tail is docked and carried upright. Hair: 5 to 6 inches (12–15 cm.) long, fine as silk, in colors of blue and fire red, or gray, blue, and fire red.

**Personality** Lively, pugnacious, cheerful, sociable, curious, very intelligent.

**Uses** Despite its proud instincts for hunting down animals in their dens and for catching mice, this dog is considered exclusively as a companion dog.

**Note** Constant care is needed to keep its coat beautiful.

## 312 AUSTRALIAN SILKY TERRIER

**Origin** The breed was developed in Australia by crossing the Yorkshire and the Australian terrier. It was officially recognized in 1933.

**Description** It is about 10 inches (25 cm.) high and should be longer than it is tall. It weighs 10 to 11 pounds (4.5–5 kg.). Eyes: small, dark, lively. Ears: erect or folded forward. Tail: docked and carried cheerfully. Hair: silky and long. Colors: blue or silver-gray with areas of bright tan.

**Personality** It has the instincts, the liveliness, the lovableness, and the affectionate nature of the best terriers.

**Uses** A true terrier, it is always busy, so not a good choice for nervous people. It can be hard to housebreak and grooming can be a chore.

# GREYHOUNDS

# 313 GREYHOUND

**Origin** This is a very ancient breed. It is probably descended from the Arab greyhound, the Sloughi, which was brought to Europe by the Phoenicians. Over the course of centuries, English breeders have developed a fabulous hunting and racing dog embodying all the needed sporting and moral qualities.

**Description** The greyhound is robust, symmetrical, and vigorous. Dogs are from 28 to 31 inches (71–78 cm.) high; bitches are from 27 to 28 inches (68.5–71 cm.) high. Weight ranges from 60 to 70 pounds (27–32 kg.). It has a long head and a chiseled muzzle. Its skull is wide between the ears; its nose is pointed and black; and its jaws are muscular with extremely strong teeth. Neck: long and elastic. Eyes: dark, lively. Ears: small, thin, in the form of a rose. Tail: carried low and slightly curved. Front legs: long and very straight. Thighs: broad and muscular. Its hair is short, shiny, and tight. Colors: black, white, red, blue, buckskin, tiger, or even multicolored or with markings.

**Personality** It is very intelligent, but its character is often undervalued because of its reserved behavior toward its master and toward strangers. It is sensitive, courageous, loyal, aristocratic, vain.

**Uses** Its greatest gift is its speed. Centuries ago it was used in the hunting of deer and wild boar; it could catch them and pull them down without stopping. It is also an incorrigible enemy of domestic animals, especially cats and geese. Today, the greyhound is mainly used on racetracks, chasing mechanical rabbits. This sport is especially popular in Anglo-Saxon countries. The greyhound is not adaptable to apartment life. It absolutely requires long runs daily.

## 314  ITALIAN GREYHOUND

**Origin**  The Italian greyhound is a very old greyhound. A dog similar to the Italian greyhound of today was found in an Egyptian tomb of six thousand years ago. Like the greyhound, it was brought to Europe by the Phoenicians. The breed was then developed in Italy.

**Description**  Height: from 13 to 15 inches (32–38 cm.). Maximum weight: 11 pounds (5 kg.). It has a long head, thinning gradually to a pointed muzzle; a dark nose; thin lips; and a healthy scissors bite. Eyes: dark, large, expressive. Ears: small, thin. Neck: long and thin. Tail: straight, ending in a slight curve. Hair: smooth and fine. Colors: solid gray, slate gray, black, fawn. White on the chest and paws is acceptable.

**Personality**  Very meek, timid, wary, submissive, very attached to its master.

**Uses**  It is a very peaceful companion dog that must be treated gently. It flees from rough children and loves serene people.

**Note**  It is notoriously sensitive to the cold and therefore needs a warm bed and a temperate environment. In winter it should wear a jacket outside.

## 315  WHIPPET

**Origin**  The whippet was developed at the end of the nineteenth century through crossings among the greyhound, the Italian greyhound, and the terrier. Its name derives from the expression "whip it," meaning to move quickly.

**Description**  Ideal height: dogs, 19 inches (47 cm.); bitches, 17 inches (44 cm.). Weight: dogs, 18 to 28 pounds (8–12 kg.); bitches, 12 to 20 pounds (5–9 kg.). It is a greyhound in miniature, with a long, lean head; powerful jaws; and a scissors bite. Eyes: very lively. Ears: small, rose-shaped. Neck: elegantly arched. Chest: deep. Back: long and broad. Abdomen: retracted. Tail: pointed. Hair: fine and short, in black, red, fawn, tigered white, or slate blue, either solid-colored or mixed.

**Personality**  Happy, affectionate, dignified, intelligent, docile.

**Uses**  The whippet is used at the track for short races, and can reach a speed of 37 mph (60 km. per hour). Due to its excellent character, it has also become a companion dog that at the opportune moment will transform itself into an attentive watchdog. Despite the delicate looks it inherited from the Italian greyhound, the whippet is resistant to illness and is quite long-lived.

## 316 DEERHOUND

**Origin** The origin of the deerhound is not known.

**Description** Height: dogs, above 30 inches (76 cm.); bitches, above 28 inches (71 cm.). Weight: dogs, 85 to 110 pounds (38.5–48 kg.); bitches, 75 to 95 pounds (30–36 kg.). It has a long head with a pointed muzzle, a black or blue nose, and abundant beard and mustaches. Eyes: chestnut or hazel, with a sweet expression. Ears: folded back but erect, soft to the touch, and always dark in color. Neck: rather long, with mane. Chest: deep. Back: slightly arched. Abdomen: very retracted. Tail: slightly curved as it reaches the ground. Its hair is 4 inches (10 cm.) long and covers its entire body, neck, and limbs, but it is notably longer on the head, chest, and abdomen. Many colors are acceptable, but those preferred are gray-blue, dark gray, yellow, or red. White is not acceptable.

**Personality** Loyal, tranquil, affectionate, obedient, with a tendency toward timidity and laziness. The writer Sir Walter Scott described the deerhound as "the most perfect creature in the world."

**Uses** The deerhound was used for hunting deer and coyotes over great open expanses. Agile and very fast, it could rouse, follow, catch, and capture the prey.

---

## 317 IRISH WOLFHOUND

**Origin** Used by the ancient Celts for hunting wolves, this breed was later brought to Ireland by the Romans. There it was carefully bred. In the second half of the nineteenth century, the breed was revitalized by an influx of Great Dane and deerhound blood.

**Description** Minimum height: dogs, 31 inches (79 cm.); bitches, 28 inches (71 cm.). Some dogs reached a height of 35 inches (90 cm.). Minimum weight: 119 pounds (54 kg.) for dogs; 88 pounds (40 kg.) for bitches. It has a long head with a moderately pointed muzzle, a muscular arched neck, a very deep chest, and a well-retracted abdomen. Its tail is slightly curved. Its shoulders are strong. Coat: rustic, in colors of gray, brindle, red, black, or white.

**Personality** Good, patient, generous, thoughtful, intelligent. It tends to attach itself strongly to a single master.

**Uses** Because of its excellent character, the Irish wolfhound could theoretically be considered an excellent companion dog. However, it needs a great deal of space for unrestrained runs. It is still used for hunting stags, wild boars, wolves, and coyotes. It is also a formidable guard dog, since the wolfhound can kill a man by grabbing him by the throat.

## 318 SPANISH GREYHOUND
### Galgo Español

**Origin** The Spanish greyhound is a direct descendant of the Sloughi, the Arab greyhound brought to Spain by the Moors in the Middle Ages.

**Description** Height: 26 to 28 inches (65–70 cm.). Weight: dogs, about 66 pounds (30 kg.); bitches are somewhat lighter. It has a long, narrow head with a prominent nose and very open nostrils. Jaws: strong, with thin lips. Eyes: dark, with a lively expression. Ears: rose-shaped, falling to the back. Back: long. Abdomen: retracted. Tail: very long, carried low. Its hair is dense and short. Colors: fawn with a black mask, black, or tigered on a light tan ground with white muzzle, chest, and feet.

**Personality** Aristocratic, obedient, tranquil, courageous, an incomparable companion.

**Uses** In the thousand years of its existence it has been the preferred hunting dog of the grandees of Spain, a guardian of flocks, and a runner in dog races.

**Note** There also exists a variety of Spanish greyhound very similar to the greyhound. It is called the Anglo-Spanish greyhound.

## 319 PHARAOH HOUND

**Origin** This is probably an ancient Egyptian dog brought to Spain at the time of the Saracen invasions. It found its ideal climate in the Balearic Islands.

**Description** Height: dogs, 25 to 28 inches (63–70 cm.); bitches, 22 to 26 inches (57–66 cm.). It has a triangular head with a flat skull, a tan nose speckled with pink, and powerful jaws with a scissors bite. Eyes: small, amber or light brown. Ears: large and erect. Neck: thin and muscular. Chest: narrow. Back: long and slightly sloping. Abdomen: moderately retracted. Tail: carried low, curved. Hair: short and shiny. Colors: white with irregularly distributed red markings or solid red.

**Personality** Docile, loyal, affectionate, very playful.

**Uses** This is a most passionate hunter and is used for rabbits and feathered game. It is also a most pleasant companion dog, but it needs frequent and long runs.

## 320 AFGHAN HOUND
## Tazi

**Origin**  This is a very ancient dog, native to the Sinai, and mentioned several times in Egyptian papyruses as well as pictured in the caves of northern Afghanistan. The breed was kept pure for centuries, and its exportation was always prohibited. It therefore only reached Europe as contraband early in this century.

**Description**  In looks the Afghan is strong and dignified, powerful and noble. Height: 27 to 29 inches (68.58–73.66 cm.) for dogs; slightly less for bitches. Weight: 58 to 64 pounds (26–34 kg.) for males. It has a long, straight, narrow head with a slightly convex skull. Its nose is black or liver brown. Its jaws are powerful. Eyes: almost triangular, dark or golden in color. Ears: carried flat to the head, covered with long, silky hair. Neck: long and strong. Tail: ending in a ring. Its coat is made up of rich, silky hair (short on its back) with a characteristic tuft on the top of its head. All colors are admissible. The most common are white, fawn, black with areas of bright chestnut, and tricolor.

**Personality**  Courageous, indomitable, sweet, sensitive, very intelligent, dignified but not indifferent, suspicious but not hostile with strangers. It must be trained kindly.

**Uses**  In its country of origin it was an outstanding shepherd and a resolute hunter of wolves, jackals, and leopards. In Europe and America, because of its extraordinary beauty, it has become exclusively a luxury dog, loving the home and the company of its master.

**Note**  Because of the extraordinary silky richness of its coat, it has been called "a greyhound in pajamas." It needs very frequent brushing. It withstands heat well and bears cold and rain with dignity. It should, however, have the chance for long, unrestrained runs every day.

## 321 SALUKI

**Origin** The Saluki is probably the fruit of ancient crossings among Egyptian and Asiatic greyhounds. It bears the name of an ancient Arab city, Salug, and is considered a sacred gift of Allah.

**Description** The Saluki is a dog of very elegant lines. It is from 23 to 28 inches (58–71 cm.) high and weighs from 29 to 66 pounds (13–30 kg.). It has a long, narrow head, which tapers gradually toward the nose; sturdy jaws; and large, shiny eyes that are either light or dark brown with a sweet, dignified expression. Its ears are pendent and are covered with long, silky hair. Its neck is elegant and flexible. Its body is very elongated, with oblique muscular shoulders; and its tail, which begins low, is carried curved. Its hair is sleek and silky. Colors: white, cream, fawn, golden, red, gray and fiery red, or tricolor (white, black, and red).

**Personality** Affectionate, sensitive, friendly with children.

**Uses** A hunter of gazelle in its native Persia, it is today esteemed as a watchdog (it has an excellent sense of hearing) and as a pleasant, clean, and serene companion dog.

## 322 BORZOI

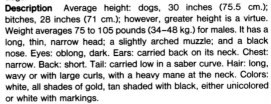

**Origin** Imported from Arabia by a Russian nobleman in 1600, the borzoi was later crossed with the collie and with Lapp sled dogs.

**Description** Average height: dogs, 30 inches (75.5 cm.); bitches, 28 inches (71 cm.); however, greater height is a virtue. Weight averages 75 to 105 pounds (34–48 kg.) for males. It has a long, thin, narrow head; a slightly arched muzzle; and a black nose. Eyes: oblong, dark. Ears: carried back on its neck. Chest: narrow. Back: short. Tail: carried low in a saber curve. Hair: long, wavy or with large curls, with a heavy mane at the neck. Colors: white, all shades of gold, tan shaded with black, either unicolored or white with markings.

**Personality** Docile, reserved, obstinate, silent, extremely loyal.

**Uses** Once a ferocious hunter of wolves, it became in the nineteenth century a noble companion dog because of its distinguished looks. It is adapted to living in the house but must be taken often for long runs outside.

## 323 MAGYAR AGÁR

**Origin** The breed was brought to Europe in the year 1000 by the Magyars, an Asiatic people. In modern times it has been improved by some influx of greyhound blood.

**Description** The standard does not indicate the dog's height; but its weight should be 60 to 68 pounds (27–31 kg.) for dogs and 49 to 57 pounds (22–26 kg.) for bitches. It has an elongated head, slight stop, and black nose. Eyes: with a gentle expression. Ears: folded back. Neck: long. Limbs: thin. Kidney area: very muscular and arched. Tail: thin and twisted. Its coat is very short and sleek; the dog therefore suffers from the cold and is prone to trembling. Colors of the coat: gray, black, tiger, dappled, or, infrequently, white.

**Personality** Affectionate but not gay, good, loyal, tenacious, and faithful.

**Uses** Although it has a poor sense of smell, it is excellent for chasing down hares and foxes. It is also used on the race track, chasing mechanical rabbits.

---

## 324 SLOUGHI

**Origin** Directly descended from royal Egyptian dogs, it may be considered a cousin to the Saluki.

**Description** The Sloughi is a dog with an accentuated bone structure and a lean musculature. It is from 22 to 30 inches (55–75 cm.) high and weighs 66 to 70 pounds (30–32 kg.). It has a moderately elongated head, a slightly pointed muzzle, and powerful jaws. Eyes: large and dark, with a somewhat sad expression. Ears: falling against the head, triangular, and rounded at the tips. Neck: lean, with folds under the throat. Tail: thin, curved at the end. Its hair is smooth and fine. Colors: sand, fawn, drab white, tigered, or black with areas of bright chestnut. Patchwork coats are not admissible.

**Personality** Docile, obedient, affectionate.

**Uses** The Sloughi is raised by many North African tribes and is used, especially by nomads, for guarding and hunting. In Europe and in America, it is used on the dog track and is also esteemed as a companion dog. Its popularity, however, is limited.

**Note** It suffers from the cold in winter. It is not hard to please so far as food is concerned.

# GLOSSARY

**Aggressiveness**   The propensity of a dog to assault and bite other dogs or people. The cause is often some sort of psychic disturbance.

**Autochthonous**   A breed of dog is considered autochthonous when it has settled in a particular area at such a remote time and developed there without bastardization that it may be said to have been born in this territory. Indigenous.

**Breed**   When one speaks of a breed of dog, one means a group of homogeneous individuals whose aesthetic and psychic qualities are transmitted unchanged from one generation to the next. Most dog breeds are the result of artificial selection by humans. With reference to purity, there are pure and impure breeds (mongrelization).

**Breeding Kennel**   The place in which matings between dogs of the same breed are accomplished with the purpose of maintaining the purity of the breed and selling the puppies. There are breeding kennels all over the world. To find their addresses, one should refer to the breed clubs. Such kennels usually guarantee their pups and will give the dog's pedigree to its new owner.

**Club**   Associations of breeders, owners, developers, and fanciers that further the knowledge about and the improvement and diffusion of a particular breed of dog. Most countries have national kennel clubs. Acceptance of a breed by a kennel club constitutes official recognition.

**Coat**   One of the most important anatomical character-

ring

sickle

squirrel

curved

corkscrew

erect

feathered

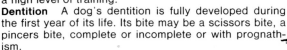

sabre

otter

istics in the standard of a breed is its coat——the hair that covers the dog's body. Its coat may be very short, short, sleek, long, hard, soft, straight, wavy, woolly, silky, or curly. A dog's coat is referred to as unicolor when it is all one color, bicolor when it is of two colors, and tricolor when it is of three colors. The coat may also be shaded, tigered, harlequin, speckled, trout marked, and so forth.

**Conditioned Reflex**   A physical-psychological phenomenon determined by the combination of a certain stimulus and a certain reaction. A dog has a noteworthy associative memory: it learns quickly to connect a word, a gesture, or a sound made by its master with a reaction of its own. For example, the sight of its leash corresponds to the pleasure of a walk; the appearance of its bowl is quickly associated with the pleasure of eating. Conditioned reflexes are very helpful in a dog's reaching a high level of training.

**Dentition**   A dog's dentition is fully developed during the first year of its life. Its bite may be a scissors bite, a pincers bite, complete or incomplete or with prognathism.

**Dewlap**   A fold of hanging skin at the base of a dog's throat. It is characteristic of some breeds.

**Dog Shows**   All over the world, there are dog shows. To qualify, dogs must be pedigreed members of recognized breeds. In these expositions, judges, expert in a particular breed, examine the dogs carefully in light of the breed's standard. They examine the dog in detail, from the color of its coat to the consistency of its hair, from its dentition to the verticality of its limbs, from the color of its eyes to the shape of its ears, its bearing, and its gait. Then the judge gives each competitor a mark. By accumulating qualifying marks obtained in various shows, a dog can reach the title of champion.

**Ears**   The ears, too, are an important part of a breed's standard. They may be short, long, set high or low, large, small, natural, docked, batlike, folded, hanging, erect, semierect, rose-shaped, and so forth.

**Education**   While training refers to getting a dog to learn particular and difficult operations connected with its "job," education (which must be undertaken by every owner) refers to teaching a dog the norms of civilized be-

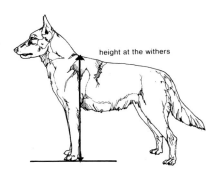

height at the withers

havior: not to soil in the house, not to bark, to sleep in its bed, to walk on a leash, and to endure a muzzle.

**Estrus**   See Heat.

**Eyes**   Depending on its breed, a dog's eyes may be of different shape and color, such as round, almond, protruding, oblique, deep-set, and so forth. Their color may be darker or lighter shades of chestnut (the majority), black, yellow, red, or amber. The color of the eyes is often influenced by the color of the coat.

**Flesh-colored**   A reddish, delicate meat color. A dog's nose when it is without pigmentation is flesh-colored. Some standards demand that the dog's nose be unpigmented—that is, flesh-colored.

**Gait**   A dog's more or less characteristic manner of walking or running. It is part of the personality of the animal and is especially important for hunting breeds, which must spring, race, and leap, often over difficult terrain.

**Gestation**   The period of time it takes an embryo to develop in its mother's body. For dogs, the gestation period averages sixty to sixty-five days, depending on the age of the bitch, the breed, the environment, and the number of puppies.

**Grooming**   The shearing of a dog for aesthetic purposes, usually following the indications of the breed's standard.

**Heat**   The brief period of fertility in the bitch. Beginning for the first time when the bitch is eight to ten months old, it recurs twice a year. Duration is about twenty-one days.

**Heredity**   The biological characteristics that are transmitted from parent to offspring. The transmission of characteristics from one generation to another, however, does not have proven rules, because the puppies may inherit all their characteristics from the sire or the dam or half from each, sometimes even exhibiting the influence of the grandparents or great-grandparents. Since bad characteristics can be transmitted as easily as good ones, breeders must always arrange matings wisely, excluding sires and dams with undesirable temperaments. Special care should be taken to avoid too close a relationship between dam and sire.

**Hocks**   The point of articulation on the back legs between the tibia and the metatarsal.

**Hygiene** Refers to the personal cleanliness of a dog, such as the bath, the combing, the brushing, the elimination of parasites, the proper feeding, and walking.

**Instincts** Natural inclinations that are inherent and independent of reasoning or teaching and that influence a dog "instinctively" to perform acts of hunting, guarding, or herding. Good instincts facilitate training greatly.

**Kennel Club** See Club.

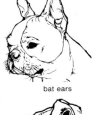
bat ears

**Limbs** Legs. The front legs, rectilinear and vertical, are used mainly for support; the back legs, oblique and muscular, are used for propulsion. When buying a puppy, it is advisable to examine its legs carefully. Swollen legs may be a sign of rickets.

**Pedigree** The written genealogy of a dog. In this document, which is granted by the official canine association of each country, are listed several generations of the animal. When a purebred puppy is bought, the breeder should give the pedigree to the new owner.

folded

**Pigmentation** The natural chemical coloration in the tissues of an animal.

**Plumb** The verticality of the front legs. This is specified in the standards for some breeds.

**Pregnancy** See Gestation.

**Prognathism** The forward protrusion of the underpart of a dog's muzzle with consequent poor occlusion of the dental arch. When not specifically indicated in the breed's standard, prognathism (which is hereditary) is a serious defect.

hanging

**Pug** A term used to describe the flattened lines of the muzzles of certain breeds.

**Roan** The coat of a dog in which light and black or reddish hairs are thickly mixed.

**Speckles** Tiny dark or black markings on a light coat.

**Standard** The collection of precise norms established by the club responsible for the care and raising of a particular breed to describe the ideal aesthetic and psychic characteristics of that breed. Each officially recognized breed has its own standard. In it, the dog is described to the last detail: height, weight, consistency of hair, color of coat and of eyes, skeletal conformation, carriage and length of tail, shape of skull, muzzle, ears and limbs, musculature, and gait. The standard also details the character and attitude of the breed and indicates the defects that will cause penalties or disqualification at dog shows.

erect

'semi-erect

**Stop** A technical term indicating the step down from the skull to the muzzle of a dog; that is, the more or less evident indentation between the eyes where the skull and nasal bone meet. The stop is very important in determining the beauty and character of many breeds, for example, the pointer.

rose-shaped

**Stripping** A form of grooming used for various wire-haired breeds (when indicated in the standard). It should be performed by a specialist and consists of pulling out excess hair with the fingers and a special little knife. This thinning operation, especially if done during the season when the hair is "dead," is completely painless.

**Tail** The shape and carriage of the tail is one of the characteristics of each particular breed. The tail may be short (either naturally or through docking), long, thick, thin, carried high or low, curved over the back or the flanks; it may be a gay tail, a ring tail, a sickle tail, a squirrel tail, an otter tail, a screwtail, a saber tail, or a plumed tail.

**Toy** The smallest-sized members of a breed that also has larger subjects. For example, there are toy poodles; but Chihuahuas, which are about the same size, are not "toys."

**Training** The sum total of various lessons taught a dog by a trainer. A dog, assuming it has the predisposition, may be trained in defense, guarding, herding, ferreting out contraband and drugs, and so forth.

**Trout Marks** Small reddish markings like those of a trout on a light background. They are characteristic of the coats of some breeds.

**Withers** The point on a dog's back (and that of quadrupeds in general) corresponding to the first dorsal vertebra. The height of a dog is always measured from the withers to the ground.

**Working Breed** In the parlance of dog fanciers, a working breed is one that is of concrete help to man, especially in the guarding of herds or property.

# INDEX OF ENTRIES

# PHOTOGRAPHIC CREDITS